THE METROSEXUAL

GENDER, SEXUALITY, AND SPORT

DAVID COAD

SUNY
PRESS

Published by
State University of New York Press, Albany

For information, contact State University of New York Press, Albany, NY
www.sunypress.edu

Production by Kelli W. LeRoux
Marketing by Susan M. Petrie

Library of Congress Cataloging-in-Publication Data
Coad, David, 1958-
    The metrosexual : gender, sexuality, and sport / David Coad.
        p.   cm.—(SUNY series on sport, culture, and social relations ; 283)
    Includes bibliographical references and index.
    ISBN 978-0-7914-7409-9 (hardcover : alk. paper)—
    ISBN 978-0-7914-7410-5 (pbk. : alk. paper)
1. Sports—Sociological aspects. 2. Sports—Social aspects.
3. Masculinity in sports. 4. Gender identity. I. Title
GV706.5.C58 2008
306.4'83—dc22   2007035438

10 9 8 7 6 5 4 3 2 1

Contents

Part Three

Acknowledgments

I would like to thank Michael Hollington for a discussion on metrosexuality at a conference in Portugal, David Halperin for his interest and kind assistance, and those who offered helpful remarks on draft work, especially Andrew Leverton, Michael O'Rourke, and William Dow. I express a special note of gratitude to John Chandler, who closely followed the text as it progressed into its present form. I would also like to thank Mark Simpson for his comments on my work and an anonymous reader for the State University of New York Press, who offered pertinent and useful advice. James Bennett, Louise Catchpole, Momin Rahman, and Eithne Quinn kindly assisted in research, and I am grateful to Carmel Bond and Stephen Bond. For permission to reproduce photographic material, the author would like to gratefully thank: aussieBum International, Getty Images, Timothy Greenfield-Sanders, HOM, Karim Ramzi, Ali Mahdavi, Millivres Prowler Group and *Gay Times* (www.gay times.co .uk), and Triumph International.

Part One

1

Sports Sex

The intersection between metrosexuality, gender, sexuality, and sports is the principal focus of this book. Chapter 1 addresses three of these elements, leaving the concept of metrosexuality to be defined in the next chapter. In order to bring the remaining concepts together, I explore "sports sex" here. By this term I refer to how sports culture conceives of gender and sexuality. I have closely examined an extreme facet of sports culture which goes by the name of "jock culture." Here we find a vivid representation of traditional gender and sexual mythologies. These mythologies circulate in the macrocosm of society and are reflected in the microcosm we designate as sports culture. After explaining what I mean by jock culture as well as gender and sexual mythologies, I explore four aspects of sports sex in order to better grasp the world of sports. These features are sports rape, homosocial desire, and homosexual and heterosexual outings.

Two American studies published in the 1970s attributed names to sports culture, "SportsWorld" and "jock culture." In 1975, columnist and novelist Robert Lipsyte coined the term SportsWorld to characterize "the values of the arena and the locker room [which] have been imposed on our national life" (*SportsWorld* ix). Lipsyte identified these values as toughness, playing by the rules, and an overemphasis on both winning and team spirit. Inspired by Lipsyte's work, Neil D. Isaacs published *Jock Culture, U.S.A.* in 1978. Isaacs's term "jock culture" has remained helpful as a critique of sports culture. He uses it to refer to aggressive drives, dysfunctional players, and violent, destructive behaviors. Thirty years after his initial work on the subject, Lipsyte was still warning readers about the values of jock culture. In *SportsWorld*, he noted that "these values, with their implicit definitions of manhood, courage, and success, are not necessarily in the individual's best interests" (ix). Similar arguments can be found in *Jock: Sports and Male Identity*, a collection of essays dating from the 1970s and edited by Donald F. Sabo Jr. and Ross Runfola. One of the critical assumptions of this book, that "sports shape many undesirable elements of the male role and perpetuate sexist institutions and values" (xvi), effectively summarizes the general reflection of the time on jock culture.

Gender and Sexual Mythologies

It was unusual for the time and perspicacious of Lipsyte to see gender as part of the debate on sports culture. Isaacs noted that "In general, sports serve the political function of maintaining the order of the status quo" (22). Part of this status quo or conservatism, as Lipsyte sensed, concerns respect for a normative definition of manhood. When Lipsyte made reference to "playing by the rules" in his critique of sports culture in the 1970s, he had in mind gender rules as an example. Jock culture offers males normative gender rules. Metrosexuality, on the other hand, proposes nonnormative guidelines, which is why the sports world and metrosexuality seem on the face of it to be diametrically opposed. They offer divergent gender and sexual mythologies. These differences can best be observed by addressing the excesses of jock culture. The great metrosexual paradox is that despite all these seeming incompatibilities, the most celebrated metrosexuals of our time come from sports culture.

Chapter 2 of Brian Pronger's *The Arena of Masculinity* explores the notion of sexual mythology. Pronger designates power as central to differentiating sex from gender. Stating that sex refers to a physiological distinction between male and female, Pronger then makes it clear that "gender is a cultural distinction that divides power between men and women" (48). Such a distinction is expressed by the use of "masculine" to describe the exertion of power and "feminine" to signify the state of disempowerment. This fundamental structuring of patriarchal power leads Pronger to observe that "Gender is a myth that justifies, expresses, and supports the power of men over women" (52).

In his analysis of the sex/gender binary opposition, Pronger borrows the notion of "myth" from Roland Barthes's *Mythologies*. The term refers to "a form of communication, a way of transmitting meaning that fuels the understanding people have of themselves and their culture" (50). Pronger allies myth to what seems "natural, ahistorical, universal" (51). Sexual mythology is therefore a set of beliefs and cultural practices about sexual differentiation, which in Western culture relies on patriarchy. It is through patriarchy that power is attributed to males and withheld from females. Maintaining the idea of a "natural" hierarchical order between the "opposite" sexes, patriarchy grounds itself in the gender myths of masculinity and femininity. The myths respectively designate certain acts, gestures, and behaviors as being "natural" for males or females. Pronger argues that "The gender categories of masculine and feminine are fundamental to the structure of patriarchal power" (52).

After identifying gender myths (accepted beliefs of what constitutes appropriate behavior for males and females), Pronger then introduces the "heterosexual myth," which is based on heteroeroticism and defined as an "erotic interest in gender different from one's own" (64). Like gender itself, the erotic arrangement which enables the mythic power differentiation between males and females to take place is another cultural invention. This is evidenced by the orthodox quality generally attributed to heteroeroticism and withheld from homoeroticism. Pronger defines the latter as "the eroticization of basic gender equality" (70).

As Pronger suggests in his title, sports inhabit a dominant arena where the gender and sexual myths are enacted. For Pronger, the gender myth combines three axes: "physical sex (male/female), sociocultural status (man/woman), and signs of gender (masculine/feminine)" (54). Sports tend to segregate the sexes into distinct teams. Insofar as it is commonly believed that sports help produce "men," there is a close connection between athletic proficiency and masculine gender status. Furthermore, codified rituals on and off the sports terrain are either perceived as "normal" signs of masculinity or, on the contrary, interpreted as feminizing.

Jock Culture

Jock culture allows a close-up look at how sports help reproduce gender myths. Robert Lipsyte is right in specifying that jock culture is a particular problem in sports and that it is not synonymous with sport itself. Using the term "SportsWorld" in 1975, he claimed that jock culture is "a grotesque distortion of sports" (*SportsWorld* xiv). Its values "create a dangerous and grotesque web of ethics and attitudes" (ix). After noting that a boy is initiated into jock culture through sports, Lipsyte specifically defines the culture in terms of behaviors which are physically and mentally unhealthy. These behaviors include machismo, desperate competition, bullying, violence, and being "tough, stoical, and aggressive" ("Surviving" 178). In May 2004, Lipsyte argued before the American Psychiatric Association that "Psychiatry has not taken enough interest in jock culture as a window into other American pathologies" (Hausman 19).

Lipsyte's 2004 text, "Surviving Jock Culture," defines some of the codes of jock culture which are damaging to the individual and society. Here he criticizes the win-at-all-costs imperative, the hypermasculine rituals, and the "bad boys" who are in need of psychological help. Also under fire is the jock's sense of entitlement and the feeling that he is above the law. This is a consequence, no doubt, of blind adulation from fans, coaches, and the media. Lipsyte singles out jock culture's use of homophobia to shame and humiliate players as particularly reprehensible. Going beyond Lipsyte's perspective, Ken Hausman affirms that "The only people that jock culture disparages as much as homosexuals [. . .] are women—an attitude that is fostered early and becomes an entrenched part of life by adulthood" (19).

Using Pronger's analysis of gender myths as a base, I interpret jock culture as a phenomenon which endorses, sustains, and justifies the myths of masculinity and femininity in contemporary Anglo-American cultures. It is a culture founded on the supremacy of males and the subjection of females. It propagates the gender myths, insisting on the "natural" differences between men and women and, finally, it relies on the heterosexual myth, attributing naturalness to heteroeroticism and unnaturalness to homoeroticism.

Sports Rape

A small but not negligible number of athletes attempt to obsessively carry out the gender and sexual myths endorsed by jock culture. Particularly since the turn of the century, sports commentators have been struck by how an increasing number of athletes defy the law with impunity. The codes of jock culture, taken to an extreme limit, are dangerous, antisocial, and occasionally illegal. Jocks who subscribe to its values feel the constant necessity to prove their manhood, masculinity, and heterosexuality. According to jock culture logic, the best way to provide simultaneous proof of all three is for a male athlete to have sexual intercourse with a woman. The more athletes have sexual relations, the more masculine they seem to themselves and to others. Heterosexual conquests are thus equated with manhood, even though such conquests may include rape.

Rape, a particular excess of jock culture, may be seen as an enactment of what Pronger terms the masculinity myth. Pronger argues that "The violent rape of women is the ultimate consummation of the violence inherent in the myth of gender" (65). Pronger links rape to Western culture's gender myths in general by arguing that "It is in [rape] that the mythic power difference between men and women is most clearly realized. It is the debasement of a woman, wherein she is not only made subordinate and brutalized, but is also reduced to a mere object" by a man "in his pursuit of the erotic incarnation of his mythic, masculine power" (65).

Sports rape (rapes committed by athletes) has already been well documented in the United States. One of the major contributors to this documentary effort is lawyer and investigative journalist Jeff Benedict. He is the author of three books outlining the cases, background stories, and sexual abuses inflicted on women by a minority of overpaid and oversexed jocks. His first book, *Public Heroes, Private Felons* (1997), exposes cases of sexual and domestic violence carried out by athletes. Published a year later, *Pros and Cons* provides two substantial sections on rape, while examining the criminal behavior of NFL players. More recently, *Out of Bounds* (2004) explicitly depicts what the subtitle calls "the NBA's Culture of Rape." These three texts provide detailed descriptions of a global phenomenon. A significant number of athletes are taking advantage of their status, money, high prestige, and immediate legal aid to harm or have forcible sexual intercourse with spouses, female partners, or total strangers.

Media coverage of celebrity athletes such as Mike Tyson, O.J. Simpson, and Kobe Bryant has been particularly extensive. This reporting, however, tends to cover up rather than expose the extent of sex crimes perpetrated by athletes. As Benedict discovers in his inquiry into football criminality, it is a phenomenon which is more widespread than commonly imagined. Benedict found that in 1996–1997 over a third of NFL players (509) had criminal histories that he was able to access. Of these 509 players, 109 had been arrested a total of 264 times, mostly for domestic violence and aggravated assault. Benedict thus concluded that one in five NFL players had been charged with a serious crime including rape.

Benedict's 2001–2002 study of the NBA's culture of rape, violence, and crime revealed that 40 percent of all players had been the object of a formal criminal complaint for a serious crime. He checked the criminal records of 177 nonforeign-born NBA players (of a total of 417) and found 71 had been arrested for felonies or misdemeanors. It is a figure which doubles the criminal rate of NFL players. Offenses included rape, assault, and domestic violence. Benedict observed in the case of rape complaints filed against NBA players that "Usually, when a police complaint is filed against an NBA player for rape, the player never ends up being charged, much less convicted" (81).

In Britain there has been similar negative reporting on jock culture's sexual excesses manifested through rape. In October 2003, readers of the *Independent* found an article on soccer titled "No Flowers, Please, for a Game That Lost Its Soul." The author, James Lawton, also added a subtitle which provides a description of the state of the game in early twenty-first-century Britain: "Drink, drugs, violence, cheating, orgies, obsessive gambling, alleged gang rape." Lawton's piece was published shortly after a seventeen-year-old girl accused five soccer players of rape and two others of sexual assault. The case was later dropped due to insufficient evidence.

Equally, in October 2003, a Leeds soccer player allegedly raped a twenty-year-old girl in a car. This was followed by an article in the *Observer* the same month which deplored the culture of excess behind a practice called "roasting" whereby a girl performs oral sex on one partner while another partner has intercourse with her. The article claimed that "Modern footballers are now seen as drunken, debauched and out of control" (Burke, Campbell, and Asthana 16). This claim received further confirmation in March 2004 when several Leicester City soccer players were accused of sexually assaulting three German tourists. All charges were subsequently dropped. Following this renewed media interest in allegations of sports rape, James Lawton returned in 2004 to vent his rage against what he called "this most pampered generation of sportsmen" who were disfiguring a national game ("Football" 56).

In Australia the following year, sports rape aroused similar media interest. After Australian articles described the alleged sexual habits of six rugby players, Peter English in the *Guardian* informed British readers of the "macho culture in Australian sport" (25). It is worth noting that the term "macho culture" is the British and Australian equivalent of the American "jock culture." English drew attention to rape and sexual assault allegations dating back to 2000. Soon afterward, *Independent* journalists Kathy Marks and David Randall titled a March 2004 article "And They Call It the British Disease." The article, later republished in the *Canberra Times*, was subtitled "Jock Culture Is Turning Elite Sportsmen into Animals" ("Why Do Good Sports Turn Bad?"). The journalists condemned the "unquestioned adulation of elite sportsmen" in Australia and the status accorded to British soccer players which "now borders on the religious" (Marks and Randall, "Good Sports" A35). A revealing illustration of the entrenched nature of jock culture in Australia is a statement made by the country's prime minister, John Howard, who was quoted as saying: "At a time like this, I stick up for the game, not put the boot in" (A35). This comment was made after more than twenty rugby and Australian football players had been accused of rape or sexual assault.

Commentators on the global rise of rape, violence, and crime in jock culture all agree on one thing: when society gives inordinate, unquestioned adulation to young, spoiled, testosterone-filled, ego-obsessed athletes, such hero worship is bound to be problematic. If professional sportsmen were not automatically granted star status, paid gross salaries, courted by advertisers, and surrounded by avaricious agents and expert legal teams, perhaps there would be less risk for the women they meet. Whatever the case may be, it remains that jock culture, at its most extreme, objectifies women, condones nonconsensual sexual congress, and congratulates sexual criminals for their aggression. Metrosexuality, on the other hand, sees no reason to objectify women or to render them submissive. Male domination is not prized as a distinguishing characteristic of metrosexual masculinity.

Homosocial Desire

In sports culture, nonnormative sexualities are highly problematic, since sports sex is synonymous with heterosexism and homophobia. Numerous studies have investigated the presence of homophobia in areas such as education and the military. One text published in 2005 also brings sport to the center of the debate. Eric Anderson's *In the Game: Gay Athletes and the Cult of Masculinity* argues that "Sport manages to maintain and reproduce orthodox notions of masculinity that are based on homophobia and misogyny" (74–75). In order to justify the claim concerning homophobia, Anderson offers a number of hypotheses demonstrating "how sport has remained behind the times" (65). This is achieved by reinforcing a single-track vision of sex, gender, and sexuality. Anderson claims that "Sports are a near-total institution in which athletes find it difficult to escape a single-minded way of viewing sex and gender" (66). The "single-minded," exclusionist view espoused by athletes, coaches, and commentators justifies and propagates hatred of difference. It also motivates a rejection of nonheteronormative behaviors.

Paradoxically, sports can also encourage sexual ambiguity. This is because homosocial desire, deprived of the athletic context, can easily be confused with homosexuality. Defined by Eve Kosofsky Sedgwick as "social bonds between persons of the same sex" (1), homosocial desire is reflected in male bonding, a phenomenon typically observed in team sports. Sedgwick, however, posits a "potential unbrokenness of a continuum between homosocial and homosexual" (1), a continuum which sports seek constantly to disrupt by separating the homosocial from the homosexual. Such a disruption, however, is difficult to produce because of a double-bind situation. Sedgwick believes that "For a man to be a man's man is separated only by an invisible, carefully blurred, always-already-crossed line from being 'interested in men'" (89). This double bind helps explain, according to Sedgwick, why football "can look, with only a slight shift of optic, quite startlingly 'homosexual'" (89). This sort of claim has been heard before. In a 1974 interview, Gore Vidal opined: "I can't imagine anyone who was not largely homosexual wanting to be a baseball or a football player, having to live with other boys so much of the time" (237). Vidal's humorous quip concurs with Sedgwick's double-bind theory and suggests they share a similar interpretation of sports sex.

It is useful to compare Sedgwick's work on the homosocial with chapter 6 of Pronger's *The Arena of Masculinity*, "Sex and Sport," which explores the specific domain of sport and what is termed "the homoerotic paradox" (182). Pronger explains this paradox as the encouragement of homosocial behavior in an environment where homophobia is usually rampant. Paradoxically, according to Pronger, "the hierarchy of gender difference compels men to find satisfaction in one another" (178–79), and sports are a principal arena where such pleasure can be found. Jock culture, especially, is bent on trying to disrupt the homosocial/homosexual continuum by forcefully denying that there is a homoerotic dimension in sports and by vilifying the homosexual.

In order to have access to an insider's view of jock culture and the homosocial in sports, it can be helpful looking at Dennis Rodman's first autobiography, *Bad as I Wanna Be*. Here Rodman explores some of the codes of jock culture that he perceived to exist around him during his NBA career. Masculinity for Rodman (as Pronger and Lipsyte theorize) is restricted to being "tough and macho. Everyone's a man's man, tough and mean" (*Bad* 210). In other words, he conveys a gender myth concerning masculinity which has two important consequences for sport: it excludes less virile behaviors and stigmatizes such behaviors as signifying weakness, femininity, or homosexuality. Yet Rodman also underlines the close bodily contact between players on the court by observing that "Man hugs man. Man pats man on ass. Man whispers in man's ear and kisses him on the cheek" (*Bad* 211). Rodman reminds his reader that in the late 1980s Isiah Thomas and Magic Johnson used to openly give each other such kisses before a match. Interpreting these acts as "classic homosexual or bisexual behavior" (*Bad* 211), Rodman endorses academic discourse concerning sport's single-minded way of viewing sex and gender (where in the public imagination such bodily contact is not supposed to erotically arouse, as the male athlete can only be heterosexual). Rodman thus explores the slippery line between being a "man's man" and being "interested in men," while helping us understand how a gay athlete could disturb the heteronormativity of sports sex. Furthermore, Rodman reminds us that a principal technique employed in keeping the homosocial nonsexual is to vilify homosexuality. And, finally, given that jock culture's extreme interpretation of the masculinity myth is indicative of society in general, *Bad as I Wanna Be* suggests why only such a small number of professional male American athletes have declared their homosexuality in the last quarter of a century.

Homosexual Outing

In the three major American team sports, football, basketball, and baseball, only six professional players have stepped forward to be counted as homosexual. Football has three names (David Kopay, Roy Simmons, and Esera Tuaolo), baseball two (Billy Bean and Glenn Burke), and basketball one single name, John Amaechi. All these athletes came out after retiring, thus demonstrating how difficult it is for a gay professional sportsman to be open about his sexuality.

The most recent case of a homosexual outing in the world of American professional sports reveals the seething homophobia that hampers gay athletes from publicly acknowledging their homosexuality during their professional careers. The former NBA player, John Amaechi, played professionally until 2003 when he left the Utah Jazz team. In February 2007, after the launch of his autobiography, *Man in the Middle*, the media relayed comments made by Tim Hardaway, another former NBA player, during a radio interview. Hardaway's vilification of homosexuality is shocking for its hatred and bigotry. He told the radio journalist: "Well, you know I hate gay people, so I let it be known. I don't like gay people and I don't like to be around gay people. I am homophobic. I don't like it. It shouldn't be in the world or in the United States" (Zeigler). This vitriolic excess caused Hardaway to be banned by the NBA from participating in an All-Star event; he lost his job as a sports advisor and a coach. Still, this anti-gay invective provided a message, especially to young people, that homosexuality should be eradicated from sports.

In Britain, a very similar history of ignominy and shame has been attached to gay sportsmen. Only one professional British athlete, soccer player Justin Fashanu, has revealed his homosexuality. In 1990, he sold his story to a tabloid after having successfully sued another newspaper in 1982 for printing gay rumors. Fashanu left Britain in 1995, and then found a job as coach with the team Maryland Mania. He fled the United States in 1998 following allegations of sexual assault. A month later, he hanged himself in London, leaving behind a suicide note containing the words: "Being gay and a personality is so hard" (Clark 124). Not surprisingly, no other active or retired professional athlete has come out in Britain.

The case of another soccer player, Graeme Le Saux, is representative of British sports homophobia. In 1999, a fellow player tried to insult Le Saux by wiggling his bum at him during a match. Le Saux, who was married with a child, persistently attracted "poof" and "faggot" insults. He is said to have been singled out for homophobic vilification ever since he "went away on a camping holiday as a teenager with a male friend, collected antiques and read *The Guardian*" (Stanford 6). The British journalist who quoted this list of "crimes" referred to homophobia in soccer as the "sport's ugliest taboo" (6).

There is every reason to believe that jock culture's homophobic rituals are similar in Australia and Canada. Rugby player Ian Roberts is the only professional athlete to have come out in Australia. This 1995 case has been analyzed elsewhere in discussions of masculinity and sport (Coad 144–48; Miller 72–78). Unlike some of the tragic ends which marked the lives of nearly all the gay professional athletes who outed themselves in the United States and Britain, Roberts's career after leaving the world of rugby has not been marred by ignominy. At last report, he was going his own path after a three-year course in acting and dance at the National Institute of Dramatic Art in Sydney. Olympic gold medalist Mark Tewksbury made his outing in Canada in 1998 after retiring from swimming. He later became copresident of the 2006 World Outgames held in Montreal.

This cross-cultural survey suggests that in different English-speaking countries where metrosexual athletes have been observed, there is a strong reticence on the part of professional sportsmen to publicly identify themselves as homosexual. Such silence concords with the generalized homophobia of the sports world. If we consider that metrosexuality has often been confused with homosexuality, sports culture would logically be an unlikely place to harbor metrosexual males. At the same time, it could be pointed out that the prevalence of homosocial desire in sports is conducive to the development of metrosexuality.

Heterosexual Outing

A sign of jock culture's fear of confusing a man's man and being interested in men can be detected behind the urge that some athletes have to initiate a "heterosexual outing." Modeled on homosexual outings, this recent phenomenon involves high-profile figures who claim heterosexual identity in a public context. Duke Blue Devil center Christian Laettner (who had been taunted by chants of "homo" at games during his university career) started the trend in

1991 by referring to gay rumors in a *Sports Illustrated* article. He later told a news service that he was "definitely straight" (Montre 1C). More assurances about his heterosexual identity were given in an article in *People Magazine* as well as in an ESPN interview.

The Laettner case reveals what can happen to a successful young athlete who rebels against the gender myths of jock culture. Curry Kirkpatrick, the *Sports Illustrated* interviewer, traces rumors of Laettner's reputed homosexuality to the fact that "As a vaguely weird joke designed to shock a few football players, Laettner walked around holding hands with a fellow freshman" (73). The journalist also provides statements made to the press by Laettner and his co-captain roommate, Brian Davis, which added fuel to the controversy. In March 1991, Davis told the *New York Times* that "the two most important things in my life are basketball and Christian [. . .] We know we're not gay [. . .] We [still] can tell each other we love each other" (Kirkpatrick 73). Earlier, the Raleigh *News and Observer* had quoted Christian as saying: "I spend 95 percent of my time with Brian. I don't want anything else; I don't need anything else [. . .] All I want to do is be with Brian" (Kirkpatrick 73). The unusually affectionate language of the two ballplayers effectively draws attention to the difficulty the sports world can have in distinguishing the homosocial from the homoerotic.

During his interview with Kirkpatrick, Laettner highlighted this difficulty through his carefree (some might say "careless") disregard for the expectations of jock culture by observing that "The stereotype of a bigtime athlete is that he's supposed to be able to get a date with anyone he wants and that he 'gets around.' It's stupid. I wasn't doing any of that. I had male friends. I wasn't seen with any females. I had bigger and better things to do. So now it's I 'get around' *and* I'm gay" (73). High-profile jocks (as Laettner and his fans all know) are expected to provide constant visible proof of heterosexuality. And in the absence of girlfriends, a public statement asserting that one is not sexually interested in men is increasingly being judged necessary to offset same-sex suspicions.

While not commenting on the rumors, the *Sports Illustrated* journalist includes in his text a series of descriptions of the "devilishly different" Laettner (the title given to the article), which go against normalized gender expectations concerning a college athlete. From the "moussed curls" (63) of the "sensitive fellow" (64) to the interrogative "Are we talking screaming diva here?" (64) Kirkpatrick's choice of language persists in distancing Laettner from the jock stereotype. Furthermore, the reader is informed that Laettner's roommate introduced him to silk shirts and hairstyling. According to his roommate, Laettner "spends an hour posing in front of the mirror. He knows he's the prettiest man walking" (64). For want of a behavioral term such as metrosexual in the early 1990s, Laettner's stylish good looks and effusive passion for another athlete were interpreted as signs of homosexuality.

In November 1991, Earvin "Magic" Johnson continued the heterosexual coming out trend when he instigated a double outing on the *Arsenio Hall Show*. While publicly announcing his HIV status, Johnson also felt the need to distance himself from some other victims, telling viewers: "I'm far from homosexual. Far from it." The studio audience proceeded to applaud. He reiterated the denial to *Sports Illustrated*: "I have never had a homosexual encounter. Never" (Johnson and Johnson 22). In *Are We Not Men?*, a study of masculine anxiety and African American identity, Phillip Brian Harper provides a detailed reading of the reactions of the media and other NBA players at the time of Johnson's declarations. Harper is right to argue that "the greater purpose of that denial" helped in the "establishment and maintenance of proper masculinity" (23). Likewise, Randy Boyd, a writer for Outsports.com, a Web site devoted to homosexuality and sports, scoffed: "[Magic] had just reassured the straight world that [. . .] he was still a Man."

Johnson gave an interview to the gay and lesbian magazine *The Advocate* in April 1992. He explained his public denial of having had a homosexual experience: "I wanted everybody to know that it wasn't just a gay disease" (Brigham 36–37). He then went on to describe homophobes as "stupid people" (37). However, when asked how NBA players would react to a gay ballplayer, Johnson seemed to proffer homophobic suspicions by suggesting that he believed all homosexual men were sexual marauders on the lookout for prey. He told *The Advocate* interviewer: "It would be tough, I'm sure, because they've always got to shower [together] and that whole thing. They wouldn't know if the guy's going to come on to them or not" (37). This fear of sexual advances from a gay player suggests a negative stereotyping of homosexuality that Johnson seems to have internalized.

Three NFL quarterbacks (Troy Aikman, Kordell Stewart, and Jeff Garcia) and baseball player Mike Piazza have also made public statements insisting that they be identified as heterosexual. Rumors about Aikman's sexuality appeared in a book written by a sports columnist in 1996, prompting the player to characterize such allegations as criminal. In 1999, Stewart reportedly told his fellow players: "You'd better not leave your girlfriends around me, because I'm out to prove a point" (Silver, "In Control" 44, 46). The object of homophobic abuse, Garcia told an interviewer in 2004 that such "knocking" was a sign of jealousy (Buzinski). New York Mets catcher Mike Piazza called a press conference in 2002 to announce his heterosexuality. Piazza's public act seemed to be linked to the suggestion of a newspaper columnist that a top player for the Mets was gay.

The British sports world seems to exert the same type of unrelenting pressure on athletes which ultimately leads to the need for heterosexual outings. Subject to multiple insinuations concerning his sexuality, British world heavyweight champion Lennox Lewis provides a striking illustration of both this need as well as the perfidious extremes of jock culture expectations. (Hasim Rahman, for example, an opponent in a 2001 world title fight, referred to an attempt by Lewis some months before to take legal action over a fight decision as a "gay move"). Annoyed by a succession of homophobic slurs, Lewis retorted in a manner which is as comic as it is degrading. In a desperate attempt to distance himself from homosexuality, the boxer plaintively asked an interviewer, "How can they call me gay? I'm 120 percent a man's man" (Tatchell). Understandably, the confused innuendo arising from what it means to be a "man's man" tended to substantiate the very accusation that Lewis was trying to dispel. Yet his attitude was far less ambiguous when he denigrated homosexuality as being synonymous with weakness and effeminacy.

Human-rights campaigner Peter Tatchell wrote to the boxer to ask him to stop denying these rumors, arguing that this gave the impression that homosexuality was something shameful and degrading. Instead, he advised Lewis to treat homophobes with the contempt they deserved, rather than fall into their game of demeaning homosexuality. Observing the extent to which British sports were homophobic, Tatchell also told the *Guardian* in November 2001 that "There are, today, several top British sports stars who are gay. They worry constantly about being found out [. . .] They lead lonely, miserable lives. Some go to absurd lengths to project a straight image, even to the extent of having phoney girlfriends." The case of Lewis suggests that jock culture always demands a girlfriend in order to "prove" a heterosexual orientation and therefore establish beyond doubt an athlete's manhood.

The tendency in sports culture over the last fifteen years to witness heterosexual outings from certain athletes may point to insecure sexual identity from these players, but more significantly it suggests generalized homophobia, a lack of tolerance concerning nonnormative sexualities, and a confusion between the normative and the normal. In contrast, metrosexuality does not discriminate against homosexuality or insist on heteronormativity. Here we have yet another incongruity in bringing together sports culture and metrosexuality.

The great paradox of jock culture and its interpretation of sports sex is that while subscribing to heteronormativity, it keeps women at bay and keeps the boys together. Jock culture encourages close homosocial contact between males, but will not countenance homosexuality. In order to deflect suspicions of same-sex interests or practices, jock culture constantly denigrates homosexuality as a means to insist on its heteronormativity. This obsessive need to conform and be normative explains why an athlete who is openly homosexual is still a taboo subject in sports culture. Heterosexual outings are strident attempts to subscribe to the gender and sexual mythologies which determine societal norms. Such conformity suggests that sports sex is not just a microcosm of attitudes and behaviors confined to athletes. Sports sex transmits homophobia and misogyny. It highlights and exacerbates ambient gender and sexual mythologies, the function of which is to establish behavioral norms and stigmatize certain gender performances and sexual acts as abnormal. This is the culture which produced the most important models of metrosexuality in the twenty-first century.

2

Metro Sex

The object of this chapter is to begin to explore the possible meanings of metrosexuality. Like other complex concepts, metrosexuality defies easy explanation. A short and concise definition would be inevitably partial and only provide a limited vision of the subject. I propose therefore to analyse the first mention of metrosexuality in the media, trace its pedigree, describe the marketing launch of the concept, and then examine the ensuing backlash it provoked. Following these steps allows us to gain a comprehensive picture of the theory behind metrosexuality. The meanings of the terms "metrosexual" and "metrosexuality" are extensive and multilayered. Consequently, each time these words are used in this book, they necessarily refer to a single aspect or a combination of different aspects, rather than the complete overall picture. It is also helpful to know what metrosexuality is commonly thought to be, but in fact *isn't*. One widely held but mistaken assumption will be addressed in this chapter: the idea that metrosexuality reveals the feminine side of a male. Finally, examining the antimetrosexual backlash can be useful insofar as it allows us to see more clearly what is potentially disturbing about metrosexuality.

Mirror Men

The metrosexual male was first identified and named in November 1994 when the British cultural critic Mark Simpson published "Here Come the Mirror Men" in the *Independent*. This inaugural text gained a wider readership when it reappeared under the new title

"Metrosexuals: Male Vanity Steps Out of the Closet" in Simpson's essay collection *It's a Queer World: Deviant Adventures in Pop Culture* (London 1996; New York 1999). Simpson's article was written to promote another collection of essays, *Male Impersonators: Men Performing Masculinity*, published a short time before. One of the chapters of this volume, "Narcissus Goes Shopping: Homoeroticism and Narcissism in Men's Advertising," bears a close relationship to the contents of the mirror men text. The subtitle of this chapter, as we will see, provides an extremely helpful nexus of ideas that capture some of the possible meanings of metrosexuality.

"Here Come the Mirror Men," as Simpson's title suggests, foregrounds male vanity and male narcissism as two fundamental characteristics of metrosexuality. These qualities are encouraged by activities such as shopping for clothes, accessorizing, and using body products. For Simpson, attention to appearance and self-care are central to metrosexuality. He saw advertising and the men's style press playing an important role in enticing males to become consumers. A partial definition is provided in this initial exploration to show the pertinence of the prefix "metro." Simpson defines a metrosexual male as a "single young man with a high disposable income, living or working in the city" ("Metrosexuals" 207). This attempt to describe metrosexuality brings together consumerist males under the age of thirty and the metropolis, a site where the mirror man can show off and attract attention.

For the next six years, discussion about metrosexuality lay dormant until Simpson revitalized the term in July 2002. He posted "Meet the Metrosexual" on Salon.com, an extremely popular American online magazine. Repostings of this article over the Internet thrust metrosexuality into the limelight internationally. This widely read text firmly and irrevocably attached the phenomenon to one particular individual, David Beckham. In so doing, Simpson also linked metrosexuality to one particular domain, sports culture. In designating the then captain of the England soccer team as "the biggest metrosexual in Britain," Simpson importantly drew attention to the potential compatibility between sports and metrosexuality.

In the Salon.com text, two facets of metrosexuality previously mentioned in the 1994 article were again highlighted, thereby consolidating their significance. The first links metrosexuality with homosexuality, not in terms of sexual preference, but as a lifestyle. This all-important distinction between sexual orientation and lifestyle became lost in the minds of many future critics of metrosexuality. By "gay lifestyle" Simpson meant commoditizing masculinity to vain urban males who were single. This is why he stated in the Salon.com text that "Gay men did, after all, provide the early proto-type for metrosexuality." He was referring to the accessorizing of masculinity through the clone look in the 1970s. Careful not to imply that metrosexuals were all gay men, Simpson clearly stated in the same article that metrosexual males might be "officially gay, straight or bisexual." Even if the sexual orientation of metrosexual males was immaterial for Simpson, he still believed that metrosexuality was inspired from a commercial model previously tested with success on gay men.

The second idea reiterated in the Salon.com posting emphasizes the extent to which metrosexual males especially liked being looked at. Beckham was nominated as the country's most prominent metrosexual "because he loves being looked at and because so many men and women love to look at him." By highlighting the looked-at-ness of metrosexual males, Simpson again moved metrosexuality away from heterosexuality and helped establish another commonality with homosexuality. In the 1994 *Independent* article Simpson contended that "the metrosexual man contradicts the basic premise of traditional heterosexuality—that only women are looked at and only men do the looking" ("Metrosexuals" 209). Because metrosexuality and homosexuality both hold up the male as the object of desire and the gaze, Simpson saw in metrosexuality something even queerer than a heterosexual version of the "gay lifestyle."

The links between metrosexuality and homosexuality had already been examined in chapter 5 of *Male Impersonators*. This is arguably Simpson's most extended reflection on metrosexuality, despite the fact that it predates his first use of the term. In analyzing Narcissus as he goes shopping, the author concentrated on the implicit homoeroticism of men's advertising from the mid-1980s to the mid-1990s. Pursuing this line of enquiry allowed Simpson to demonstrate that metrosexuality was *already* in operation during this decade. He was also further consolidating the underlying queerness of metrosexuality.

Simpson's chapter on Narcissus shopping begins with the Nick Kamen Levi's television commercials, "Bath" and "Launderette," first shown on Boxing Day 1985. These ads inaugurated a new way of looking at the male body in British advertising. At the time the Kamen Levi's commercials were broadcast, other writers noticed their revolutionary innovation. After observing Kamen flaunt his body, strip to his boxers, and immerse his jeans in a bath, television critic George Melly claimed that the model was "really pushing it" (41). He situated the advertisement as part of a recent trend by noticing that "Lately, however, a totally new development has surfaced—the use of men as passive sex objects" (41). The overtly erotic use of a male body in publicity led Melly to conclude that "These ads are aimed equally at both sexes. Either way, there is no question that this method of presenting beefcake is strongly voyeuristic" (41).

Melly's comment is significant because ten years before the term metrosexuality was coined, he was inadvertently helping to formulate some of its defining qualities. Like Simpson, Melly is intrigued by the looked-at-ness of males. The use of the term "beefcake" (meaning a sexually attractive denuded representation of a male body) instead of Narcissus, or "mirror man," draws attention to the male subject as the object of the desire and the gaze of women and other men. Simpson's assertion that Kamen "is single, unafraid, flouting responsibility and passively inviting our gaze: he is 'queer'—his sexuality is outside regulation" (*Male* 99) confirms and extends Melly's observations. It also provides a useful starting point to discuss metrosexuality in general.

These texts published by Mark Simpson in 1994 and 2002 constitute the theoretical cornerstone of metrosexuality. They contain the major themes that reappear throughout his future reflection on the subject. Simpson's principal standpoint is clearly expressed in "MetroDaddy Speaks," an article posted on Salon.com in January 2004. Here the author forcefully reaffirmed that metrosexuality "'queers' all the codes of official masculinity of the last hundred years." This queering can be demonstrated in three ways: "It's passive where it should always be active, desired where it should always be desiring, looked at where it should always be looking." In this formulation we possibly have Simpson's most successful attempt at grasping the essential characteristics of metrosexuality.

Dandies

If we turn from the birth of metrosexuality as a term of cultural debate and begin to examine its pedigree, we find that one of the most common words used by journalists to help explain "metrosexual" has been "dandy." Press coverage of males who have been described as metrosexuals continues to describe them as dandies. This overlap suggests that the terms are synonymous. Consequently, their partial commonality will be analyzed here with the intent of better understanding not only what makes a metrosexual athlete, but how the very nature of being an athlete makes him different from a dandy. The parallel with dandyism is useful in order to demonstrate how a dandy and a metrosexual are *not* the same thing despite obvious similarities.

Historically, dandyism was cultivated in England and France. Regency England produced the template for modern dandyism, George "Beau" Brummell (1778–1840). Dandyism had previously blossomed in England during the Elizabethan Age, flourished in the Restoration Period, and in the 1770s bore fruit with the arrival of macaronis (fashionable men with an extravagant hair style). Regency dandies, other than Brummell, included the Prince Regent, Lord Byron, and a host of eccentric aristocrats. Across the Channel, prominent nineteenth-century dandies were French literary figures such as Balzac and Baudelaire. Dandyism was revived on both sides of the Channel during the decadent *fin de siècle* when Oscar Wilde and some of his coterie turned the lifestyle into an art. The twentieth century had its own notable dandies, among whom we find Ronald Firbank, Cecil Beaton, and Noel Coward.

Authority George Walden defines dandyism as "vanity, frivolity, hedonism, a preoccupation with externals and above all a posture of ironic detachment from the world" (35). For Walden, the three essential dandiacal characteristics, impertinence, nihilism, and provocation, depend on male autonomy. Stephen Robins's *How to Be a Complete Dandy* also helps to define the concept through a compilation of quotations on the subject. Subtitles in chapter 2, "The Rules of Dandyism," provide a useful guide. Robins lists, for example, artifice, lying, taste, originality, style, self-love, idling, hedonism, wit, dress, and fashion as typical tenets of dandyism.

When journalists use the term "dandy" to describe metrosexual males, they are undoubtedly using a meaning restricted more or less to the idea of sartorial elegance (as in the case of David Beckham). Walden explains that this is due to a dandy's being "most immediately recognisable by the fanatical care he or she takes with their appearance" (36). Walden goes on to describe the modern dandy as "a stylish creature, ultra-conscious of clothes" (46). While these definitions

Loan Receipt

Library Services
Liverpool John Moores University

Borrower: Traynor, Thalia LSATTRAY

Loaned today:

The metrosexual : gender, sexuality and
sport /
31111012251649
Due Date: 02/03/2020 23:59:00 GMT

Total items loaned today: 1

Library charges: £0.00 GBP
Overdue items: 0
Total items on loan: 1

23/02/2020 17:12

Please keep your receipt in case of
dispute.

apply to dandyism, the same may be said for metrosexuality, thereby accounting for some of the present confusion between the two terms. This fanatical concern for appearance, shared by the dandy and the metrosexual, is at times expressed as vanity. Barbey d'Aurevilly began chapter 1 of *On Dandyism and George Brummell* (1844) with an attempt to reclaim vanity from its place among the minor vices. He pithily apostrophizes dandyism as "that child of vanity" (Walden 70) and, careful to differentiate it from fatuity, simply states that dandyism is "English vanity" (72). This characteristic helps explain why some athletes known for their preoccupation with appearance (such as Jim Palmer and David Beckham) have been occasionally asked by journalists if they are vain.

The stem of the word "metrosexual" foregrounds the city, a site where males can indulge in self-display and gazing. This urban environment provides a descriptive element of both dandyism and metrosexuality. One explanation for this can be found in the opportunity the city provides its dwellers for *flânerie*. This French term, usually translated as "strolling" or "loafing," is favored by the idle, tasteful male. Walter Benjamin, the German philosopher and cultural critic, described the *flâneur* leisurely walking in the Haussmann-designed arcades and spacious boulevards of Paris. In *The Painter of Modern Life* (1863), Baudelaire combined the figure of the dandy (he who displays himself) with the *flâneur* (he who gazes upon others). In this context, Jon Stratton is correct to privilege gazing as best defining the urban stroller. He argues that "Whilst the *flâneur* was sometimes also a dandy, the key difference to *flânerie* was the activity of gazing" (94).

There is a general suspicion that both the dandy and the metrosexual are homosexual. Regency dandies exhibited predominantly heterosexual inclinations, although this was not the case for many subsequent famous dandies. Walden attempts to allay suspicions concerning sexuality by declaring that "Dandyism in its essence is not a homosexual condition" (45). The same claim might be made for metrosexuality. However, despite the fact that metrosexuality caters to multiple sexual identities, there is always a hankering suspicion that metrosexualization and same-sex practices go hand in hand, like Oscar and Bosie. Simpson himself comments on the "relaxed, faggoty, submissive metrosexuality of David Beckham," which he finds "a trifle distasteful," when it is not "downright nauseating" ("Meet"). Critics of metrosexuality often interpret it as a euphemism for homosexuality.

A major characteristic not shared by the dandy and the metrosexual is found in the role of sport. The idling and *ennui* of the confirmed dandy prevent him from indulging in any kind of athletic
competition. Oscar Wilde supposedly said that "Football is all
very well a good game for rough girls, but not for delicate boys."
In *How to Be a Complete Dandy*, Robins similarly claims that "The
dandy detests soccer" (55). There would seem to be a significant
problem in identifying athletes as dandies, since, according to
dandy rules, sports are to be eschewed. This incompatibility partly
explains why Walden, unlike many journalists, disqualifies David
Beckham from being a fully fledged dandy. In *Who Is a Dandy?* he
opines that "Beckham enjoys dressing up, but this family man and
team-player is too straightforward a fellow to be a dandy in the
true sense" (53). According to Walden, other characteristics defining the dandy are also markedly absent in the soccer player's behavior, notably wit, ironic detachment from the world, and good
taste. All the same, Beckham's spectacular vanity and narcissism
induce others to feel that he justifies the label dandy. Furthermore,
he exhibits favorite dandiacal characteristics such as rapid upward mobility, conspicuous consumption, and appreciation for extravagant luxury.

Outwardly, there are numerous characteristics shared by traditional dandies and contemporary metrosexual males: sartorial elegance, vanity, and urban *flânerie*. Both groups also tend to exhibit an
extravagant lifestyle. However, when it comes to describing a stylish
athlete, despite its seeming appropriateness, the term dandy remains inadequate. A dandiacal sportsman is a contradiction in
terms. Metrosexual is a far more suitable word to use than dandy to
describe an elegant sportsman, since metrosexuality has no problem
with athletic competition. Rather than give pride of place to nonath-
letic aesthetes, metrosexuality holds up the sportsman as a hero and
a behavioral model.

Playboys

Although the lexical and dandiacal origins of metrosexuality are located in the lavender land of Wilde and Simpson, it is in the United
States that we find the most influential early precursors of today's
metrosexuals. It is useful to analyze the American pedigree of the

metrosexual male in order to foreground the notions of leisure and hedonism, two more characteristics of metrosexuality.

In 2003, Bill Osgerby contributed a chapter to a study of masculinity and men's lifestyle magazines in an attempt to correct the somewhat restricted focus of the 1990s British debate on male consumerism. This debate implied that Britain pioneered an innovative approach to male urban consumption. The chapter entitled "A Pedigree of the Consuming Male: Masculinity, Consumption and the American 'Leisure Class'" (Osgerby 57–85) is inspired by the writer's full-length study of masculinity, youth, and leisure-style in twentieth-century America, *Playboys in Paradise*. In both these texts, Osgerby convincingly argues that the idea of the consuming male "had already taken shape a hundred years earlier and had become clearly recognized in America by the 1930s" ("Pedigree" 58). Osgerby provides historical American consumer models, which include the urban bachelor (dating from the end of the nineteenth century and embodied by the "dude" figure), the "Arrow Man," the Jazz Age Gatsby buck, and the gangster. All these types of consumption need to be included in an examination of the origins of the hedonistic American consumer who, after Simpson, would be dubbed a metrosexual.

Twenty years before Thorstein Veblen theorized notions of conspicuous leisure, conspicuous waste, and conspicuous consumption in his 1899 classic, *The Theory of the Leisure Class*, the dude was satirized in American 1880s trade cards for his effete flamboyance and "foppish vanity" ("Pedigree" 62). Osgerby defines the dude as "a young man, upwardly mobile and debonair, who sauntered through the bustling city streets" (62). Similar to the European *flâneur*, the dude even gave his name to Chester Allan Arthur, the American president from 1881 to 1885, who was known as "Dude President." At the turn of the century, an image used in advertising known as the "Arrow Man" symbolized a new leisure-oriented male intent on wearing stylish shirts which had previously only been worn for sport. This was the beginning of the "Ivy League" style of dressing, characterized by a "smart-but-casual combination of button-down shirts, chino slacks, letter sweaters, cardigans and loafers" (65). After the First World War, the gangster image introduced a new sartorial model represented by "expensive suits, tuxedos, spats and jewelry" (64). In the 1920s, Gatsby-style playboys incarnated what Osgerby refers to as "a new masculine style defined by a sense of youthful and narcissistic hedonism" (65).

Metrosexuality perpetuates this long tradition of stylish, pleasure-loving American playboys. When Michael Flocker, the author of *The Metrosexual Guide to Style* (2003), went on to publish *The Hedonism Handbook: Mastering the Lost Arts of Leisure and Pleasure* in 2004, he was highlighting the playboy ethic as one of the facets of metrosexuality and showing its continued relevance, especially in an American context.

Feminine Side

Now that Simpson's theorization of metrosexuality has been examined and the metrosexual pedigree situated in the figures of the dandy and the playboy, I want to approach the meaning of metrosexuality from a different angle. Since June 2003, when the media took an intense interest in metrosexuality, it has been common to find a shorthand summary of the phenomenon which has circulated widely and gained general acceptance as a trustworthy definition. This attempt to identify the essence of metrosexuality and reduce its meanings to one easily understandable phrase began when two simultaneous studies were released by the global marketing and communications agency, Euro RSCG Worldwide. The results were made available in a twenty-page report under the title "The Future of Men: U.S.A." An almost identical survey "The Future of Men: U.K." was carried out in Britain at the same time. These studies are of prime importance for two reasons. First, this agency was the principal commercial driving force behind metrosexuality, thus demonstrating metrosexuality's strong ties with finding profit in new markets. Second, the agency offered a nonacademic definition of metrosexuality which quickly gained credence everywhere. Reproducing the simplified and distorted claims expressed in the agency's surveys, many journalists worldwide unwittingly helped to propagate ideas about metrosexuality which were based on popular psychology. When Simpson wrote *Male Impersonators* and the follow-up article "Mirror Men," he was influenced by gender theory, not popular psychology. Euro RSCG fabricated a new and highly problematic meaning of metrosexuality, which bore little resemblance to Simpson's original theorization.

Although Simpson's name appears nowhere in the RSCG reports, its authors later informed the British writer that their source of inspiration had been the Salon.com text "Meet the Metrosexual." In this article, Simpson clearly stated that a metrosexual male might assume a variety of sexual orientations. However, this fundamental feature of the meaning was ignored by the communications agency. It seems clear that the principal idea behind the RSCG reports was to target male heterosexuals. Metrosexuals, the agency believed, were exclusively heterosexual males with money to spend (like David Beckham, mentioned early on in the British report). This preoccupation with heterosexuality explains why Euro RSCG Worldwide restricted the meaning of metrosexuality to characterize "men [who] are primarily urban, heterosexual, well educated, and on easy terms with women and feminine ways" (Euro U.S. 3). This definition shows a desire to link metrosexuality with a monolithic normative sexuality and in so doing iron out anything queer as being irrelevant to the subject. A comparison with earlier definitions of metrosexuality reveals that Simpson and Euro RSCG agreed on only one thing, the urban framework. RSCG excluded the nonheterosexual from its frame of reference and ignored or at least failed to recognize the underlying queerness of metrosexuality. In contrast, this is exactly what Simpson had been so intent on pointing out.

Excluding the queer from metrosexuality is especially discernible in the fact that some journalists, reporting on the RSCG findings, incorrectly informed their readers that "metrosexual" was a combination of "metropolitan" and "heterosexual." *Le Monde,* a major French newspaper, offered such a spurious definition in January 2004 (Lorelle 26) as did the September 2005 issue of *Femme en Ville,* a magazine offered to shoppers in one of Paris's largest department stores. Gina Scala's article informed readers that metrosexual males exhibit their femininity, before blithely announcing that the new term derived from a contraction of "metropolitan" and "heterosexual." Scala was justified in explaining that these "new men" express attitudes which hitherto had been seen as exclusively feminine, but she overstepped the mark by claiming that metrosexuals were "*100% hétéro*" (28). Reducing metrosexuality to straightness is not just "slightly silly," as Simpson commented in "MetroDaddy Speaks." It is also slightly homophobic.

The last part of the RSCG definition, "on easy terms with women and feminine ways," is more succinctly expressed elsewhere in the reports by the enigmatic expression "feminine side." The first sentence of the American study declares that "American men in 2003 are embracing their feminine sides" (Euro U.S. 2). After crediting Beckham with having explored "the feminine side of his nature" (Euro U.K. 3), the British report affirms that the sentiments of the male population in general mirror what is happening in the United States. It asserts that "British men in 2003 are feeling comfortable [. . .] with their feminine sides" (Euro U.K. 4). This observation constituted for Euro RSCG Worldwide *the* defining characteristic of the "new type of male" (Euro U.K. 3) who was identified as metrosexual.

RSCG vastly reduced the potential cultural importance of metrosexuality by inventing a "feminine side" theory. This fable credited by the marketing agency was picked up globally and afterward served up as the principal meaning of metrosexuality. From New York to London, passing by New Delhi, the message was repeated that the metrosexual male was a feminized male. Writing for the *New York Times*, Warren St. John referred to "this new type of feminized man" (1). Angelique Chrisafis endorsed the same point of view in the *Guardian* when she wrote that a metrosexual male "struggles to take on feminine characteristics" (6). Himanshu Verma published a pamphlet in India, *The Metrosexuals*, which reiterated the dictum, informing readers that the metrosexual "is not afraid to embrace his feminine side" (3). Beckham provided RSCG with ammunition in his 2000 biography by stating: "I'm not scared of my feminine side and I think quite a lot of the things I do come from that side of my character" (95). Even Michael Flocker's successful, prometrosexual guidebook, *The Metrosexual Guide to Style*, repeats the same idea. Just inside the front cover, Flocker offers a "man willing to embrace his feminine side" as the final definition of his subject. The "feminine side" theory became so widespread that Mark Simpson addressed the issue in "MetroDaddy Speaks." For him, this expression was simply a euphemism, or "polite version" of yet another "laughably mistaken notion," the idea that "gay men are by definition in touch with their feminine sides."

A 1997 interview with Dennis Rodman published in *The Advocate* provides evidence of this widespread conflation between homosexuality and femininity. It also demonstrates a commonly held belief in gender "sides." Before transcribing the conversation, Peter Galvin muses, "Who among us doesn't imagine being able to explore the depths of both our masculine and feminine sides, without fear of oppression?" (28). This rhetorical question prepares the reader for a series of queries aimed at Rodman, who is asked, "Why do you have the courage to explore your feminine side so openly in public?" (28).

Rodman falls into line by replying that "Every man has a feminine side. Any man that says he don't is a liar" (28).

Part of the problem with the expression "feminine side" appears when we look at the prevailing tendency of this conversation. Apart from an almost incidental interest in cross-dressing in the interview, the main subject is Rodman's homosexual inclinations. This explains why the *Advocate* cover promises "The GAY interview." Most of the conversation concerns the athlete's homoerotic fantasies. Given the subject of discussion, the reader is left to deduce that homosexuality must also be the expression of a man's feminine side. Interviewer and interviewee imply that the dyed hair and flashy clothes are as much a manifestation of Rodman's homosexual desires as his femininity. This is more than problematic, since it presupposes that femininity and homosexuality are synonymous. To consider same-sex desire as an indication of a male's femininity reflects a century-old discourse that no longer finds credibility, except in the most backward of quarters. Despite Rodman's clear-sighted observations in his biography concerning the nonnormative behaviors of athletes, his *Advocate* interview reinforces the stereotypical association of femininity and cross-dressing with same-sex desire.

There are two main problems attached to this continued use of the word "side" in combination with gender. One difficulty is that it is far too concrete a term to describe what is more aptly perceived as a performance or a citing of rituals. Gender is a "doing," not a state of inner being. The word "side" makes the acquisition of gender too biological by implying that there are two sides of the brain or psyche, one masculine, the other feminine. The other problem is Euro RSCG's parallel claim that no athlete, or any male for that matter, need prove his manhood. In this light, we understand why Beckham served as a perfect model of metrosexuality. As Beckham was married, had fathered children, and shown skill on the soccer pitch, it was easy, contends RSCG, to amass a series of "proofs" asserting the uncontested masculinity of the star.

In a key 1991 essay later anthologized as a cornerstone of queer theory, "Imitation and Gender Insubordination," Judith Butler describes gender as a "performance" or an "effect," rather than a preexisting psychic reality. Butler claims that "all gendering is a kind of impersonation and approximation" (21). She argues against "a predisposition to think of sexuality and gender as 'expressing' in some indirect or direct way a psychic reality that precedes it" (24).

Following this argument, masculinity and femininity are based on the compulsive repetition of rituals, or can best be explained as "theatrically produced effects" (21). They are not ontological realities. Gender is not something you *are*. Instead, it is a process, an act, a *doing*. If this is the case, speaking about gender in terms of a "side" is inappropriate for two reasons. First, it assumes that masculinity and femininity are preexisting psychic or somatic realities. Second, it presupposes that there is a stable connection between males and masculinity, or between females and femininity. Butler questions this naturalized relationship between sex and gender.

The RSCG reports imply that after performing a sufficient number of masculinity rituals, a male can by common accord be declared a "man." This explains why RSCG can announce that Beckham has no need to prove his manhood. Butler, however, argues just the opposite. All males, especially athletes, need to prove their masculinity through a compulsive and compulsory citation of various acts, performances, or rituals. A "man" is a becoming, not an achievable end result. To suggest that a male who has achieved sufficient confidence in his "masculine side" can then give expression to his "feminine side" is untenable from Butler's point of view. There are no "sides" and such confidence in manhood is a delusion.

For RSCG, metrosexuals are exclusively heterosexual males who exteriorize their feminine sides by spending "a lot of time getting themselves to look, smell, and feel attractive" (Euro U.K. 6). Like women, they "take pleasure in shopping" (Euro U.K. 6). According to the advertising agency, all these characteristics are naturally feminine. This amounts to what is known as "essentialism." Such a term signifies the belief in inherent traits which acquire a fixed masculine or feminine connotation over the generations. For RSCG, shopping *is* feminine and men who shop *are* feminized because everyone agrees that shopping is essentially linked to women. While such an activity can acquire a gendered meaning in a particular place at a particular time, to assign one specific gender to a ritual denies historical and cultural differences.

The supposition that shopping has historically only been carried out by women is questionable. Bill Osgerby's texts address a binary opposition informing previous cultural studies. According to this opposition, production, work, and responsibility have traditionally defined masculine identities, while consumption, display, and pleasure are the hallmarks of conventional femininity. Rachel Bowlby's work on consumer culture would seem to concur with this perspective. She argues that "the history of shopping is largely a history of women, who have overwhelmingly been the principal shoppers both in reality and in the multifarious representations of shopping" (7). Osgerby, on the other hand, is careful to point out that despite such a historic association, "it would be misleading to see [consumerism and its pleasures] as a field from which men have been totally (or even largely) excluded" (60). Osgerby's critique is also justified by other research. One representative case is *The Hidden Consumer*, Christopher Breward's study of masculinities, fashion, and city life in Britain from 1860 to 1914. Like Osgerby, Breward argues that "masculine consumption habits have been effectively obscured by an uncritical explanation of the separate-spheres ideology" (9). It would be more exact then to consider the list of "feminine" traits given by RSCG as signifying *human* characteristics. They do not constitute femininity.

In 2005, the authors of the RSCG reports together published a follow-up to their reflections expressed two years earlier. In *The Future of Men*, Marian Salzman, Ira Matathia, and Ann O'Reilly acknowledge that they have a conception of metrosexuality which diverges from Mark Simpson's formulations on the subject. Everyone agrees that vanity is an essential characteristic. However, Salzman and her team accuse Simpson of pairing it with pretense. This is unwarranted as Simpson suggested no such thing. Salzman and her marketing team posit instead that metrosexuality is "more about the strength to be true to oneself" (55). This comment subsequently provokes another observation concerning metrosexuality, which is unusually acute given the previous simplifying of the subject by the authors of the RSCG reports. Sensing that metrosexuality has strong links with revising gender mythologies, Salzman, Matathia, and O'Reilly suggest that "Rather than adhere to the strictures of their father's generation, [metrosexuals] are willing to move beyond rigid gender roles and pursue their interests and fancies regardless of societal pressures against them" (56). This observation, as I will later demonstrate, is more than justified as an appraisal of the wider repercussions concerning metrosexuality.

Despite this ability to see that metrosexuality can signify a desire to go beyond binary oppositions based on gender, the authors of *The Future of Men* persisted in propagating two limiting and mistaken ideas: metrosexual males embrace their femininity and metrosexuality is synonymous with heterosexuality. Metrosexual males do attempt to be true to themselves, even if this means a disregard for gender norms. But this defiance of convention should not be equated with feminization. Choosing David Beckham to typify metrosexuality, the writers of the RSCG reports hoped to attach metrosexuality exclusively to heteronormativity and deprive it of any links with homosexuality. Using exactly the same athlete, I will demonstrate the underlying queerness of metrosexuality in chapter 8.

Backlash

Almost as soon as the New York media storm informed the world about metrosexuality in mid-2003, metrophobic sentiments were relayed by grumbling, sometimes irate die-hards of both sexes. These people yearned and yearn for a premetrosexual paradise where you can supposedly tell the difference between a "real" man and a male who owns a moisturizer. It can be useful to analyze antimetrosexual feeling, as it helps extend the definitional parameters of metrosexuality.

A representative example of the antimetrosexual backlash was posted in September 2003 on the Web site Cruxnews.com by executive editor Michael S. Rose. This was just three months after the news broke that America had been visited by metromania. Rose's "Metrosexual Goes America" contained a mostly fair summary of the roles played by Simpson and RSCG in bringing metrosexuality to the attention of the world. However, when Rose came to his "bottom line" conclusion, he protested with vigor against what he saw as a serious cultural threat. He stated that "the metrosexual is nothing more than a feminized man—effete, insecure, and socially emasculated—seeking to re-empower himself in a world in which the sexes are artificially converging." Rose also contended that metrosexuality was "specifically an assault on masculine integrity, but no less an assault on human sexuality in general." He proceeded to voice his final objection by deploring that "the complementarity [*sic*] of the sexes, male and female, is being eroded by cultural influences in the world of fashion marketeering."

In order to address Rose's objections to metrosexuality, it is useful to recall chapter 1 where I analyzed the gender and sexual mythologies critiqued by Brian Pronger. Such mythologies, as Pronger demonstrates, are built on and encourage the subjection of women.

If, as Rose implies, all males are strong, rational, natural providers (and poor shoppers), while females are natural mothers, cooks, and "mindless consumers" overconcerned about their appearance, the next step is to attribute power and privilege to all men. Let the ladies get on with the housework—and their shopping. Rose's objections to metrosexuality thus rely on a sexist vision of the world. This attitude accounts for his dislike of any convergence between the sexes and explains his need to insist on sexual and gender differentiation. Resemblances between men and women and gender trouble are seen to threaten the "natural" hierarchy which gives power and authority to one sex, males. Following Rose's logic, when men turn into metrosexuals, they start acting like women. This is why he uses words such as "effete" and "feminized." The "natural" gender order is thus disturbed. Rose subscribes to a stable alignment between sex, gender, and sexuality. In objecting to metrosexuality's disruption of this alignment, he supports a sexual politics which privileges the power of men and discriminates against women who are deprived of power.

It is ironic that Rose thinks it appropriate to attack metrosexuals for being socially emasculated. This is because popular style guidebooks show how metrosexuality can be quite the opposite. Michael Flocker's *The Metrosexual Guide to Style* is a notable example. This guide advises the metrosexual wannabe in the following domains: general etiquette, wine and cocktails, dining out, art and culture, music, books and films, fashion and personal style, good grooming, body and fitness, sex and romance, home décor, and what is called "the metrosexual mindset." Likewise, the guidebook produced by the *Queer Eye for the Straight Guy* Fab Five team, published in New York and London, advises readers on food and wine, grooming, decorating, fashion, and culture. These manuals of manners demonstrate an aspect of metrosexuality that seems to have gone unnoticed by Rose.

In the introduction to his guidebook, Flocker counters Rose's "insecure" accusation by arguing just the opposite. He contends that "The new breed of man [. . .] is just as strong and confident as his predecessor [. . .]. Secure in his masculinity, he no longer has to spend his life defending it" (xiii). It would seem that Flocker has not read queer theory either. Like Rose, he implies that gender security is possible. But this is untenable if we consider, along with Butler, that all gender acquisition is based upon more or less failed imitation and approximation of an unattainable ideal. Flocker also indirectly suggests that a metrosexual is a male who has already convinced himself and others that he is a "man" (contra Butler who considers this to be a cultural fantasy) and then branches out on the gender smorgasbord by dipping into femininity. To equate metrosexuality with optional femininity for males is to vastly restrict its multifarious meanings and implications.

Rose's criticism concerning an assault on masculine integrity is helpful, as it highlights what I see as an essential characteristic of metrosexuality. Along with others, Rose is uneasy about the objectified and passive looked-at-ness of metrosexual males. As Laura Mulvey notes, such characteristics destabilize a sexist subject position that insists on men's status as bearers of a gaze traditionally directed at women. Mulvey made this important distinction between women as objects looked at and men as bearers of the gaze in her 1975 essay "Visual Pleasure and Narrative Cinema." It is in this essay that the idea of "looked-at-ness" was first theorized. Mulvey addresses the traditional, exhibitionist role of women, who "are simultaneously looked at and displayed, with their appearance coded for strong visual and erotic impact so that they can be said to connote *to-be-looked-at-ness*" (27). Mulvey further argues that in the cinema, "the male figure cannot bear the burden of sexual objectification. Man is reluctant to gaze at his exhibitionist like" (28) because of the homoerotic implications of an all-male gaze.

Metrosexuality, as Simpson stated right from the start, is about upsetting the heterosexualized visual norm that Mulvey identified as traditionally operating in films. Metrosexuality offers males roles which the likes of Rose have ascribed exclusively to women: vanity, narcissism, exhibitionism, and passivity in front of the male gaze. Rose is uncomfortable with the idea that males can also be desired. This exhibitionist, spectacularized display of masculinity goes further than males simply offering their bodies to be looked at or photographed. The metrosexual male is not just desirable; he is fuckable. In "Meet the Metrosexual," Simpson similarly argued that "the exhibitionism of male metrosexuality is literally asking to be fucked." He is absolutely right on this point. The horror of male sexual passivity and men as potential objects of the male gaze explains Rose's fear that the metrosexual is an assault on masculine integrity and an assault on "human sexuality," by which he means heterosexuality.

✑

Although it can be argued that metrosexuality concerns gender and sexuality in the general senses of the terms, it can also signify an attempt to go beyond the constrictive bipolar categorizations created by the masculine/feminine and hetero/homo divides. From this point of view, metrosexuality can be unhinged from gender and sexuality to become an asexual personal aesthetic. In other words, it is a lifestyle or an art of living. This explains why metrosexuality lends itself so easily to men's lifestyle magazines and constitutes the basis for makeover or "make-better" television programs. In this sense, metrosexuality can be practiced by both sexes.

The introduction to the *Queer Eye* guidebook makes clear the nongendered and asexual aspects of metrosexuality. It affirms that "knowing how to dress better, how to behave better, how to look, cook and live better . . . these aren't girly topics. They're *human* topics" (Allen 12). The executive producers of the show share this opinion. In the foreword to the guidebook, David Metzler and David Collins state that "It's not gay or straight to want to look good and feel good about yourself" (9). In an attempt to dissociate metrosexuality from homosexuality (demonstrating at the same time how it can apply to women as well), the Fab Five explain that "A queer 'eye' doesn't mean a queer look. It's a point of view, a receptiveness to looking at what works and what doesn't [. . .] It's an openness to what's stylish and fun" (12). It is noteworthy that this definition of metrosexuality uses terms such as "receptiveness" and "openness" which, because of their sexual connotations, take us back to the passivity so dreaded by Rose. This demonstrates the difficulty and the necessity of dissociating metrosexuality from gender and sexuality.

Paradoxically, it is study of sexuality that allows us to perceive the historic breadth of metrosexuality and at the same time observe its status as an asexual art of existence. The third volume of Michel Foucault's unfinished history of sexuality is entitled *The Care of the Self*. The second part of this book is devoted to the Hellenistic idea of "The Cultivation of the Self," a philosophical tradition that can be traced back to Socrates. Foucault examines links with the Roman practice of *cura sui* (taking care of oneself) during the first two centuries of the Christian era, a "golden age in the cultivation of the self" (45). Metrosexuality can be seen as a modern version of this human desire for care and cultivation of the self. The glaring difference when comparing modern metrosexual adaptations of self-care with their ancient equivalents is, of course, the absence of any spiritual dimension. Care of the soul was a vital component of the Hellenistic and Roman conceptions of self-cultivation. In contrast, metrosexuality is restricted to a corporeal and commodity-centered interpretation of the age-old injunction to cultivate the self.

Part Two

3

New York

Mark Simpson wrote his "Mirror Men" piece for the *Independent* after having visited the London style exhibition for men called "It's a Man's World," held in November 1994. Sponsored by the men's style magazine *GQ*, this exhibition featured five pavilions full of consumer items, from fashionable clothes and grooming products to gadgets and health ideas. Obviously, this exhibition was not the first grouping together of such metrosexual interests. Encounters between advertisers, commodities, designers, and what Simpson calls "mirror men," have been common fare in the men's style press for years. The difference between the style press and the "Man's World" exhibition lies in the visible and concrete evidence of metrosexuality at the exhibition, in contrast to the words and pictures which make up a magazine. *GQ*'s British marketing director was conscious of this difference when he commented to the *Times* that "the point is to bring the various elements of the magazine to life" (Kay). In 1994, metrosexuality became a living reality in London.

In order to see if metrosexuality was a living or represented reality before this London exhibition, research was carried out on various editions of the men's fashion magazine *GQ*. I wanted to find out if there were figures from the sports world other than Beckham who could perhaps also be classed as metrosexuals. The following two chapters reveal my findings. Art Cooper's editorship of *GQ* in the United States (lasting from 1983 to 2002) was a crucial period for developing strong ties between the worlds of fashion and sports. During this period, *GQ* featured an impressive number of athletes who manifest a special interest in style, clothes, and fashion. When David Beckham, Britain's principal metrosexual, posed on the cover of the

British *GQ* in 2002, he was perpetuating a tradition that had already been operating in the United States for twenty years. Some of the highlights of this tradition are elucidated in this chapter.

Since the early 1980s, *GQ* covers, articles, and photo spreads have been featuring high-profile professional athletes. This coverage provides a venue for discussion about fashion between athletes and *GQ* journalists. Competitions organized by *GQ* to nominate the best-dressed athletes are another example of how the men's style press reinforces the connection between sports and style. The designs of Ralph Lauren were on display at the London "Man's World" exhibition. The background of this designer will be examined here insofar as it helps show how he pioneered the bringing together of the worlds of sports and fashion. The contribution of fashion photographers will also be analyzed. We can now start to find out the names of the major celebrity style jocks that *GQ* helped to reveal over a twenty-year period. If the term "metrosexual" had been available, it is likely that many of these athletes would have been labeled as such.

GQ

As soon as Art Cooper took over the editorship of *GQ* in 1983, he decided to revamp the magazine and extend its readership. He wanted to satisfy preexisting homosexual readers, but at the same time attract a larger heterosexual audience. In a 2002 interview, Cooper recalled his early editorial decisions:

> When I first started editing *GQ*, it gave the impression of being, and in fact was, a gay magazine [. . .] What I wanted to do in repositioning the magazine was make it very clear very quickly that this was a heterosexual magazine [. . .] But the message I wanted to send was that it's not aimed at a gay audience. (Beland)

Rather than draw on the usual professional male models, the editor chose well-known faces from film, television, and the world of sports. *GQ* pioneered giving coverage to sports celebrities as part of a conscious editorial decision to try to attract young heterosexual consumers. Athletes interested the New York fashion world because of their perceived heteronormativity. The very fact that they were sportsmen seemed to imply hypermasculinity and unquestionable heterosexuality. This generalized perception has always been essential in motivating designers and magazines to choose them as cover models.

Another notable way *GQ* contributed toward establishing a tie between sports and fashion was to transform athletic competition into aesthetic competition. This idea can be observed in two representative articles, "Jock Style" and *"GQ's NBA All-Star Team."* In January 1986 *GQ* ran "Jock Style," in which sports columnist John Schulian celebrated and derided what he called the "sartorial wonders" (Schulian 110) of contemporary professional sportsmen. Schulian formulated a list representing the five most style-stunted athletes. They included a designated hitter for the Oakland Athletics whom he outed for owning "slacks that barely reached the top of his socks" (113). A forward for the Portland Trail Blazers owned only sweatshirts and jeans, a fullback for the Washington Redskins lived in camouflage fatigues, and a New York Knicks player was simply "rumpled, unbuttoned and scuffed" (113). More generally, professional tennis players were accused of wearing the same clothes on and off the court. No one had a crease in hockey except Wayne Gretsky, while golf was replete with yellow sweaters and green pants. Blue jeans, flannel shirts, and camouflage gear were the only items of clothes owned by most professional sportsmen. When a men's fashion magazine interests itself in comparing individual sportsmen in terms of how they dress or compares athletes' fashion sense generally according to their sport, this contributes to establishing style off the terrain as a potentially important factor when discussing professional athletes. During the years that followed the publication of "Jock Style," the idea of naming and praising a country's worst and best-dressed athletes has continued to interest the media and readers of the style press.

As well as making public the names of athletes who do not care about their personal appearance in off-the-field clothes, the men's style press has provided an avenue of expression for style-conscious sportsmen who feel comfortable about publicly expressing their interest in fashion and clothes. The consequence of this coverage has been to normalize such discourse and gradually make it commonplace. Such discussion helps turn athletes into style models for each other and for males outside the sports world. An example of style talk from a jock can be observed in the 1986 "Jock Style" article. Here two-time All-Star Reggie Theus, a thirteen-year NBA veteran, spoke easily about his attention to sartorial detail. He told the *GQ* journalist:

> Well, I have a very large distressed-leather vest with double-rope
> sleeves, and I wear it with a sweater that has all the colors of the dis-
> tressed leather plus a few leather stripes of its own. Or I wear the
> vest with a black-and-taupe-colored sweater, black leather pants and
> black boots. Both outfits look very clean, yet they have a tremendous
> statement to them. (Schulian 113)

This exemplary taste for colors and a clean image was outstripped
by another potential role model, Jim Rice, left fielder for the Boston
Red Sox from 1974 to 1989. "Jock Style" carries a full-page photograph of Rice wearing a Gianfranco Ferre nail-head-patterned wool
suit, a Paul Stuart Sea Island cotton shirt, and a Rooster silk polka-
dot tie. A cotton pocket square completed the image of the second
most well-dressed style jock. The first was Los Angeles Laker coach
Pat Riley, who starred at the top of Schulian's list of well-dressed
sportsmen. In *Queer Eye for the Straight Guy* terms, Theus, Rice, and
especially Riley were the *GQ* "Fab Three" for the latter part of the
1980s. Together they were set up in the style press as models for
other men. An innovation was taking place that would be vital to
changing expectations and habits in the sports world. Certain professional and high-profile athletes were adulated in the media as
proficient style leaders. How an athlete looked when not participating in sports became an element of media interest when judging him.
This change in attitude concerning how athletes were perceived
demonstrates new priorities in both sports culture and in the world
outside sports. Brawn mattered, but increasingly what was worn
around the brawn mattered as well.

This perception that men can compete on the style front, not just
in sports, is confirmed by *GQ's* return to the subject of well-dressed
sportsmen in February 1991, five years after running the "Jock Style"
piece. The magazine polled over fifty experts (players, coaches, refer-
ees, and sportswriters) in order to identify "*GQ's* NBA All-Star Style
Team." Before announcing the winners of the vote, sportscaster Marv
Albert relates a story about Nuggets guard Walter Davis. Walking
down the street with friends one day, Davis heard gunshots. Instead
of diving for cover, the guard is purported to have refused to hit the
ground. According to Albert, Davis did not want to ruin his silk trousers. Such "sartorial courage" and "silken grace under pressure"
("*GQ's* NBA" 184) is then lauded by a *GQ* editorialist. Despite such
heroics, it was Houston Rockets center Akeem Olajuwon who was
declared by the same editorialist as the almost unanimous winner of

the poll. An elegant Olajuwon is pictured wearing a custom-made wool suit and cotton shirt by the Italian designer Ermenegildo Zegna. These items are accessorized by a Hermès silk tie. Atlanta Hawks teammates Dominique Wilkins and Kevin Willis also feature in the photo spread. The remaining two NBA style star winners were one of the 1986 "Style Jocks" (Reggie Theus in a Paul Stuart dress shirt and silk tie) and Laker legend "Magic" Johnson.

By the time *GQ* ran their NBA All-Star Style Team competition in 1991, Magic Johnson already had a reputation as a style jock. He had appeared on the March 1987 *GQ* (U.S.) cover wearing a Perry Ellis single-breasted linen sports coat, a cotton dress shirt, a dotted silk tie, and a pair of pleated cotton trousers set off by a Paul Stuart lizard belt with a gold-tone buckle. Living it up in true Hollywood style, Johnson was ensconced in a Bel Air mansion with a Rolls Royce, a Mercedes-Benz, and a Jeep in the driveway. Diane K. Shah's piece, "Magic's Kingdom," described what she called "the good life" (253), enjoyed by this twenty-seven-year-old sports star. Part of this material success manifested itself in Johnson's sense of style, a trait he inherited from his father. Every square inch of his wall-to-wall bedroom closet was, she wrote, "packed with magnificent clothing—suits, sports coats, fine wool sweaters, and a dozen hats he has never been seen in" (253).

These representative *GQ* competitions point to one important characteristic of style jocks. The continued media coverage of the same faces suggests a sincere interest in fashion and the sartorial by the athletes who were designated as style winners. Dressing up is not just something that has been imposed. Instead, it signifies a conscious and continued desire for elegance. This priority became more generalized in sports culture as more celebrity athletes were nominated and lauded by the men's style press throughout the 1990s and into the new century. In this way, the public was kept informed about which celebrity males deserved admiration for their sartorial elegance.

Ralph Lauren and His Models

New York fashion houses have played a vital role in turning athletes into style leaders. For decades, designers have been exploiting the youth, good looks, manly and heterosexual reputations of sportsmen as marketing incentives. Ralph Lauren is a key pioneer figure in the total picture of normalizing relations between sports and the fashion industry. More than any other designer, he has been able to exploit sports in his collections. He is the first designer to have realized that sports and style can make a perfect match. In 1969, Lauren established his first designer boutique for men in the New York City Bloomingdale's. Since the 1970s, Lauren's items of clothing have represented the preppy Polo lifestyle. The use of the word "polo" helped establish his name in the world of American fashion, thereby demonstrating an early use of a sport to enhance a fashion label. In 1993, Ralph Lauren launched the Polo Sport line, thus reinforcing his dependence on sports as a commercial strategy. He was also making the most of the 1990s personal fitness craze in order to promote his original idea that a healthy nation wears his designs not only for exercise, but for leisure activities as well. Each successive appearance by athletes in the fashion press added credence to the marketing strategy adopted by Lauren decades before—that sports and style easily went together. Thus, when the designer launched the Rugby lifestyle collection in 2004, he continued to seduce customers from around the world, inviting them to believe in the American dream based on sports and success.

Since the late 1990s, a number of athletes have modeled for Ralph Lauren in *GQ*. Longtime NFL receiver Jerry Rice modeled Lauren's formalwear Purple Label in the September 1997 *GQ* (U.S.). Rice's "Savile Row–worthy physique" (Corsello, "Quiet Man" 351) is revealed by a double-breasted pin-striped suit, a French-cuff shirt, and a silk satin tie. The fact that a football player's build could be admired as suitable for high-class formalwear, rather than just athletic skill, demonstrates a change in how athletes are perceived. Increasingly, they were being prized for their natural ability to wear and help sell middle- and high-range clothes. This was also the case for Mike Piazza, who wore the same high-end label for a *GQ* (U.S.) cover in April 1999. In a pose inspired by a 1933 portrait of Clark Gable, the All-Star catcher donned a navy suit and a white shirt. Piazza's silk tie and pocket square were chosen from Lauren's Polo line. In the same issue, the glamorous Mets star posed in more Polo items for a photo shoot carried out at Shea Stadium. Piazza is a good illustration of an athlete whose public outings in the fashion world interest the media. He was photographed, for example, at a New York showroom for the Hugo Boss Fall 2002 collection and later at the launch party for a new fragrance in September 2003.

Tiki Barber is another athlete who has modeled for Ralph Lauren. He demonstrates how interviews published in fashion books also contribute to reinforce the worlds of fashion and sports. Twin brothers Tiki Barber (New York Giants running back) and Ronde Barber (Tampa Bay Buccaneers defensive back) posed for a series of shots featuring double-breasted suits from American and European stylists in the October 2001 GQ (U.S.). One of the suits is a wool and mohair pin-striped, double-breasted Ralph Lauren creation. In 2002, Barber was interviewed by Lloyd Boston for his book *Make Over Your Man*. There is a strong suggestion in this interview that Barber's interest in fashion came principally from his wife, a publicist for Ermenegildo Zegna. Boston affirms that the running back "says he's learned to see the sweet and sartorial things in life" (37). Such an impression is justified by Barber's realization that wearing a suit made him "feel good" (38) and caused people to look at him. He admits, though, that it is his wife who always chooses his wardrobe and that he does not like to spend a lot of time in shops. Barber has been photographed at different New York events, suggesting that his wife's influence has been effective. In 2003, for example, he attended the Men's Health New York Fashion Week, which celebrated the magazine's Guide to Style, and later the same year he was present at a New York launch party for a men's skin care line. In April 2004, the football player was photographed at the opening of Ermenegildo Zegna's flagship store on Fifth Avenue.

Protometrosexuality

A perusal of *GQ* issues covering the last twenty-five years in search of style jocks reveals an athlete who especially deserves to have his name remembered as a metrosexual precursor. Ozzie Smith, Hall of Fame shortstop for the St. Louis Cardinals from 1982 to 1996, demonstrates how cover status, articles, interviews, and fashion photography can effectively publicize metrosexuality. This early metrosexuality can perhaps best be termed protometrosexuality. As well as giving an idea of the large number of narcissistic masculinity rituals which would later be grouped together and classified as metrosexuality (purchasing impeccable outfits from foreign couturiers, personal grooming, and coordinating colors), Smith also provides ample proof that professional athletes in the same sport can imitate each other sartorially. All it needs is one catalyst and peers can then follow the example of a style leader. Such imitation is essential in the propagation of metrosexuality.

On the April 1988 *GQ* cover Smith adopts the pose of a beaming dandy, one hand in his suit trouser pocket, the other daintily pulling on the corner of his pocket square. The inside caption shows another photograph of Smith in the same Italian, custom-made, mini-checked wool suit, worn over a Christian Dior cotton dress shirt. Here Smith throws back one hand with fingers extended, while he lightly grasps the French cuff with another. Such stylized poses justify the adjacent editorial comments describing the baseball player as the "Wizard of Ooohs and Ahhhs" and "the incarnation of ineffable style."

This pronounced sense of style is partly achieved by personal grooming. Thomas Boswell's article "The Wizardry of Ozzie" draws attention to the player's grooming habits. "If you dragged Ozzie Smith out of a plane wreck," the cover story begins, "he'd probably be filing his nails" (246). The introductory paragraph concludes that "This is a man who's made himself, polished himself, down to the cuticles" (246). There is a full-page photograph of Smith wearing a body-length leotard. No explanation is offered as to the choice of garment or where it comes from. The journalist simply subtitles his article with the words "Balletic Grace" (246) to insist on the player's style, achieved with the help of a heightened sense of personal presentation.

In his "Mirror Men" founding text on metrosexuality, Mark Simpson wrote that "Metrosexual man [is] everywhere, and he's going shopping" ("Metrosexuals" 207). Love of shopping is highlighted in another article on Ozzie Smith published in the same issue of *GQ*, Loren Feldman's "A Cardinal in Peacock's Plume." A picture of Smith's walk-in twenty-foot deep closet, lined wall to wall with suits and enough shoes on the floor to satisfy the most spendthrift of shoe fanatics succinctly illustrates the piece. The caption reveals disbelief by the male shopper in having purchased all the items piling up in his closet: "Even Ozzie admits, 'I look at some of my things and say did I actually buy that?'" (249). For the *GQ* interview with Feldman, Smith decided to make a style statement by turning up in a shiny, sharkskin suit, a Stefano Milano silk tie, a diamond tie-pin, and a gold collar bar. Unexpectedly for the time, given the sports context, the interview concentrates on the topic of clothes. It has become common for athletes to speak to the men's style press about their personal tastes in clothes. Here, however, Smith was setting a precedent.

An intense interest in clothes is demonstrated by the opening question and answer of Feldman's interview. Asked if the Cardinals are still wearing polyester, without hesitation Smith replies that "We're still with the double knit" (249). It may seem surprising that a shortstop from Mobile, Alabama knows what "double knit" means. However, more surprises await the reader. The pair speaks about who have the ugliest uniforms in the league, the players who look good, and those who do not. Characteristically for a protometrosexual, Smith equates a fashionable uniform with a tight one because it shows off the body's contours. Such statements reveal that this athlete is not only concerned about his own personal presentation. He is also interested in what other males are wearing. Observation of other men (how they look, who is worth imitating, and who is not) is evidence of metrosexuality. The discussion also reveals that the shortstop travels to Montreal to buy French-cut suits. This demonstrates a desire to travel long distances, even abroad, in order to satisfy sartorial requirements. When asked about other players in the clubhouse, Smith replies that "We are always asking each other about where we shop. Guys come to me all the time, so there are a lot of shops now that most of us go to when we go to certain cities" (249). Smith illustrates that baseball players can equate urban environments with wardrobe extension, not just as sites to play sports. Furthermore, his comments demonstrate the progressive normalization which would take place over the coming years of male athletes shopping for themselves and seeking advice about shopping from other males.

Narcissism, fetishism, and an interest in color-coordinated underwear are evident in Smith's comments. Smith offers this explanation as to why he became interested in fashion, "Probably just looking in the mirror one day and saying, 'God that looks good'" (249). This explanation shows that Simpson's phrase "mirror men," used to describe metrosexual males, is not just a metaphor. Smith also freely admits to having a fetish for clothes, although he draws the line at pink pants. When questioned about the underwear-buying habits of other players, Smith reveals that he had closely observed other players in the locker room, so much so that he knows that the Cardinals team members have a penchant for Calvin Klein designer briefs. The player also demonstrates an interest in color coordination by stating, "I think it's very fashionable to wear underwear that's the same color as the clothes you've got on" (300).

Ozzie Smith's poses and comments may come across as somewhat camp. His protometrosexuality would seem to be more in the
tradition of Franco-British dandyism than the American playboy
ethic. From evidence provided in *GQ,* other members of Smith's
baseball team were only too ready to take advantage of their style
guru by discussing clothes and shopping. Correcting all the contents of Feldman's article which might be misconstrued as pertain-
ing to a man with same-sex tastes, Boswell's piece is accompanied
by a photograph of Smith with his wife and two sons. Besides illus-
trating ahead of its time some typical aspects of metrosexuality,
GQ's coverage of a baseball player's deep-felt desire to be noticed
off the pitch perfectly highlights a contentious issue faced by metrosexual males: is it possible to draw a line between looking good and
looking like a queen?

Fashion Photographs of Athletes

Fashion photography is another important element contributing to
publicize jock style. Bruce Weber's work particularly needs to be acknowledged. It is notably the February 1982 "Sporting Style" issue
of *GQ,* published a year before the beginning of Cooper's editorship,
which has remained unsurpassed for its sheer concentration on bodies, athletes, and sports fashion. Weber pioneered this early association of sports and fashion by photographing anonymous gymnasts
for the "Sporting Style" issue. These gymnasts modeled shorts, tops,
and jogging pants. Unidentified half-naked wrestlers modeled nylon
wrestling pants. Photographs of swimmers in Speedo racing briefs
and swim briefs were also included. A fourteen-page photo spread
taken in Sardinia featured suave models clad in European shorts,
sweatshirts, and swim trunks.

Photographic evidence of the heterosexual status of American
style jocks in the men's style press abounded during the 1980s, suggesting the importance at that time of controlling readers' perceptions of dressed-up athletes. Without this heterosexual contextualization, professional athletes modeling clothes could have been
judged as suspect. One strategy that *GQ* employed to broaden the
appeal of the magazine by targeting a heterosexual readership is the
insistence on the heteroeroticism of athletes dressed in designer
clothes. The first page of a 1985 article on Dan Marino featured a

small photograph of dapper Dan and his wife Claire. Bachelors sometimes received a similar treatment. In 1993, for example, Troy Aikman was photographed arm in arm with a noticeably blond and curvaceous Nashville warbler.

Such heterosexual contextualization was not always as clear as the above examples. An interesting case of erotic ambiguity concerns photographs of New York Mets player, Ron Darling, featured in a suit for the August 1986 *GQ* cover. While this shot is completely conventional and unnoteworthy, the article on Darling is illustrated by a full-page shot of the pitcher, naked from the belt up. The hairy forearms and chest, the inviting stare at the camera lens, and the lack of a designer's name for the trousers situate this picture in the tradition of physique photography, a style which is particularly appreciated by a gay readership. This photograph emphasizes a possible homoerotic connotation and thus invites the spectator to see fashion and clothes as homosexual preoccupations. In contrast, the following page shows a half-naked Darling with his fully clothed and newly wed Irish wife resting on his shoulders, thereby insisting on the model's heterosexual credentials. As the half-naked picture is obviously not used to model clothes (or to advertise a designer), one can only wonder about the intent of including this photograph. Manifestly, the pitcher is not modeling anything except his bare body. Despite the smaller-sized shot of the happy couple, there would seem to be a desire to offer an item of interest to *GQ*'s gay readers, who according to publisher Jack Kliger in 1988 "are still considered very important readers at *GQ*" (Belsky). More generally, providing an inset image of a sportsman's partner served to counteract any fears that jocks dressing up (especially together) might provoke a homoerotic reading. Yet, at times, as the case of Ron Darling demonstrates, despite the presence of an adoring spouse, a certain ambiguity remains. This ambiguity points to and reinforces prevalent notions concerning male models, especially half-naked ones. *GQ* was faced with two conflicting objectives after Cooper took over its editorship: satisfy gay readers with the occasional partial nudity, but refrain from giving the impression that fashion was an exclusively homosexual interest. The problem became more acute when athletes were used to exploit this double intention.

The implicit heteroeroticism of fashion photographs, especially those featuring athletes, sent out a specific message to *GQ*'s straight readers: dressing up in stylish clothes was not a masculine ritual that threatened a heterosexual image. Providing proof of a model's children or a recent marriage helped transmit this message. This is why, from the 1980s onward, athletes who showed unusual interest in their tailoring were frequently shown in romanticized or domestic poses. Examples include Isiah Thomas, who was portrayed alongside his wife Lynn on a bed of autumn leaves. The dandified Ozzie Smith appeared with his wife and two children in the playroom of their home amid a sea of balloons. Jose Canseco struck a loving-couple pose in the arms of his recent bride Esther. All these heteronormative cases consolidated the idea that dressing up could be perceived as a normalized masculine gender ritual.

Not surprisingly, all-male configurations of athletes run a greater risk of making fashion veer toward the homoerotic and therefore they reinforce the stereotypical idea that dressing elegantly signifies a homosexual orientation. Despite this reservation, by the twenty-first century such configurations were commonplace. The October 2001 article "Bring on the Buffet" features football players all dolled up in leather and fur. The "Hungry Half Dozen," as the players are called, are divided up into two trios on as many pages, sitting and standing together in their luxurious attire. Another story in the same issue, "We've Got Game," features six young NBA draft picks who are clasped together in arm-over-shoulder poses, while showing off their casual clothes. A third article from this issue presents a "Dream Team" of three NHL players wearing tuxedos, referred to as the season's best "holiday" clothes. They give the impression of attending an expensive all-stag event. These more recent editions of *GQ* demonstrate a break with the traditional technique of providing an article centered on only one athlete and the accompanying preoccupation with insisting on heteroeroticism by featuring a family photograph. The necessity to include a heteronormative context thus seems to have decreased over time. This suggests that the homosexualizing stigma attached to an athlete's interest in clothes and fashion was far less powerful by the twenty-first century.

It is revealing that in the first major American newspaper article concerning metrosexuality, "Metrosexuals Come Out," no mention is made of any American athlete. The author, Warren St. John, could only come up with models taken from Hollywood, such as Cary Grant, Humphrey Bogart, and Harrison Ford. England's reigning metrosexual, David Beckham, was named as the sole candidate representing the sports world. This is odd since there was consistent media coverage of style jocks in the pages of *GQ* from the early 1980s onward. In naming a few movie stars and one foreign soccer player, St. John would seem to be oblivious to an already existing reality in the American sports world, or else he sees it differently. This chapter provides some idea of the impressive number of potential metrosexual candidates from sports culture. Many more examples will become apparent in later chapters.

Still, St. John's *New York Times* piece is important in two ways. It shows the reliance on film stars as an easy means of providing the public imagination with representative metrosexuals. Such a tendency is still evident in the world press, which continues to find in Hollywood and Bollywood a ready supply of narcissistic and well-dressed males. The article also demonstrates the specific difficulty in the United States of identifying national sports heroes as typical metrosexuals, whereas in Britain and Australia, for example, this is common practice, despite the novelty of the concept. Such reticence to name celebrated American metrosexual athletes was partially redressed shortly after St. John's June 2003 article. An ESPN list of top metrosexual men in sports compiled in September 2003 nominated Oscar De La Hoya, Derek Jeter, Mike Modano, Dennis Rodman, Alex Rodriguez, and Jason Sehorn.

Finally, I would like to offer a tentative explanation to help account for this seeming reluctance. The concomitant feminization seen by many to be synonymous with metrosexuality might be preventing American athletes from publicly making statements about fashion which could be interpreted as compromising their manly status. The same could be said concerning doubts that metrosexuality is a euphemism for homosexuality. Before 2003, the style jocks examined in this chapter did not risk such a strong feminizing and homosexualizing label due to the absence of a term which can be used as both a compliment and an insult. Suspicions about gender and sexuality might have been raised, but there was no single catchphrase circulating in the media to describe style-conscious males. Dubbing an athlete a metrosexual can be judged as questioning status as a jock and as a hypermasculine heterosexual.

There is added evidence to account for the reluctance of some athletes to claim status as metrosexuals. The cases of sportsmen previously alluded to in this chapter suggest a relatively high proportion of African Americans in the overall picture of metrosexuality. The cases of African American athletes examined throughout this book far outweigh their percentage in the national population. Black metrosexual candidates might have an especially heightened reluctance to embrace a term often confused with homosexuality. This hypothesis is confirmed by scholars working in the fields of black and queer studies who point out the particular problem of associating blackness and homosexuality. E. Patrick Johnson, for example, sums up the dilemma thus: "True Niggers Ain't Faggots" (36). In *Appropriating Blackness*, Johnson argues that "The representation of effeminate homosexuality as disempowering is at the heart of the politics of hegemonic blackness" (51). If an interest in clothes, fashion, and external appearance is stereotypically and constantly linked to homosexuality, identification as a metrosexual for an African American would seem to be particularly problematic. If heterosexuality is seen as "authentic" and if "black masculinity secures its power by repudiating the (homosexual) Other" (55), as Johnson contends, then we have here a compelling explanation to account for the unwillingness of black athletes to see themselves and be seen as metrosexuals.

4

Armani

The gradual publicizing of ties between sports and fashion in the New York men's style press did not reveal many celebrity names in sports culture. Nor did it expose any outstanding metrosexual candidates, except perhaps Pat Riley, the winner of *GQ*'s 1986 "Jock Style" competition. The most convincing explanation for the relative absence of illustrious cases is simple. New York fashion houses mostly offer middle-of-the-range sportswear. Sportsmen with less subdued sartorial tastes are attracted by the narcissistic delights of European ready-to-wear clothes and customized haute couture.

The designer who occupies the focus of attention in this chapter is Giorgio Armani, described by Colin McDowell as "the undisputed genius of male fashion in the second half of the twentieth century" (183). He is in a league of his own and a central piece in the metrosexual puzzle. Just as Armani stands out in menswear fashion, similarly, some of the most prominent award-winning athletes in the United States, Europe, and Brazil have chosen to wear Armani labels for the status the name projects worldwide. In the United States, celebrated megastars in basketball, tennis, and baseball are attracted by Armani's designs to express their personalities. High-profile soccer celebrities from many countries do likewise.

My objective in concentrating on Armani is to help account for the astonishing success of metrosexuality in Europe and in the United States. The key factor in the transmission and normalization of metrosexuality adheres to the male role models who typify a realignment of masculine gender rituals and the ways these rituals are made to signify normative or nonnormative sexualities. If it were not for the names of particularly high-status athletes who have systematically been pigeon-holed as metrosexuals, it is doubtful whether this cultural process would have achieved the same amplitude and attention as it has in the last few years. This chapter attempts to show that metrosexuality gained recognition and popularity through a specific sort of encounter. This meeting concerns perhaps the most highly admired Italian designer and a number of immensely wealthy stellar athletes who are all extremely proficient in their field. It is this assembling of acknowledged talents in fashion and sports and its extensive coverage in the media which helped to create the conditions necessary for the identification and generalized proliferation of metrosexuality.

Armani's Stellar American Athletes

During the late 1980s, the beginnings of a major change took place in sports culture when one of its influential figures, Laker coach Pat Riley, turned to Armani's power suits as a means of enhancing his image. At the same time, Armani was seeking out American celebrities to wear his designs as a way of associating his labels with illustrious and influential names. Ever since Richard Gere wore impeccable Armani shirts and suits for his role in *American Gigolo* (1980), Americans have considered Armani as the incarnation of understated European chic. His unstructured men's "power suits" with their broad shoulders and wide lapels became the symbol of status and luxury in the 1980s. The power suit was inspired by the glamorous attire worn by Hollywood actors during the 1940s. It epitomizes comfort, elegance, and exquisite tailoring. After having successfully attracted a stable of Hollywood actors (some of whom continue to don Armani jackets for award ceremonies), the couturier decided to include megastars from the sports world as potential walking publicity. Over the next twenty years, this reciprocal meeting of talent and stardom assembled European style and America's highest-paid and most prominent sportsmen in basketball, hockey, and tennis. It laid the foundations for providing the world with a select group of perfectly dressed role models whose influence has been a major factor in identifying and disseminating metrosexuality.

Pat Riley is the first American from sports culture to have attracted Armani's attention. As mentioned in the last chapter, in 1986 *GQ* was responsible for putting him at the top of a list of sportsmen who represented "jock style." According to *GQ* writer John Schulian, Riley set himself apart from sartorial primitives who had a liking for bell-bottoms, gold chains, and lizard-skin cowboy boots. Instead, Riley looked "supremely elegant" and could pass as "the unofficial captain of dishabille" (111), so much so that the coach's dress shirts with crescent-shaped collars brought him more fan mail than his basketball strategies. It seemed only a matter of time before the stylish coach appeared as a cover model in the fashion press. This event took place in January 1989 when one of Herb Ritts's photographs featuring Riley in an Armani power suit was chosen for a *GQ* cover.

The Armani power suit splashed on the cover of *GQ* drew attention to and reinforced the fact that Riley's name was linked to an extremely successful and powerful sports team. Here we have the beginning of a reason to explain why leading figures from sports culture express the desire to be seen in public wearing prestigious fashion labels. This act enhances the perception they have of themselves as powerful and influential figures, while favoring exactly the same impression in the minds of others in and outside sports culture. As an example of Riley's success, we can note that just six months before his first *GQ* cover, he had taken the Los Angeles Lakers to their second world championship in a row. Diane K. Shah's cover story, "The Transformation of Pat Riley," revealed a Hollywood-style magnate basking in the glory of his winning team. For Shah, Riley exemplified to perfection a "winner with pizzazz" (137). Such Showtime excitement and world success were reinforced in the coach's appearance; "his Armani suits, the stylishly collared shirts, the slickback hair," encapsulated "the GQ look" (137). A native of New York, Riley had transformed himself into what Shah termed "the perfect laid-back Californian" (138). One major effect of the Armani wardrobe was to make the coach indistinguishable from the Hollywood celebrities occupying front-row seats at championship matches in Los Angeles.

Riley's taste for Armani was one aspect of a fanaticism about clothes which was sometimes taken as a sign of narcissism. Hollywood director and screenwriter Robert Towne referred to Riley as possessing "putative narcissism, down to the knot in his tie" (Lapointe 1). For the duration of his coaching career, Riley carried the tag "Armani" like one of the designer's jackets. Speaking of the couturier in the *New York Times* in 1990, the coach expatiated that "The man understands exactly what it is that people want. His fabrics really are to die for. I like to feel my clothes" (Lapointe 1). This desire to dress immaculately and feel the comforts of "fabrics" provides a neat résumé of what some men linked to sports culture were demanding, sensuous self-satisfaction through the sartorial. Armani was able to satisfy such a characteristically metrosexual requirement better than New York fashion houses.

The coach's fidelity to Armani is a sign of a successful marketing strategy on the part of the designer. It also indicates that the association between the two men, even if initially motivated by commercial concerns on the part of Armani, transformed into a friendship. The relationship was so close that Riley even paid Armani summer visits in Italy to talk about basketball and fashion. The coach attended a New York Giorgio Armani Party in 1996 before repeating his *GQ* cover status in January 1998. This time he appeared alongside NBA players Tim Hardaway and Alonzo Mourning, wearing an Armani custom-made suit and shirt. Peter Richmond's piece "Pat Riley Is Still Looking for a Fight" portrayed the fifty-two-year-old (who had thrice earned the award Coach of the Year) as a faultlessly dressed control freak. His fanaticism about looking and dressing better, typified by the Armani wardrobe, showed his determination to motivate his team to be the best by winning. Dressed in Armani's power suits, Riley exuded the power and success of the whole Lakers team.

Riley may have inaugurated the now generalized appeal of European fashion within professional basketball, but stellar tennis players have also been associated with Armani. This tendency for tennis champions to be seen showing their style off the court is an international phenomenon and not restricted to the United States. At times the exhibitionism takes place on the court, as Andre Agassi once demonstrated by playing in the finals of a tournament held in Florida wearing lipstick, eyeliner, and an earring. Given the intense media interest in high-profile tennis tournaments and the presence of only two players competing at one time, it is not surprising that some of these celebrities enjoy dressing up for the camera.

Andre Agassi, an early sartorial role model from the world of tennis, achieved *GQ* (U.S.) cover status at the age of nineteen. He was photographed in September 1989 wearing an Armani double-breasted suit with peaked lapels, a straight-collared, cotton-chambray shirt, and a silk tie. At this time, the controversial teenager had a reputation more for divesting himself of clothes on the court (and throwing them to screaming female fans) than for donning designer garments. Confirming his sex appeal for women, the *GQ* article includes a small photograph of Agassi with his "steady girlfriend" (Hirshey 420). All of Armani's stellar athletes possessed generalized appeal because of a perceived heterosexual status. The sexual orientation of straight sportsmen has always been a major drawing point in establishing their exemplarity as role models.

From the days when Agassi sported a mullet cut (short blond-streaked hair on top, long in the back, a buzz cut near the ears) to his more recent shaved head and now discarded dangling single earring, the tennis champion has continued to attract the attention of the fashion press and influence the perceptions of males concerning grooming. Although Agassi cannot be pigeonholed as solely an Armani fan, he is America's youngest and earliest athlete to have adopted the Armani look for the men's style press. In 2003, Agassi launched "Aramis Life" for the Estée Lauder perfume company. Since then, his image advertises the cologne as "the fragrance for men" on buses, billboards, and in the fashion press globally, thereby encouraging the acceptance that all men need grooming products.

Pete Sampras is another world-renowned tennis champion who has been used by the fashion press to advertise designer clothes. Before attending the 2000 Armani Retrospective at the Guggenheim Museum, Sampras had his photograph taken for *InStyle*. Dangling a cherry over a trophy, he wore a black Armani suit and white shirt. The combination of the trophy with the Italian label suggested that success and Armani made a perfect pair. This combination was further emphasized when, surrounded by friends such as Wayne Gretsky and Elton John, Sampras wore an Armani tuxedo to his wedding. Photographs in the press of Armani-clad grooms such as Sampras considerably reinforce an association in and outside the sports world between fashion, masculinity, and heterosexuality. In August 1998, eight full-page photographs further emphasized this link when Sampras graced the pages of *GQ* as part of a fall preview. The many fashion designers modeled by the tennis player included Gucci, Versace, and Armani. Representing the latter, Sampras wore a stretch-wool pin-striped suit and a silk crewneck. Each time Sampras donned European designed clothes for a public occasion or for magazine photo spreads, it highlighted his status as one of the country's elite sportsmen. His exceptional prowess on the court was thus emphasized and enhanced by the wearing of exceptionally tailored garments.

Baseball wonder Alex Rodriguez has taken over from Riley the role of the megastar model from sports culture who wears Armani. His annual salary of over $27 million is the highest in Major League Baseball. Already in 2000, A-Rod (as the player is widely known) made sports history by signing a ten-year $252 million contract with the Texas Rangers. He has twice won the American League Most Valuable Player award. His talent, wealth, physical appearance, and stellar reputation are the factors explaining his appeal to designers as a marketing tool. Like his predecessors in the sports world, Rodriguez's heterosexual status has been determinate in his appropriateness as a metrosexual model.

Armani's decision to endorse Rodriguez draws attention to how jock style crosses ethnic lines. Although Rodriguez was born in New York City, his parents are from the Dominican Republic. The April 2000 *GQ* (U.S.) cover featured what was known at the time as the "Holy Trinity" of shortstops: Alex Rodriguez, "baseball god" Derek Jeter, and Nomar Garciaparra. Rodriguez wears a cashmere crewneck and wool gabardine trousers signed Armani. A photo spread features Jeter running in the street, decked out in an Armani suit, shirt, tie, and belt. Next to him, dressed in similar Armani attire, Rodriguez is also running. And behind them, admiring female fans are seen trying to catch up with their fleet Italian-suited idols. Part of the heteroerotic appeal of these wealthy sports idols relies on the sensuality implicit in the Armani name.

In a Canadian newspaper interview in March 2004, Rodriguez was reminded of a declaration he had once made which clearly demonstrates the importance he attributes to the sartorial. He said "I'm not impulsive at all, except about buying clothes. You can take my cars and my house, but don't mess with my clothes" (McCarron 4). This privileging of the sartorial above other material possessions is a typical metrosexual characteristic. Asked if he was a clotheshorse, the baseball megastar replied that he had a positive relationship with Armani: "We've had an arrangement for about five years and it's good" (McCarron 4). Both parties benefit from reciprocal superstar status. An aura of overwhelming success, wealth, and sensuality attached itself to designer and athlete. This underlying sensuality was picked up by a *Newsweek* article in 2001. Here Rodriguez was described as "a tall, buff, soft-spoken charmer with caramel skin, shimmering, hazel eyes and a boyish smile" (Samuels and Starr 54). Little wonder that Rodriguez was able to walk into any Armani store and leave with anything for free. Though burglars divested A-Rod's Miami home of $43,000 worth of Armani designs in 2000, baseball's highest-paid player continues to wear Armani.

Coverage of A-Rod in a women's magazine showed readers what could be normal preoccupations for men. In May 2004, a photograph of Alex Rodriguez and his wife Cynthia was used to begin a feature in *Vogue* after the player had been traded to the New York Yankees. With his wife's head resting on his torso, *Vogue* shows Alex lying on the grass wearing a Robert Talbott white shirt and Armani trousers. Robert Sullivan's article "Dream Team" is based on conversations with Cynthia Rodriguez at the time the couple was moving to Manhattan. Cynthia speaks enthusiastically about her husband's natural knack for clothes shopping. She reveals that Alex "chooses color combinations that I would never dream of. He chooses patterns that I would never think of. He does much better than I ever could" (266). It is evident that in this couple the roles of fashion-conscious wife and reluctant, drag-along-to-the-shops husband have been reversed. This gives readers the impression that attention to color and pattern in clothes can be considered as normal preoccupations on the part of a heterosexual male. Furthermore, it is Rodriguez who is eager to take his wife shopping on Madison Avenue (where the Armani store is located) and not the contrary, to the point where shopping is described as Rodriguez's one vice. A description of his closet reveals that "[There are] stacks of shirts, racks of suits, and rows and rows of shoes—[it] looks like the men's wing at Barney's" (Sullivan 267). Rodriguez is a perfect model of an urban *flâneur,* who not only takes pride in his image and appearance, but actively takes charge of extending his wardrobe by indulging his "vice" for shopping.

Taking their cue from a succession of Lakers coaches such as Pat Riley and Phil Jackson, an increasing number of NBA stars also dress in European designs. Two representative examples of such role models are ballplayers Kevin Garnett and Carmelo Anthony. Garnett appeared on the cover of the 2002 *GQ* (U.S.) sports issue, wearing diamond ear studs and an Armani white shirt, unbuttoned to reveal his smooth chest. Here we catch a glimpse of erotic display which is generally underplayed in American cover shots of athletes wearing Armani. Before Rodriguez's contract, Garnett's $126 million five-year contract with the Timberwolves made sports history in 1997. Matthew Teague's article compares Garnett with Allen Iverson who joined the NBA one year after Garnett. Iverson gained a reputation as the "bad boy" of basketball. In contrast, Garnett, the "genuinely nice guy" (245), is described as "suave and natural" (298). His taste for Armani helped justify the impression that Garnett was conscious of how external appearance mattered. He further demonstrated his flair for exhibitionism and fashion in December 2003 by posing for an NBA photo call for which he wore a suit with a hat and an umbrella. The Timberwolves champion appeared stunningly comfortable in front of the camera. That same month, guru observed disciple when Armani was one of the celebrities present in the front row watching the Timberwolves play against the New York Knicks. Later, Garnett attended the *GQ Magazine* 2004 NBA All-Star Party held in West Hollywood. In extending his list of fashionable sports engagements to Los Angeles and modeling in Italian-designed clothes, Garnett provided the country with yet another visible and attractive model to help project an image of athletes as style-conscious aesthetes.

Carmelo Anthony was one of three draft picks who featured in a *GQ* (U.S.) article on custom-made suits in October 2003. "Melo," as the braided Denver Nuggets' star forward is known, twirls a basketball for the *GQ* photograph while wearing a made-to-measure Armani suit, cotton shirt, and silk tie. Interviewed by Peter Richmond, Melo reveals how dressing up can be a long-term lifestyle desire, not just a fad. Since the age of ten or eleven the player had been interested in color coordination on and off the court.

> "When I'm dressing, everything's got to match. I will color-coordinate. From the stitching in the pants to everything. I'll be in my house: 'What am I going to wear?' I'll match this with that. I'll be dressed about twenty-five minutes after I start. They always say I'm late because I've got to see what I'm going to wear. Because everything has to match." (Richmond, "Height" 240)

Melo's discourse on clothes demonstrates a high-profile athlete who takes Carson Kressley's advice from *Queer Eye* to heart, "Repeat . . . After . . . Me: 'I am worthy of couture'" (Allen 163). This taste for Armani does not prevent Melo from donning hip-hop garb in public. He therefore has cross-over appeal extending from couture to street styles, which arguably could serve to increase his effectiveness in influencing sartorial habits across a broad spectrum. As a sign of his loyalty to the Italian designer, Melo traveled from Denver to the New York Emporio Armani store in May 2004 for the official launch of Armani's book, *Faces of Sport*.

The United States has been a fertile ground for Armani's marketing strategy to sell his designs using athletes as models in the style press. In exceptional cases, endorsement ties or even ties of friendship were created. However, for most athletes interested in Armani, the initiative came from them and they continue to wear his designs at prestigious public events. Their status as talented and rich celebrities participates in extending the aura associated with the Armani label and vice versa. Their perceived normative sexuality has been vital in creating the perfect conditions for the generalized dissemination of metrosexuality.

Armani's Superstars in Europe

Extensive media coverage by the European fashion press has put many more fashion-conscious athletes into the public eye. After the turn of the century in Milan, Armani began to attract a coterie of faithful soccer players who have continued to occupy front-row space at his men's fashion shows. A select group of superstar European soccer players, together with some Brazilians, have become regular fixtures when new collections are presented. Factors which facilitate Armani's marketing strategy to use and attract soccer players include the geographic proximity of fashion runways for athletes who live in and near Milan as well as the Italian normalization of dressing stylishly.

Europe is of particular interest because this is where Armani published the photograph album *Faces of Sport* in 2004. In the preface, Armani praises the "relaxed athleticism" and "exceptional physical prowess" of men and women who "are really the modern day gladiators." Speaking in 2004, Armani offered another observation about athletes which was quoted in many newspapers around the world. He claimed that "Footballers are today's new style leaders but, unlike the movie stars and pop stars who they now join as fashion icons, they have to show an acute combination of mental and physical discipline which makes them genuinely heroic" (Williams 46). Armani went out of his way to attract celebrity sports superstars who were all exceptionally gifted in order to turn them into "fashion icons." As simultaneous sports and fashion icons, they easily attract the attention of the public, just like their American counterparts.

The one specificity of Armani's marketing strategies concerning athletes in Europe is the international composition of the European residents he attracts. The innermost circle of Armani's coterie in Europe reads like a checklist of superstar sportsmen from around the world who have been recognized for their outstanding sports skills. Names in this select elite group include Ronaldo (1996, 1997, and 2002 FIFA World Player of the Year), Figo (winner of the 2000 European Footballer of the Year Award and the 2001 FIFA World Player of the Year), Shevchenko (2004 European Footballer of the Year), and Kaká. With such award-winning talent in close proximity, Armani had a perfect instrument to arouse sartorial emulation from sports fans everywhere in the world.

A combined characteristic concerning athletes who model Armani in America and Europe is a noticeable eroticization by the style press. As already observed, attempts to eroticize Alex Rodriguez and Kevin Garnett are evident in American style magazines. Another example of this tendency is a full-page shot of Andre Agassi which appeared in *GQ* (U.S.) in 1989. The player is shown reclining on an open-air lounge in just shorts, socks, and sneakers (Hirshey 416). The one arm crooked behind his head imitates a pin-up gesture. There is a constant fascination concerning the female companions of athletes. They invariably tend to be top fashion models, since this profession is now the prime choice of celebrity athletes who are looking for wives. In the American and European style press, the heterosexual identity and desirability of Armani's athletes are emphasized by providing accompanying girlfriends and by revealing semi-clad bodies. Such heteronormative appeal is an important factor in normalizing an interest in fashion for heterosexually identified males.

Armani's earliest superstar working in Europe is the Brazilian Ronaldo Luíz Nazário de Lima, known as "Ronaldo," and nicknamed "The Phenomenon." In March 2000, Ronaldo appeared in the British and Italian versions of *GQ*. The twenty-three-year-old athlete who played for Inter Milan at the time is shown naked from the groin up, wearing Armani Jeans green trousers. After helping Brazil win the World Cup, Ronaldo filled up eight pages of *GQ* (Italy) in October 2002. Such was his attraction for the magazine that he returned beside Brazilian model Fernanda Lima in December 2003 wearing an Armani unzipped-to-the-chest white sailor shirt. This outfit is accessorized with an array of hip-hop jewelry from Doc Dog (three silver chains carrying the word "DOLLS" plus a playboy bunny) and a pair of Christian Dior sunglasses poised on his shaved head. Photographs of Ronaldo and Lima exemplify the sort of heterosexual pairing that has been normalized in American and European representations of Armani-clad sportsmen. It also illustrates the playboy pedigree of metrosexuality that was discussed in chapter 2.

Another member of the privileged inner circle of Armani's international superstars is the Portuguese soccer player Luís Figo. Accompanied by his wife, Swedish supermodel Helen Svedin, Figo modeled in Armani for *GQ* (Italy) in March 2001 and again in May 2006. Wearing an Armani black leather jacket, he also was featured alone in fashion pages for both *Esquire* (UK) in December 2001 and *GQ* (Germany) in July 2003. The designer's admiration for the player was made plain during a 2004 interview when Armani confessed, "When I see [Figo] at shows, I can always visualize him as a matador. He's so dark and hairy and has this great tough presence" (Deeny 42). For Armani and for other fans, Figo's appeal seems to have been strongly physical and based on the player's overt hypermasculinity. Such an image is influential in transmitting the idea that men's fashion and virility are not incompatible. This amounts to a revision of stereotypical, preconceived ideas that there is something feminizing or suggestive of homosexuality about a male posing in Italian designer menswear.

The tattooed Ukrainian Andrij Shevchenko, popularly known as "Sheva," who spent seven years with A.C. Milan, is a sports superhero of a different kind. In 2002, Shevchenko modeled on the runway for Armani and signed a franchise for the first Armani Collezioni store in Kiev which extended to include an Armani Jeans store two years later. An advertising campaign similar to Beckham's Police sunglasses campaign turned the soccer player into the symbol of Armani Occhiali sunglasses. In November 2003, *GQ* (Italy) ran a ten-page article and photo spread showing Sheva and his future wife, American model Kristen Pazik in various states of undress. The overt eroticization here is another typical representation of the semi-naked body of a male athlete as a desirable heterosexualized object. The cover shot of the couple shows the top model in black underwear and the soccer player looking like a rap singer: low-hipped jeans, underwear showing, and a conspicuous tattoo on his arm. Intimate bedroom scenes illustrate the interview, featuring a partially denuded Shevchenko clad in Armani designs. A solitary, less bare Sheva returned to the pages of *Vogue Sport* (Italy) in January 2005.

Wearing a combination of Emporio Armani garments (oversized linen pants, a black V-neck sweater, a hooded top, and a made-to-measure black suit), the soccer player demonstrates that both high and lower Armani lines can be worn alternately. A subtle message is being sent out to soccer fans and other males who are invited to imitate their hero. Fabia Di Drusco's accompanying text broached the subject of the designer's fascination for the Ukrainian. For her, Sheva's features resembled those of the classic models used by Armani in the 1980s and his gracious confidence before the camera seemed both "military and ballet-like" (Di Drusco 205). In summer 2004, the designer explained his choice in the sports fashion magazine *Sepp* by stating that "Shevchenko is a great player, we all know that. But he is also a very handsome, assured guy. I felt attracted to his personality right away, which is one reason we began working with him" (Deeny 41). The athletic proficiency, physical appeal, and personality of Shevchenko account for Armani's sustained interest in exploiting the player's image. Together with his wife, Shevchenko was chosen to model for the Fall/Winter 2006 Armani Collezioni campaign.

In 2004, Armani began to use A.C. Milan player Ricardo Izecson dos Santos Leite (more usually referred to as "Kaká") as the new face for Armani Jeans (AJ). Two years later, Kaká began to pose for the Emporio Armani label. The first campaign coincided with a portrait of the twenty-two-year-old Brazilian on the cover of *GQ* (Italy) in October 2004. Kaká is sitting with his arms folded, wearing two necklaces, a jacket, and a sweater unzipped to below the chest. His disheveled hair, slightly parted lips, and plunging neckline help to constitute a highly eroticized image. In a moment of exuberant praise for the model, Armani once expatiated that "Kaká is molto bello! He has this other-worldly, hard to describe quality. Plus he's naturally elegant" (Deeny 41). The "hard to describe quality" would seem to be a certain androgyny quite unlike the hard-muscled masculinity of his AJ predecessor, David James. This may help to explain why a British journalist in 2004, impressed by Kaká's "chiselled jaw and toned buttocks," referred to him as a "pretty boy" (Guidi 68). Terms used to refer to the physical attributes of this player (for example "bello" and "pretty") alert us to a potential problem in choosing an adequate vocabulary to describe metrosexualized bodies.

From this survey of athletes featured in the European fashion press, it can be seen that after the turn of the century, Armani attracted around him a select group of international soccer superstars who attended his runway shows, modeled for his advertising campaigns, exhibited his creations in the style press, and in the case of one player, entered into a commercial operation. These superstar athletes provided the designer with excellent marketing tools. The influence of Ronaldo, Figo, Shevchenko, and Kaká has been invaluable in giving soccer its reputation in Europe for attracting celebrity players who share a similar interest in fashion, conspicuous consumption, and sartorial display. They have been central to providing the public with images of masculine elegance and style. Such athletes exist in the United States and in Continental Europe, but the one glaring exception where Armani has not been able to shine and establish role models is England. This final meeting between Armani and sportsmen needs now to be addressed because it lies at the origin of the designer's initiative to concentrate on sports.

The Great Masculine Renunciation

It is paradoxical that Armani has not been influential in British sports culture, since it was the commercial use of a British athlete on the runway in Milan which first gave the designer the idea of exploiting sportsmen as models. The appearance of Liverpool soccer player David James at one of Armani's 1995 men's fashion shows was a deciding moment for the history of metrosexuality and sports. Nearly ten years later, British fashion editor Peter Howarth recalled the event.

> Then the lights dim for a new passage and when they go up again something has changed. Instead of a 20-year-old kid from the American Midwest called Brad or Joe with regular features and slicked-back hair, there's a giant on the catwalk. At well over 6 ft and with cropped peroxide hair, he saunters the length of the raised stage, stripped to the waist in a pair of jeans, and disappears [. . .]. The big man is David James, the young goalkeeper [. . .] who had just made history by bringing football to fashion. ("Beautiful Game" 10)

Before this event, a photo shoot for the Autumn/Winter 1995 issue of the British men's fashion magazine *Arena Homme Plus* featured James wearing an Armani tank top, wool trousers, and a V-necked sweater. Upon advice from the *Arena* photographer, Armani decided to continue to use the same sportsman in order to model his creations on the runway. Previously, like other designers, Armani had contented himself to use the services of professional models not only on the runway, but also in his advertising and promotional work. Needing a new source of inspiration, Armani turned to athletes to further enhance his image and with their endorsement sell a style to a wider public. He therefore set about using sportsmen's bodies and athletic prowess as profit-making tools. Armani's encounter with James was a central moment in the designer's exploitation of sports and sportsmen.

In the spring and summer of 1996, advertisements featuring the Liverpool player appeared throughout the world promoting Armani Jeans and Emporio Armani Underwear. The bleached, tattooed, and half-naked Anglo-Jamaican is featured wearing a pair of dark Armani jeans. One photograph for Armani's underwear line shows James crouching, heels raised and hands spread, as though he were about to begin a race. Although there is a glimpse of black and white Armani underwear, James's naked musculature is the center of focus here and not the item of hardly visible clothing. The James publicity campaign based on exhibiting the energy and force behind an experienced athlete was an instant success. Armani had found an excellent marketing strategy based on the spectacle of a partially denuded athlete wearing his creations.

James's perspective acts as a stark contrast to the attitudes of American athletes who wear Armani in the style press. Interviewed in 2003, James disclaimed any desire to follow up this advertising success of the mid-nineties. He claimed that "Armani used the photographs everywhere, and all of a sudden model agencies started ringing up saying they wanted me to join them. I just said 'I can't be stuffed.' What was I going to do? I wasn't into fashion, and I'd already done Armani anyway" (Thomas, "We All Knew" 24). Despite the strong reluctance expressed here to rework as a model, James returned to have his body used in fashion promotion. After completing an Armani photo shoot for the British magazine *Hello!*, he was featured in the January 2005 issue of *Vogue Sport* (Italy) which contained a photograph showing the athlete in an Armani Jeans blue hooded top. James has also modeled in Britain for the Swedish multinational menswear label H&M. This national and international coverage demonstrates that ten years after his first parade, James was still modeling. The disdain for fashion the athlete expressed in 2003 needs to be reconsidered. Furthermore, James's presence the same year at both the Armani Retrospective and the 2004 launch party for Armani's book *Faces of Sport* supposes reasons (commercial or otherwise) pushing the athlete not only to publicly demonstrate some sort of fidelity to the Italian stylist, but to want to accept continued commercialization of his body. Whatever the case, James's engagement with the fashion industry does not constitute a lifestyle. It is a successful one-way marketing venture between fashion companies and a model.

This is certainly not the case concerning David Beckham, the most notable exception to the general British disinterest in Armani. The LA Galaxy star first met the Italian stylist in London in 2003 when Armani designed the formal and casual official "off-field" outfits for the national soccer team. One Armani design was even dubbed the "Beckham jacket" in honor of the then captain of the England team. Since their first meeting, Beckham has continued to be fascinated by Armani's sense of style. Their mutual esteem reached a high point in the Spring/Summer 2008 advertising campaign for Emporio Armani underwear that featured several shots by fashion photographers Mert Alas and Marcus Piggott. The official Emporio Armani Web site displaying the highly eroticized Beckham ads promises men sexy briefs and boxers that offer "the utmost in luxurious comfort." Beckham's bulge on public show has been a huge commercial success for the Armani brand. Soaring sales in the United States and in Europe demonstrate the efficacy of bringing together sports and fashion.

Notwithstanding the dissimilarity separating the sedate James and the ostentatious Beckham, the two Davids were photographed for *GQ* (UK) in October 2003 alongside two other soccer players for the England team and their manager. The five men are standing in their official traveling outfits next to their smiling style guru, Armani. A navy suit, a cardigan jacket, and casual trousers make up the principal items in the wardrobe. Shirts, ties, overcoats, and accessories complete the attire. A full page of nine photographs shows the three-day-long fitting process. Speaking about the England team, Armani opined that "These men don't need extreme fashion" (Sullivan, "Forza" 184). Instead, the designer saw the exercise as an "opportunity to do something beautiful and elegant" (184). This exhibition of pure Armani suggests that collectively the England sports team is conscious of the imperative to compete internationally on the fashion front, but that individually there is not the same attention given to unofficial clothes.

There may be historic reasons to account for this relative disinterest in Italian fashion. Historically, Englishmen who returned from France and Italy dressed in a European style were at times ridiculed for their effort. In the 1770s, fashionable Englishmen who had acquired foreign tastes in their wardrobe were referred to as "macaronis." Horace Walpole described these fops with an extravagant hairstyle as "young Men of fashion who returned from their Travels" (McNeil 380). According to Peter McNeil's study of macaroni masculinities, when used as a mockery the word implied "transgressions of status, gender and sexuality" (398). A macaroni could even be synonymous with a sodomite. Continental fashion in the minds of some would seem to be still linked to excess, effeminacy, and sexual depravity, characteristically imagined to be absent at Savile Row. Jon Stratton is surely correct when he blames the scandal surrounding Oscar Wilde and his trials for making British male display synonymous with homosexual desire. He explains that "From this time on, in Britain at least, male display in costume or manner was associated with effeminacy and with same-sex sexual activity" (Stratton 140). Since the late nineteenth century, such characteristics in Britain have come to be associated with the dandy. As the British press after 2003 constantly used the word dandy to help explain the new term metrosexual, the specter of Wilde appears to have hovered and unconsciously convinced a nation that metrosexual males were sexually dubious.

Another explanation to account for English indifference toward masculine sartorial glamour can be found in what fashion historians have termed "the great masculine renunciation," an English cultural phenomenon usually thought to have started at the end of the eighteenth century and to have continued into the early nineteenth century. Renouncing extravagance and ostentation, this style is based on an ideology of inconspicuous consumption and sartorial modesty. David Kuchta finds an even earlier precedent to this masculine renunciation than the Oscar Wilde scandal. Toward the end of the seventeenth century a similar renunciation of masculine display replaced luxury and lavishness. Foreign observers have often noticed this great English masculine renunciation. Ralph Waldo Emerson, the American minister who toured England in 1833 and 1847, commented on the "studied plainness" of English clothes. He was struck by the "low tone in dress" (Kuchta 164–65). This subdued tone is still observable in the country, notably in upperclass dowdy chic.

If men who give importance to appearance, dress stylishly, and have a taste for European style are still equated with effeminate homosexuals in Britain, it is little wonder that it is safer to remain drab in a country where masculine display has been periodically disdained since the Glorious Revolution of 1688. The near absence of Armani followers in British sports culture is thus partly a direct consequence of historic factors. This is in marked contrast to Continental Europe and America where masculine display has not been the object of national renunciations and where normative masculinities do not preclude conspicuous and colorful attention to the sartorial.

Reiteration in the media across the world of Beckham's name as the most visible case of a metrosexual male tends to take attention away from the many other celebrity athletes who also demonstrate signs of metrosexuality. Investigating the role played by Armani in attracting custom among wealthy sportsmen reveals Pat Riley to be a serious contender for possible metrosexual status. Since the turn of the century, the European men's fashion press, especially the Italian edition of *GQ*, put into the media spotlight a group of stellar athletes who all manifest personal ties with the world of European fashion. This is insufficient to justify calling them metrosexuals. The accumulation in Milan of so many fashion-conscious and high-profile athletes acts as a powerful instrument in providing a positive portrayal of metrosexuality. In the United States, there are also a number of well-known athletes from different sports whose passionate interest in Armani sends out a signal that male self-care can be taken to luxurious heights. All the athletes mentioned in this chapter, and the preceding one, represent the tip of the metrosexual iceberg in the world of sports. The next chapter shows how metrosexuality is gradually touching the lives of people everywhere.

Fig. 1. Baseball
Hall of Fame
winner Jim Palmer
advertising
"élance" Jockey
underwear. (1980)

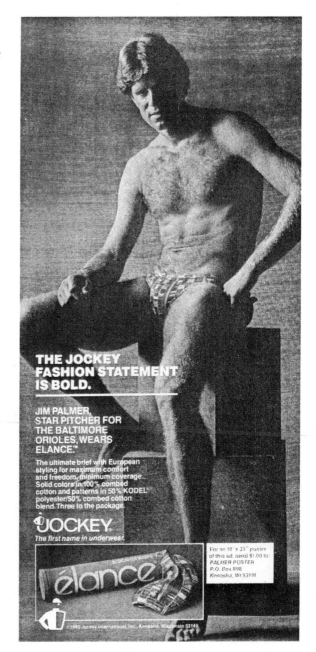

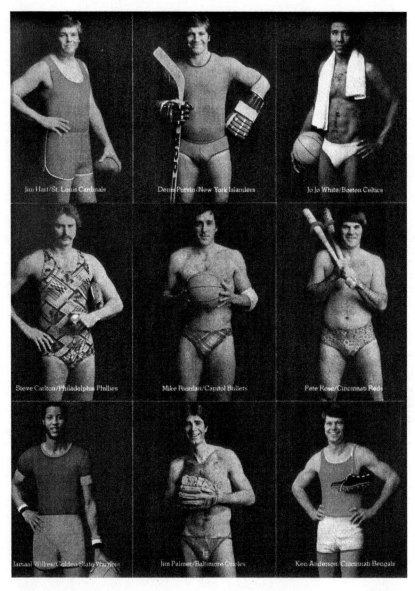

Fig. 2. "Take Away Their Uniforms and Who Are They." *Jockey underwear advertisement.* (1977)

Fig. 3. Swedish Calvin Klein underwear model and West Ham United soccer player, Fredrik Ljungberg, on the cover of *Gay Times*. (2004) *Courtesy Millives Prowler Ltd.*

Fig. 4. Australian metrosexual underwear. The aussieBum "Seven Deadly Sins" brief. (2005). *Courtesy aussieBum*

Fig. 5. French metrosexual underwear. The couture collection, HOM. (2008). *Courtesy HOM*

Fig. 6. French former professional tennis player, Yannick Noah, advertising
Sloggi underwear. (2005). *Courtesy Sloggi*

Fig. 7. French Tae Kwon Do Olympic medalist, Pascal Gentil, advertising timepieces (2004). Portrait by Karim Ramzi. *Courtesy Karim Ramzi*

Fig. 8. American professional basketball player, Marcus Fizer, wearing a Sean John fox-fur coat as originally published in *Gentlemen's Quarterly* (2000). Portrait by Timothy Greenfield-Sanders. *Courtesy Timothy Greenfield-Sanders*

Fig. 9. Portuguese Manchester United soccer player, Cristiano Ronaldo, stripping off his jersey during the Euro 2004 soccer championship. *Courtesy Getty Images*

Fig. 10. Studio portrait of Amir Khan, the British Olympic medalist for boxing. (2006). *Courtesy Getty Images*

Fig. 11. French Olympic medalist for boxing, Brahim Asloum, advertising a timepiece (2003). Portrait by Ali Mahdavi. *Courtesy Ali Mahdavi*

Fig. 12. New York Jets quarterback, Joe Namath, advertising Dingo Boots. (1972)

Fig. 13. Joe Namath advertising Brut 33 Skin Moisturizer. (1977)

Part Three

5

Undies

Examining the style press's exposure of athletes who show a marked interest in New York fashion houses or in European menswear provides a partial picture of how metrosexuality has been publicized over the last two decades, especially since the turn of the century. Not all males have the desire or means to imitate these fashion-conscious athletes. However, if we move our attention to underwear and look at an item of clothing which necessarily concerns *all* males, it is possible to trace the exponential rise of metrosexuality and see how widespread it has become. Men's underwear publicity featuring athletes as models reveals how metrosexuality has penetrated to the most intimate apparel worn by males. Metrosexuality is not just about custom-designed suits worn by rich and privileged megastars. This chapter shows how metrosexuality lies in a multitude of drawers.

An underwear poster featuring an athlete can be an excellent instrument to advertise metrosexuality. Once the first photograph of a star athlete was used to promote men's underwear, this marked a radically new conception of sports erotics. Exposing a well-known sportsman in his undies as a marketing tool is a potentially disturbing and exciting sign of male nudity and male sexuality. It also acts as a highly visible proof of male aesthetics, since it foregrounds the body beautiful in all its near-naked glory. Stripping in public can be an intimidating exercise for any male. Still, this is what some vain and virile athletes have been regularly doing since the 1970s. Photographs of athletes in their briefs and the impact of these images on undie-buying habits together constitute two very visible proofs of metrosexuality.

The history of men's underwear advertising in the United States over the last quarter of a century reveals two opposing visions of the male body. On the one hand, a marketing strategy employed by mainstream underwear brands such as Jockey and Hanes was aimed at housewives and mothers, the main undie-buyers of the period. As a secondary consideration, heterosexual males were also addressed. (According to mainstream men's underwear philosophy homosexual males did not exist). Efforts were made to eroticize men's underwear by these companies, but they were constantly faced with a difficulty linked to the very item of clothing they were promoting. Normalized gender and sexual mythologies inculcated the idea that only the female body could be denuded, objectified, and eroticized. Further, according to conventional norms, the exhibition of nude male bodies risks feminization and attracting the homoerotic gaze. Traditional men's underwear brands therefore had to tread a fine line between showing enough of a bulge to convince women to buy their products, but not too much because this could be interpreted as turning males into sex objects. Choosing to exhibit the denuded bodies of heterosexually identified athletes in advertising made perfect commercial sense for these mainstream brands as the ultimate objective was to physically attract wives out shopping for their husbands. Athletes easily managed that. Given their proficiency at sports and popularity with male fans, they also helped allay generalized fears that paying particular attention to underwear might be a sign of effeminacy or same-sex desire.

On the other hand, a different philosophy of the body is evident in high-fashion underwear advertising. Calvin Klein holds the honor of being the first and most successful designer to plug more upmarket men's underwear. Rather than only target women and heterosexual men, Klein and other designers directly addressed *all* males in their campaigns, even before the number of men buying underwear started to equal the number of female buyers. With the help of the same fashion photographers who provided glamorous portraits of athletes in the men's style press, Klein's advertising paid much more attention than mainstream brands to eroticizing and fetishizing both the male body and men's underwear. The initial result was that homosexual males lapped it up, but so gradually did heterosexual men who copied their example in droves. Athletes were also a prime tool used by high-fashion brands to advertise their creations. Women and homosexual men tended to desire them. And straight men wanted to be like them.

Two concepts used in this chapter require explanation. The first is "undie trouble." By this term I refer to the problems linked with a male looking at his underwear (this can easily be confused with fetishism and perversion) and a male who is interested in the underwear of other males (this suggests the possibility of same-sex desire). The premise of the mass-market undie-selling technique reflects and is a product of traditional gender mythology. It implies that only women look at men, only women shop, and only women are interested enough in how they look to worry about undergarments. Men's underwear designer labels adopted this series of rituals and believed in their appropriateness for males. They imagined a world in which males could look at other males (motivated by a sense of wanting to be as sexually alluring as the models, rather than marry them as before), where males shopped for their own underwear, and where they knew the difference between shapeless rags thrown on in haste and quality-made garments which enhanced natural endowments and aroused desire. The second concept I will be using is the "undie revolution." This refers to the stunning changes that have taken place in the last thirty years, but more especially since the beginning of the twenty-first century, concerning the shapes, colors, textures, and designs of men's underwear.

In tracing the history of men's underwear advertising from 1915 until the first decade of the twenty-first century, my objective is to extend preexisting academic debate on the male body and in this way broach a more extensive subject. This larger debate opposes traditional gender and sexual mythologies (according to which only women and homosexual males find unmentionables mentionable) with a revised mythology which invites all males of any sexual orientation to pay particular attention to their bodies, including what covers their genitals and buttocks. Attributing importance to men's briefs is seemingly vain, but I see analyzing this item of clothing which has been long neglected by cultural critics as the easiest way to demonstrate changes in men's attitudes toward their bodies. As we will see, athletes have been primordial in transmitting the idea that bodies matter.

Premetrosexual Undies

Before analyzing the undie revolution, it is instructive to know what the premetrosexual world of men's underwear looked and felt like.

The Montgomery Ward Catalog of Winter Underwear and Outerwear for 1915 gives an idea of this reality. The first thing to note in
this catalog is the use of line drawings to suggest the human figure.
Photographing live models had to wait until the late 1930s. In the
1950s, we even find animal shapes used in advertising Hanes underwear, an innovation which seems to be a regression from the earlier
catalog etchings. In 1915, only one item of underwear was offered,
the union suit. If in two separate parts, the top section was called a
"shirt" and the bottom part "drawers." The first page of the Montgomery Ward Catalog advertises ankle-length drawers with a three
pearl button-front and ribbed cuffs. On the same page, a union suit is
shown with an impractical "closed crotch." The predominant color
of the union suits is natural grey; however tan, scarlet, and red were
also for sale. Page 4 of the catalog advertises particularly unappeal-
ing heavyweight and fleece-lined underwear in a chocolate brown
color on the outside and a pure white fleecing on the inside. Underwear at the beginning of the twentieth century was all about function: keeping warm, preventing shrinkage, and holding on to the
same garments for as long as possible. It was also about covering up
as much flesh as possible. Sports entered underwear advertising in
the 1940s when Jockey devised a series of drawings featuring
clothed athletes next to drawings of men in underwear. Athletes featured in this way include Babe Ruth, Ty Cobb, Byron Nelson, and
Don Hutson. However, it was not until 1976 that Jockey hit on the
idea of using photographs of athletes stripped to their underwear.
This marked the beginning of the undie revolution.

The Pioneer of the Undie Revolution

Baltimore Orioles baseball player, Jim Palmer, is the first athlete
who made a significant contribution toward revolutionizing men's
underwear advertising and undie-buying habits. He is the first
sportsman advertising men's underwear to offer self-care advice to
other males, thus demonstrating that underwear is part of a more
general approach to looking at and caring for the male body. Born in
New York City in 1945, Palmer pitched for the Orioles from 1965 to
1967, and again from 1969 until 1984. He was named to the American League All-Star team six times and inducted into the Baseball
Hall of Fame in 1990. In 1976, Palmer agreed to be one of sixteen

professional athletes who posed for the Jockey advertising campaign called "Take Away Their Uniforms and Who Are They." Two full-page publicity photographs, each featuring eight athletes, launched a profusion of professional sportsmen into brief fame. Another Jockey campaign followed in 1978 around the new slogan "The Look of a Winner Starts with Jockey." Palmer was the only athlete to reappear alongside five new professional sportsmen. In the space of two years, Jockey had exposed the bodies of twenty-one professional athletes from the worlds of football, ice hockey, basketball, baseball, soccer, and pole vaulting. Another face appeared in the late 1980s when Olympic gymnast Bart Connor posed for Jockey. He was billed as "short, blond and suave," as opposed to the "tall, dark and handsome" stereotype of masculine beauty that Palmer embodied. Never before had so many athletes from different sports exposed their intimate bulges for all the country to see.

One player outstripped all the others to become the commercial face of Jockey underwear throughout all of the 1980s. Part of Jim Palmer's marketable appeal as an underwear model depended on his Mr. Clean, boy-next-door look. In 1985, at the height of his celebrity as a Jockey spokesperson, the forty-year-old Palmer corresponded to the image of a virile adult that housewives could especially find attractive. Even if they look tame now, advertisements of Palmer wearing just Jockeys created controversy in the late 1970s when the jock was exhibited on a Times Square billboard. Unused to seeing a sportsman, not only out of uniform, but almost naked, passers-by either loved it or tried to turn a blind eye. Given that about 70 percent of men's underwear buyers at the time were women, Palmer's status as an identifiable heterosexual helped turn him into a sex symbol for shopping housewives. Pictures of the baseball player in his briefs also turned up in gay bars during the clone years. This unsolicited success demonstrates the potential appeal of men's underwear models to homosexual males, not just housewives. In the case of Palmer and Jockey the homoerotic appeal was accidental. Later on, however, other underwear labels would actively seek to attract men as a marketing objective.

Jim Palmer can be associated with the trend of colored briefs topped with coordinating T-shirts. This marks a major initial step in the eroticization of male bodies, since it offered a personalized choice of hues. In 1969, the market for colored briefs accounted for just 3 percent of Jockey's sales. By 1980, one out of two American males who wore Jockey briefs had color in their drawers. A hetero-sexual male who insists on color-coordinated underwear has a tinge of metrosexual vanity about it, but this is what the pitcher promised. A magazine advertisement from 1980 announcing "The Jockey Fash-ion Statement Is Colorful" showed Palmer sitting on a bench with one hand on his hip (a stylized, somewhat camp posture) and one leg raised and resting on the other knee. He promised a broad selec-tion of styles, patterns, and colors, while wearing a matching red T-shirt and Y-fronts. A 1984 ad shows the pitcher in what became the classic Palmer pose: one leg lifted with his foot on a block, one hand covering a muscled thigh and the other resting on his briefed waist. In this picture, Palmer is wearing the same "life" red Jockeys, but without the T-shirt. The visibly hairy chest and abdomen center at-tention on the hard male body, contrasting with the soft, combed and absorbent cotton red pouch.

Beyond color, another development contributing to the eroticiza-tion of male bodies was the arrival on the market of new names for Jockey briefs. A hint of exoticism crept in to provide an erotic thrill for raunchy, undie-buying spouses. In the 1976 campaign, Palmer posed in a revealing "International Skant Tropez Brief." In 1980, he was seen wearing the "poco" model, a low-rise and Continental-styled gar-ment with a two-layer pouch and a fashion-knit waistband. A couple of years later, a more risqué variation called "élance" hit the market. Evoking images of exotic eroticism, the "élance" brief (a word mean-ing "throb" in French) promised Continental styling for maximum comfort, freedom, and minimum coverage. How the honest-to-God American male achieved maximum freedom inside minimum cover-age was a secret tightly held by Jockey International. The "élance" brief was also billed as made of luxurious combed cotton unlike the humdrum, absorbent cotton of the "life" model. This smacks of mate-rial fetishism. Paradoxically, Jockey's success in bringing an erotic French *frisson* of *luxe* and *volupté* to undie-buying was obtained through a beefy, unquestionably American sportsman. For women, the hint of sexy underwear on their husband was irresistible.

As well as color and evocative names, another logical step in the eroticization of male bodies was to make briefs briefer. The princi-pal means by which Jockey was able to get away with exhibiting more flesh was provided by the sports contextualization. The "Take Away Their Uniforms" ads from 1976 featured sports accessories such as balls, bats, cleats, gloves, and football protection gear. In a

1988 advertisement, Palmer posed in front of a large poster of himself in full baseball uniform, gloved and ready to pitch. In a Macy's ad from the same year, he lay reclined with two dumbbells, one in his hand and the other positioned so as to hide a nipple. Such props and décor provided a safety valve of decency and sports-sanctioned masculinity in a world of foreign-sounding and potentially feminizing skimpiness. The greatest single coup for the underwear manufacturer was to use a sportsman as model. Even without the occasional sports props, Palmer's athletic proficiency justified, excused, and condoned the wearing of colored, low-cut briefs with suggestive names. A Jockey vice-president remarked in 1982 that "When Jim Palmer, an all-American hero, appears in our briefs, he's telling customers that it's all right to wear them" (Meyers 23). The gradual realization by heterosexual males that it was "all right" to choose, buy, and enjoy wearing underwear constituted a major break with the past. Along with designers and fashion photographers, sportsmen such as Palmer were one of the main instruments helping to change perceptions of the denuded male body.

The all-American hero is not only memorable for his promotion of Jockey underwear. Jim Palmer is America's first protometrosexual briefed beef. His importance as a metrosexual precursor is thus twofold. First, he actively participated in the early eroticization of men's underwear. And more generally, he is a precursor of what would later be referred to as a metrosexual lifestyle. The principal means of attracting male followers was the 1985 publication of *Jim Palmer's Way to Fitness.* Illustrated chapters address subjects such as the "Palmerfit" workout program, nutrition, posture and body balance, hair and skin care, stress, and smart dressing. Two chapters especially, "The Personal Touch" and "Fashion Fit," are an attempt to metrosexualize American males, almost twenty years before Michael Flocker's *The Metrosexual Guide to Style.* Amid photographs of Palmer dressed smartly in a tie and suit, looking at his reflection in the mirror shaving, or else standing bare-chested, wearing just a towel and holding up a tie and shirt, we find a multitude of hair, skincare, and fashion tips proffered to the metrosexual wannabe. The Jockey model turned out to be an expert on dry and oily skin, recommending a "scent" (this would now be called a "fragrance"), shampoo frequency, and hairspray for men. Palmer's credentials as hair expert were made public in 1982 when he participated in a national ad campaign for Tegrin Dandruff Shampoo. The fitness book offers advice about selecting clothes according to their fit, fabric, and color for three body sizes: "endomorph" (stocky), "mesomorph" (naturally proportioned), and "ectomorph" (long-limbed). Thrown in with all the fashion hints, Palmer even admits to owning a $3,500 Russian raccoon coat.

A *Washington Post* article, appearing just after the publication of Palmer's fitness book, provides further evidence of the pitcher's protometrosexual lifestyle. Stephanie Mansfield's opening description of "His Hunkness" sets the tone by noticing that "Jim Palmer sits across the restaurant table sipping iced tea and basking in the bronze glow of his Bain de Soleil tan. His body is long and lithe, his ice-hard chest straining against the snug, white European-cut shirt. There's a dimple in his chin and a smirk on his lips" (D1). Even though Palmer normally turned to New York designers Ralph Lauren and Perry Ellis for his outfits, this vignette of a confident American in Continental garb acts as an introduction to the multiple metrosexual clues strewn throughout the rest of the text. The journalist reports, for example, that Palmer "describes himself as vain, narcissistic [and] self-absorbed." A longtime observer refers to the underwear model as "the definition of a prima donna." Mansfield asked her subject if he was vain, thus preempting a question often posed later on to acclaimed metrosexual athletes. (This question came after the comment that Palmer was "the kind of guy who probably checks himself out on the back of every spoon"). The self-confident athlete answered: "Of course. I would say I'm vain." Such a carefree admission helps to account for the American Image Award that Palmer received from the Men's Fashion Association in 1983. It was an apt recompense for such an early pioneer of the undie revolution.

The Modern Kouros

By the mid-1980s, the baseball hero had been surpassed by a sportsman who was chosen to model underwear for fashion designer Calvin Klein. While Jim Palmer was smilingly signing autographs in shopping malls for grateful, Jockey-buying housewives, Calvin Klein revolutionized the way an athlete's body could be portrayed in commercial representations of men's underwear. In 1982 he was wandering around Los Angeles looking for a new model when he spotted Tom Hintnaus, the son of Czechoslovakian refugees. The twenty-four-year-old was born in Brazil, had spent most of his life in the United States, and was preparing for the 1984 Olympics as a pole vaulter. Over six feet tall and weighing 185 pounds, Hintnaus agreed to do a sportswear commercial for Klein. Soon afterward, he launched himself into instant fame when Bruce Weber photographed him on the Greek island of Santorini.

The posters and magazine advertisements of Jim Palmer almost pale into insignificance compared with the overt display of erotics achieved by the hot Brazilian-Californian. The combined efforts of Klein and Weber produced a model for men's underwear photography that remained a source of inspiration for the next twenty years. This partnership marks the beginning of a new and divergent objective when exploiting the male body in order to sell men's underwear: attract males while keeping the attention of women. Calvin Klein had already experimented with the dangers and delights of risqué advertisements in his 1980 CK jeans campaign using the fifteen-year-old Brooke Shields, who had looked salaciously into the camera and asked: "You know what comes between me and my Calvins? Nothing." The double entendre was too much for two New York television stations and the CBS television network. The ad was banned. Exploiting the furor created by the nymphet, Calvin Klein hired Hintnaus. Helped by the technical skill of Weber, the New York designer launched the first briefed and beefed sportsman to benefit from art photography.

Weber's portrait of Tom Hintnaus wearing a pair of white Y-front briefs (the model with which Klein made millions, first as a fetishistic item of gay apparel, then as a mainstream garment) was an amazingly studied and thought-out example of fashion photography. The bronzed body of the pole vaulter provides a successful contrast with the pure, white cotton of the briefs and the white background, beyond which we see a typically Mediterranean blue. Hintnaus is standing, his eyes shut and hands extended on his legs. The standing posture, upright and rigid, distinguishes itself from Palmer's relaxed and naturalistic pose. Here everything is stylized, to enhance what Robert Aldrich has called "the seduction of the Mediterranean." Erect stationary figures, such as that of Hintnaus, are reminiscent of Greek statuary from the Archaic Period. He recalls *kouroi*, large sculptures of naked male bodies which served as devotional offerings to the gods. The closed eyes, in contrast to Palmer's blue-eyed shots, effectively suggest a god-like equanimity, distant perfection, and narcissistic self-sufficiency, far removed from the realm of admiring, worshipping mortals.

Bruce Weber manages to capture a sexual tension which is hardly perceptible in the Jockey photographs despite their vivid names. Behind this tension lies the idea that male sexuality can be exploited for commercial purposes, something that mainstream underwear brands have tended to underplay. One shoulder is raised higher than the other, foregrounding a taut torso. The manner in which the fingers of the right hand are separated and extended suggests a studied solidity and stylization. The raised neck, the head thrown slightly backward, and the camera angle invite the viewer to look up at the figure in wonder. The loose, asymmetrical briefs with their sculptured folds obviously cover a bulging form. As symbolized by the forty by fifty foot billboard of Hintnaus in Times Square, this Apollo basking in the sun on a Greek island took men's underwear advertising to new hypostatic heights. Obscene graffiti appeared on the glass covering the poster in New York bus shelters. Fetishists smashed the glass to steal the briefed Brazilian (over thirty-five cases of purloined loins were reported). Weber had turned men's underwear into an art form. In so doing, he offered a blueprint for a generation of advertisers whose conception of the male body and men's intimate clothing depended on eroticizing the male body. The challenge was to not exclusively attract the female and homoerotic gazes, but to try and capture the attention of heterosexual males who, Klein thought, were in dire need of undie satisfaction.

Football and Basketball Favorites

Four new sportsmen indulged in underwear exposure throughout the 1980s, beginning with two New York Jet football players, defensive lineman Mark Gastineau and carousing quarterback Joe Namath. The choice of heterosexually identified football players to model men's underwear is significant, as it points to underlying undie trouble. Football's image of violence and rough play as well as the assumed heterosexuality of all players were used to offset fears attached to undie interest. After Nantucket Industries hired Gastineau to launch a line of underwear and swimwear, he advertised Brut fashion briefs in *Ladies' Home Journal* in June 1982. The president of Nantucket spoke to the press about what had led the company to choose a professional football player six foot five inches tall and weighing 270 pounds. He referred to "the identification of the blue-collar worker with him. He's down in the trenches, too" (Eskenazi D27). Such muddy trenches distinguish themselves from Calvin Klein's Apollo of the same year.

As for Joe Namath, after retiring from professional football, the famous playboy married at the age of forty-one. Soon after, he signed a five-year contract with the same company that had hired Gastineau to produce a new line of men's underwear bearing Namath's name and signature. Namath not only modeled the underwear, he approved all the designs and allowed his photograph to appear on packaging. In November 1984, *Time* magazine reported Namath's marriage and underwear launch beside a photo of a smiling husband in sky-blue briefs. The *Washington Post* described the collection as comprised of·nine styles, each accompanied by a mini-poster of the athlete. According to the report, "Some look like swim trunks in Dacron printed tattersall checks, window-pane plaids and pin stripes, plus others in heathers and solids. Another group mixes jersey and mesh in running-shorts styles" (Hyde K3). Readers almost needed a degree in underwear fabrics to follow this précis of fetishism. Other patterns included subway graffiti and jungle scenes. There was a conscious effort on the part of Nantucket to appeal to females buyers, half of whom, it was thought, would purchase the item to wear themselves. Media star Joe Namath thus consolidated the tradition of using straight football players for the express purpose of tempting women to buy men's underwear, a tradition that has continued to the twenty-first century.

The Gastineau and Namath experiments were flashes in the pan episodes leaving almost no trace. However, when the major underwear brand Hanes hired sports celebrities in 1989 the effect was much more marked. Hanes reportedly spent $25 million on its most expensive television and print advertisement campaign in eighty-eight years. Though a number of sportsmen appeared in the campaign (pushing men and boys underwear, socks, and fleece wear), only two advertised briefs: Michael Jordan from the Chicago Bulls and Super Bowl quarterback Boomer Esiason of the Cincinnati Bengals. A family-friendly after-the-game approach was taken by Hanes, again in order to appeal to wives. Supposedly about to take a nap after a game, gridiron legend Esiason appeared in the TV ad clad in white underwear. Hanes went on to create the Michael Jordan

Collection of men's underwear in 1997 in which the athlete's sur-
name was printed on the waistband of each model.

Choosing such heteronormative models from sports culture may
have had the positive benefit of trying to counteract taboos linked to
males taking an interest in their own bodies. This could be achieved,
it was thought, by setting up athletes as role models for other men.
But Hanes's blatant heterosexualized imagery also reinforced the
stereotypical idea that buying and looking at men's underwear was
exclusively a woman's task and pleasure. Jockey also subscribed to
the same idea. One of their ad campaigns from 1994 featured the slogan "If a woman buys you the Jockey pouch take it as a compliment." Such a slogan ignores the possibility of men taking an interest
in their own pouches.

The All-American Metrosexual

The initiative of using athletes in order to exploit their virility and
heterosexuality has been the cornerstone of men's underwear publicity in the United States since the days of Jim Palmer. This is particularly obvious in the career of Gregory Sovell. After working for
Calvin Klein, Sovell started a new men's underwear label in 1991
called 2(x)ist ("to exist"). From the start, this line was directed at
what was perceived to be a "gay market." A publicity campaign
from 1994 used professional model Tracy James, an American who
had worked for at least sixteen underwear companies including Emporio Armani Underwear. He was chosen for a *Cosmopolitan* center-
fold in 1996. Advertisements of James relied on a pumped up, Muscle Mary body with an angelic head, traits believed to attract a
homosexual audience. One black and white photograph of James
wearing white briefs shows the model characteristically lying on a
bed, his head thrown back on a pillow. Armpits, deltoids, six-pack,
and imposing thighs all invite the homoerotic gaze.

Toward the end of 2001, Sovell's company attempted to widen
their customer base by selling their boxers and briefs to heterosexual
males. In order to attract non-gay male buyers, 2(x)ist butched up its
undies act by choosing a new spokesman from the world of football.
This had temporarily worked when eight football players were chosen by Jockey in the late 1970s and was confirmed with Gastineau,
Namath, and Esiason in the 1980s. The services of New York Giants

cornerback Jason Sehorn were bought for a million dollars. Jeff Danzer, executive vice president of marketing for 2(x)ist, explained the move away from a professional male model to a football player. He stated that "In order to get the word about us out to the masses, we had to go with someone everybody could identify with. Every guy wants to be him, and every woman wants him." Asked about Sehorn's appeal to gay men, Danzer nonchalantly added "so be it" (Walton F1). The blatant homoeroticism of previous 2(x)ist iconography was downplayed in the photographs and publicity shots of the Giants' star player. Photographs of Sehorn standing, sitting, and reclining in white briefs and boxers, avoided raunchiness. Instead, they tastefully showed a jock at ease in designer underwear. While this publicity was aimed simultaneously at two distinct targets, women and heterosexual males, it was obvious that Sehorn would also hold appeal with homosexual males.

There was an added reason to use a twice-married, heteronormative sportsman to sponsor men's underwear. In order to attract heterosexually identified males or their partners into buying more sexy, costly, and stylish underwear, it made commercial sense to have a married man exhibit himself in a Lycra piqué knit, brushed nylon, or Peruvian cotton. Without this strategy, buying underwear for luxurious softness, moisture management systems, stretch, and "breathability" might be construed as fetishistic and thus resemble homosexual shopping habits. Sponsorship of *Queer Eye for the Straight Guy* by 2(x)ist, coupled with explicit advice from the Fab Five mentioning the underwear stylist in various episodes, showed the new inseparability of the heterosexual *and* gay buying public, now rubbing shoulders at the same underwear counters.

Like his predecessor, Jim Palmer, Sehorn's preoccupation with the body extended far beyond men's underwear to include a general interest in the sartorial. Sehorn's reciprocal relationship with the world of fashion, his exposure in the men's style press and his attendance at public events in New York have all helped to publicize metrosexuality. Public interest in Sehorn as a style jock began in September 1999 when *GQ* (U.S.) ran "Jason Sehorn Is Born" with the subtitle "The hard-bodied cornerback and soft-to-the-touch cashmere make a comeback this season." Wearing a kind of wool that Carson Kressley from *Queer Eye* once described as "pornographically pleasurable to the touch" (Allen 164), Sehorn modeled for six photographs, wearing expensive garments made of cashmere. The use of the words "hard" and "soft" in the subtitle was a way to convince male readers that it was possible to be virile and stylish at the same time. One photograph shows Sehorn proudly exhibiting his six-pack by partially stripping off a Polo Ralph Lauren turtleneck. The nipples and six-pack became an invitation for readers to appreciate, fantasize about, and want to touch the athlete's body. A close-up full-page portrait of Sehorn's head may have been there to exhibit a cashmere crewneck, but the center of focus was a man's face, not his clothes. There was some obvious titillation proffered to readers who might be male or female, straight or gay.

Sehorn has multiplied public appearances in New York and in Beverly Hills as well since his retirement from professional football. After attending the Armani Retrospective at the Guggenheim in October 2000, he was present at the launch party of the Lanvin fragrance Oxygene Homme in February 2001. Demonstrating his personal engagement with the fashion industry, he was seen onstage at the 2001 and 2002 Vogue Fashion Awards in New York City. In April 2003, Sehorn attended the Metropolitan Museum of Art Costume Institute Benefit Gala, sponsored by Gucci, and in February 2004 the model was photographed at the Louis Vuitton 150th Anniversary party and store opening during Olympia Fashion week. In February 2006, Sehorn attended the 8th Annual Costume Designers Guild Awards in Beverly Hills. He typifies how attributing importance to underwear can be a small piece in a larger picture concerning body image and self-care. Sehorn's potential effect on changing perceptions linked to looking after the body tended to be restricted to the United States. When a non-American underwear model working for Calvin Klein stole the limelight in 2003 at the height of media interest in metrosexuality, the sphere of influence of one athlete standing in his briefs extended to the world.

Undie Trouble

The Jason Sehorn underwear campaign took place before metrosexuality was brought to the attention of the world media. This is why the football player's name was not immediately associated with the cultural trend known as metrosexuality. I would now like to consider Fredrik Ljungberg, an underwear model who presents two major differences from Sehorn. First, as a bachelor, Ljungberg does not benefit from the same amount of heteronormative credibility as a married athlete. As a consequence, this lack of a spouse has provoked distinctive signs of undie trouble. Second, the fact that his underwear promotion took place during the time when "metrosexual" was becoming a household buzzword and not before means that a single word was now available to try to specify the interests shared by males such as Sehorn and Ljungberg. In the case of Ljungberg, however, his bachelor status kindled fears and suspicions that fashion-conscious males who publicly exhibit their bodies in designer underwear are sexually attracted to other men. Ljungberg has had to deal with critics questioning his sexual orientation. This is a direct result of confusing lifestyle and sexuality.

Ljungberg's rise to metrosexual fame began in 2003 when Calvin Klein, not to be surpassed by his rivals, returned to the underwear foray and chose a Swedish soccer player who was identified as heterosexual. Known more popularly as "Freddie," Ljungberg joined the Arsenal soccer team as midfielder in 1998. The British *GQ* devoted an illustrated article to the Swede in June 2002. Due to his off-the-field wardrobe and penchant for dyeing his hair, he was billed in the article as the premier league's most preeminent dandy and the Dennis Rodman of soccer. When Freddie entered the Fumoir at Claridge's Hotel in Mayfair London for the *GQ* interview, he struck the interviewer as resembling someone who had just walked off the Milan runway. Ljungberg was wearing "boot-cut denims, swaggering Cuban-heeled chisel-toed boots, a huge white trash Kid Rock–style belt buckle with the legend 'DC/DC' picked out in shimmering rhinestones" (Mills 176). He also had an "an open-necked Seventies print Italian shirt, teamed with a waisted JR Ewing jacket and a neckerchief tied in a coquettish side knot" (Mills 176). For this *GQ* story, Ljungberg modeled clothes from "Vertice Uomo," a boutique owned by a designer friend in South Molton Street, London. It was not only Ljungberg's allure that created the impression of a style-conscious athlete. He counted designers among his friends, thus demonstrating close links with the fashion world.

Two months after this fashion coverage, Ljungberg gained wider media coverage when he was interviewed for the British arts and entertainment weekly *Time Out*. By August 2002, the swaggering Swede was shorn of his aubergine locks and had adopted his now characteristic buzz cut. Compared to David Beckham because of his chiseled looks, this urban *flâneur* was interested in following the latest fashion tendencies. He told *Time Out:* "My hobby is clothes. A couple of my friends know about fashion and one of the things I do in afternoons is check out catwalks before stuff makes the shops" (Davies 14). Ljungberg's interest in fashion, his uninhibited sartorial style, and imposing physique made him a perfect metrosexual candidate for the first CK men's underwear campaign of the twenty-first century.

Coinciding with Ljungberg becoming *the* CK underwear model, in September 2003 the British *GQ* published a series of photographs taken in Stockholm of the soccer star wearing various items of urban sportswear. The relaxed portraits titled "Bend It Like Freddie" (as a homage to Gurinder Chadha's 2002 film *Bend It Like Beckham,* implying that the Swedish soccer sensation had acquired equal popularity for his looks) incorporated a wide selection of American and European designers. Ljungberg explained his eclectic fashion tastes to *Room Service* in April 2005. He told a journalist: "I don't like wearing outfits from one specific designer, like you see in a shop window—I like to mix and match, mix vintage with nice, new stuff" (Raphael 29). Such tastes for clothes from a wide variety of designers show the athlete's attempts to individualize his sartorial style, rather than have it imposed by one or two fashion houses.

After being plastered over twenty-four windows of Selfridges store in London, as well as adorning the city's famous red buses, Freddie's mostly naked body was hoisted up in Times Square like his predecessors. Although he had obtained some publicity in Britain, Ljungberg's shaved and tattooed body wearing white Pro Stretch CK briefs with a red waistband brought a previously unknown face to American billboards. The twenty-six-year-old athlete evidenced a return by Calvin Klein to his initial men's underwear marketing strategy, begun twenty years previously with Hintnaus. Photographed by Steven Klein, the new CK poster featured Freddie with his arms upright, one hand behind his head, the other lying flat on his military-style scalp. These gestures accentuated his shoulder and pectoral muscles. A false panther tattoo on the right side of his abdomen, replacing a real panther tattoo on Freddie's back, added a fetishistic interest and drew the viewer's eye towards the Pro Stretch pouch. Klein's 2005 publicity poster of Ljungberg showed one arm gripping a bar (emphasizing his bicep) and another pulling down slightly on the waistband of his black CK boxer briefs to expose a part of his groin.

By mid-2003, there was a new lexical tool to describe the latest arrival to the parade of briefed jocks. Quick to comment on the sportsman, the *New York Times* judiciously referred to Ljungberg as "the dishy, slim-hipped metrosexual fashion plate for our times" (Silva 80). Whereas in the past, men's underwear models with a marked interest in clothes and how they looked were simply labeled "narcissistic," like Jim Palmer, or "flamboyant," like Joe Namath, Mark Simpson's 2002 Salon.com article and the Euro RSCG reports issued in the summer of 2003 provided journalists with another word to describe fashionable sportsmen. George Wayne's *Vanity Fair* interview with Ljungberg, published in April 2004, included the now expected question on one side of the Atlantic: "But are you metrosexual?" As Wayne merely interpreted metrosexuality in terms of pedicures, hair treatment, and nail care, Ljungberg responded with a general denial, saying "No, I don't do any of that stuff."

Ljungberg's *Vanity Fair* interview is still of interest because it suggests that the soccer player's metrosexuality lies elsewhere. Ljungberg's sex appeal is a much more convincing indication of metrosexuality than his hair rinses. The *Vanity Fair* interview is an excellent example of how an athlete's genitals can be the subject of public debate. Such a topic shows sports sex from a new angle. After Ljungberg is asked if he is a member of Foreskin Anonymous, Wayne further provokes him by inquiring what his teammates called him after his CK endorsement: "Do they call you Frédérique?" No, said the model, they all called him Freddie. He was asked if the other players in the Arsenal locker room "stuff their underwear with socks and mince around the room imitating" him. "There is a little teasing," admitted the midfielder. Wayne then feigns surprise upon learning that his interlocutor never waxes his "cho-cho." Probing questions about the size of Freddie's "lunchbox" show a male comically reduced to a bulge and put on a par with female pin-up models.

Contrasting with this lighthearted humor, in the country where Ljungberg lived, the press was still locked into stereotypical and facile equations between outward appearance and sexual orientation. Faced with the athlete's "outlandish" looks, tabloids have been obsessed with a different question: Is Freddie gay? Repeated rebuttals by the bachelor midfielder in British newspapers only fueled the controversy, which even reappeared in the February 2004 *GQ* (UK) where the object of discussion frankly admitted, "We laugh about it—because we know all these rumours are rubbish" (Morgan 114). This debate led to the printing of statements such as this by dancer and singer Denise Lopez in January 2004: "I've heard the rumours about him being gay but I can tell you Freddie is all man, 100 per cent straight" (McGee). Lopez's comment draws attention to generalized suspicions that metrosexual interests are synonymous with same-sex desire. This impression concerning Ljungberg was encouraged by the exposing of his near-naked body in publicity, his fashion photo shoots, and the importance he gave to shopping and clothes.

The Arsenal midfielder found his face on the cover of the British magazine *Gay Times* in July 2004. In this issue, his portrait was used to illustrate an article on the Euro 2004 soccer championship's ten "sexiest stars" (Smith 52). It is likely that Ljungberg was unworried about this publicity because the following month he traveled to New York in order to pose for the cover of the U.S. gay magazine *Out.* Here the "soccer stud," as he is called in the title of the short article, posed for two conventional fashion shots wearing a Calvin Klein track jacket, T-shirt, and jeans. He exposed himself in the gay press on both sides of the Atlantic and he did this without benefiting from marital status to help offset the suspicion that he, like the readers of *Gay Times* and *Out,* might also be gay.

The coverage of Ljungberg in *Gay Times* is evidence of how the gay press can use photographs of athletes without their authorization in order to boost sales and satisfy reader voyeurism. For Ljungberg this is unproblematic, as he intentionally provided *Out* with a short interview and posed for their photographer. However, it is intriguing to wonder what the succession of ten European soccer stars made of their sex-symbol status as relayed in "Game On," the *Gay Times* article which displayed their photographs and heaped praise on ten "hot, sweaty footballers" (Smith 52). Voted number one on the list, Ljungberg is described as "the mousey-blond bombshell" (52), while the Swiss Bernt Haas is complimented for being "ruggedly handsome," "broad of shoulder," and "beautifully fashioned" (52). The Frenchman Thierry Henry, shown shirtless on the pitch, is given the accolade "pretty" (58), the German Sebastian Kehl "baby-faced" (61), while the Swede Olof Mellberg invites the unusual compliment "rather tasty little bear cub" (62). The appropriation of athletes' bodies by the gay press is becoming more normalized, as demonstrated by another British gay publication, *Attitude,* which put Ljungberg on a cover in April 2006. This issue promised the "Top 10 Hottest Football Studs."

Ljungberg demonstrates a relaxed attitude about exposing his body to the gaze of women and men of any sexual orientation. In the *Vanity Fair* interview, he clearly stated that he thought the Calvin Klein publicity was "a good thing to do" (Wayne 116). One important result of such public exposure is mentioned in this interview. In the words of the interviewer, Ljungberg (like all other athletes who model men's underwear) is "lusted after by men and women all over the world." Ljungberg's acceptance and ostensible enjoyment of this attention, even at the price of having his sexual orientation questioned, demonstrates a decided distance from jock culture. In contrast, a sportsman who models men's underwear can encapsulate national fears and insecurities concerning changing gender roles for men. One such case is Pat Rafter in Australia.

Resistance to Metrosexuality

Ljungberg provides evidence of openly endorsing a revision of gender and sexual mythologies, but this is not always the case for all athletes who model men's underwear. Tennis legend Pat Rafter, winner of the U.S. Open in 1997 and 1998, demonstrates resistance to the winds of change. Even though this athlete has stripped to his underwear for publicity, he still voices traditional bipolar logic and a conservative conception of gender roles. In July 1999, the American *GQ* devoted a cover shot and article to "The Aussie Adonis." Sally Jenkins's piece, despite some gender-confused comments about Rafter's ponytail, insisted on the tennis player's attraction for lovesick females. Michael O'Neill's full-page accompanying photograph presented a pin-up style portrait of Rafter with a naked torso and a floppy ponytail. Such a pretty-boy image was somewhat attenuated by a belching Aussie who was described as "legendary for his farts" (110).

Three years after this international coverage, Rafter was hired to be the new face of Bonds, the Australian version of Hanes. Begun in Sydney by an American at the time of the First World War, Bonds adopted the cartoon character Chesty Bond as an iconographic representation in 1938. In 2002, deciding to revamp its image and replace the cartoon by a living celebrity, Hanes chose recently voted Australian of the Year winner Pat Rafter to model for posters and underwear packaging. In 2003, a television commercial campaign featuring Rafter was launched to promote "very comfy undies," hipster trunks. The following year, he was back on TV praising a "very comfy" boxer range.

Rafter has modeled briefs, boxers, T-shirts, and tank tops for Bonds. Over 250 million Chesty Bond "singlets" have sold since they were first marketed. The Bonds brand name is associated with blue-collar, no-nonsense masculinity. In order to suggest such an "authentic" masculinity, the summer 2003 Bonds television ad features Rafter wearing hipster trunks in a locker room while a tennis match is heard on a television set in the background. After friends ask Rafter why some tennis players grunt when they hit the ball, we hear the punch line: "Mate, they're not wearing comfy undies." Another locker room scenario inspired the cotton boxer 2004 television commercial showing Pat and a mate getting changed after a workout. As they put on jeans over loose-fitting boxers, they see a group of men wincing and sighing. Pat and his male friend have worked out the reason for the aches and pains. These blokes are not wearing "New Bonds Cotton Boxers, very comfy Undies."

Despite the fact that the commercial success of Bonds underwear depends on wide audience appeal, there is something suspiciously queer about Rafter's underwear ads. To assure interest from as large a public as possible, this brand of clothing has to be associated with heterosexuality. Hiring a butch thirty-year-old sportsman as the "face" of Bonds seemed to fulfill this objective, even if the tennis player announced his retirement from professional sport early in 2003. This defection was remedied by Rafter's June 2004 marriage, thus reinforcing his heterosexual credentials. However, what I find of interest in the television ads more than the typically Australian celebration of mateship is the homoerotic subtext which counterbalances and subverts the overriding keep-it-straight intention. Already there is something suspect about the all-male locker room setting, corresponding to a homoerotic fantasy of a masculine space occupied by sweaty, sometimes naked, pre- and post-showered bodies. Like Rafter, all viewers of the 2003 ad are left to ponder on the image of crotch-tight tennis players, grunting and groaning in some sort of painful pleasure as they make a hit. Having a group of males decide whether another male has "comfy" or "non-comfy" underwear demonstrates an interest in men's genital comfort that borders on the homoerotic. There was more grunting in the 2004 ad in which Pat and his mate together imagined the excruciating pain of more men suffering from uncomfortably tight hipster briefs. To add to the multiple and conflicting readings that the Bonds television ads provoke, posters of Rafter on Australian buses wearing "Guyfront Trunks" do not help dispel the homoerotic aura surrounding the Bonds campaign. Instead, these posters draw even more attention to the model's manly pouch by parading it through the country's urban bus routes for all bankers and businessmen to see.

Public statements by the tennis champion distancing himself from any inclinations that might be termed metrosexual have helped keep Bonds, and Rafter, on the straight and narrow. At the Melbourne Fashion Festival in March 2005, Rafter made a point of refusing ever to catwalk in underwear. He stated: "I'm not an expert on fashion at all. I'll be at the parade, but, God no, I won't be on the catwalk. No amount of money in the world would get me in my undies on the catwalk" (Hurt 40). He also made it clear that attending fashion festivals and fashion in general was not his cup of tea. Such diehard comments are an attempt to resist metrosexuality by shunning activities perceived as compromising a virile and heterosexual self-image. Oblivious to the queer subtext of his commercials, Rafter may have imagined that "undie talk" among mates was innocent and being filmed in underwear was unproblematic. He was comfortable with the idea of showing himself in briefs or boxers to the nation's men on television, being plastered over buses and displayed in the printed press, but decidedly ill at ease having to show his bulge to a live male audience. The reason is simple. At a fashion parade he could *see* the reaction of other males.

Metrosexual Undies

As outlined at the beginning of this chapter, the premetrosexual world of men's undergarments was grim. Function and durability as well as a restricted choice in materials and colors meant that wearing underwear was more of a chore than a pleasure. The main concern of premetrosexual men's underwear manufacturers was to provide cheap, long-lasting garments. Since 1976, a revolutionary change in attitude has been taking place in both mainstream and designer men's underwear labels. In the space of thirty years, a radically new vision based on eroticizing the male genital area and men's buttocks is transforming the ways men look at their bodies. Four locations (Australia, New Zealand, the United States, and Europe) will now be

examined in order to compare variations in how underwear manufacturers offer males body satisfaction. The scope of the undie revolution has been vastly helped by modern technology. Web sites such
as International Jock and International Male post underwear to any
destination in the world and thus create a global community of men
interested in how their bodies look and feel.

The Sydney-based aussieBum brand of underwear and swimwear was set up by surfing and swimming enthusiast Sean Ashby.
Since 2001, aussieBums have turned into a cult fetish, attracting
customers worldwide. The success of the aussieBum label partly
lies in the commercialization of the Australian beach and open-air
lifestyle. Videos from the aussieBum Web site have featured life-
savers and water polo players. The aussieBum brand brings fun to
men's underwear. Vibrant patterns and pastel colors, playful collection names (Flaunt, Animal, Seven Deadly Sins, Tutti Frutti,
Commando, and Cool), and expert advertising campaigns have
helped to turn this brand into a success story. The launching of the
Wonderjock at the end of 2006 in the underwear line caused a
media stir. Like the Wonderbra it referenced, the Wonderjocks were
meant to lift and separate. Efficient sales via the Internet and enticing photography to market the brand have helped export carefree
Aussie hedonism everywhere.

Nearby in New Zealand, twenty-two-year-old Daniel Carter
from the All Blacks team was chosen in 2004 to model a new Jockey
Dri-Y trunk and tank top, seam-free trunks, and sport mesh boxers.
New Zealand had used sports celebrities in men's underwear advertising since the beginning of the 1990s. Jockey's targeting a male-
buying public with a young rugby player made sense in a country
where the sport is so pervasive. Billboards and buses in Auckland
and Christchurch brought Carter instant celebrity in his native New
Zealand where he at once attracted girly groupies. Perhaps it is the
way Carter crosses his hefty arms like a construction worker in publicity shots that stopped the media from stirring interest in the
model's sexuality. Jockey's intention was to have a body which
would equally appeal to both sexes. A spokesperson from the company informed an online fashion Web site that "Men know the importance of good support and the new Jockey range as modeled by
Daniel has plenty of that in all the right places" ("Rugby Hero"). Despite this cocky assurance, Carter told the British press that after
having found the posters, his father had said, "What the hell are you

doing? Get your trousers back on" (Foy 100). The rugby player him-self admitted that there were drawbacks by stating, "I don't mind a bit of attention, but at times it can get out of hand" (Foy 100). The at-tention, it seems, came principally from men. According to a 2004 online survey called the "Great Revealing Undie Debate," 76 percent of New Zealand males bought their own underwear ("NZ Guys"). A new term was coined to describe this cultural realignment, the "retro-metro-undie-sexual," defined as "a guy who likes to think he doesn't care about what undies he wears, but really does" ("NZ Guys"). American fashion designers had been preparing for this turnaround since the beginning of the 1980s. Twenty-first-century metrosexuality and a New Zealand rugby player made it lexically and culturally possible.

While New Zealand was setting records in the undie revolution, back in the United States the men's underwear war continued. After Calvin Klein attacked with Ljungberg in 2003, the creative designer of 2(x)ist, Gregory Sovell, counterattacked by leaving the company he had founded and creating a new one under the label C-IN2 ("see into"). New York saw the 2004 launch of this new underwear and swimsuit collection which later hit international markets in South America, Europe, and Japan. Unlike so many previous underwear campaigns, no sportsman was visible to excuse the blatant sexuality and raciness of C-IN2. It was confrontational, daring, and intention-ally provocative. In the past, athletes had been used as underwear models to appeal to customers of both sexes and to supply some jus-tification for transgressing the taboo concerning male nudity in ad-vertising. The C-IN2 publicity campaign is based on the assumption that cultural norms have changed and that there is no longer a need to use sports to disguise the objectifying, exhibition, passivity, and sexploitation of the male body.

According to the company's philosophy outlined on its Web site, this new brand of underwear and swimwear is a fantasy of fabric and construction variations destined for every man's wardrobe. Un-like previous underwear campaigns which were addressed princi-pally to women and heterosexual males, C-IN2 is a clear call princi-pally addressed to all males. One swimwear item features a patented, sling built-in support, described by the company as an ad-justable microfiber strap sewn into the crotch that lifts, brings for-ward, and improves the profile of the wearer. Underwear innova-tions such as this one encourage males to be proud of their pouches.

Other variations invented by C-IN2 include briefs that are fly-front, lo-no-sho, contour-pouch, active sport, and a profile boxer. There is also a jockstrap, a thong, a lo-no-sho trunk, an engineered tank, and a deep V T-shirt. Gone are the days of Jim Palmer's so-called "life" briefs, since a whole new vocabulary of voluptuousness now caters to vain males. It is fascinating to realize that these garments are destined for mainstream consumption rather than for the satisfaction of a fringe of fetishists.

The C-IN2 philosophy makes its objective clear in two ways. First, all males of any sexual orientation are targeted, and second, men's underwear is envisioned as a lifestyle item, not just an insignificant encumbrance. This second aspect is evident in the Web site claim that "our underwear products have been designed with a man with an active lifestyle in mind." The intriguing and somewhat paradoxical means adopted by C-IN2 to promote this so-called active lifestyle is to insist on the passivity of the underwear models in their publicity. Steven Klein's photographs, which are visible on the company's Web site, capture the spirit of the new collection. One features a muscled model in white C-IN2 briefs, with his pants down, handcuffed and held by one police officer, while a second officer is about to draw his pistol. A second shot shows two briefed males being manhandled by as many police officers. One is forced to bend over the front of the police car in order to be handcuffed from behind. Such poses show the powerful turnaround that has taken place since Palmer's smiling shots.

Based on conventions of gay porn, Klein's images manage to respect and break two rules of traditional masculinity norms. One of these norms equates masculinity with power. Klein respects this norm since the hypermasculine sports heroes who are normally the fodder of men's underwear ads are transposed into two police officers. These uniformed "athletes" are shown disempowering two tattooed and accessorized males who have a penchant for designer underwear. While paying lip service to normative notions of masculinity, Klein also subverts them because the center of focus in each photograph is a disempowered and denuded male, not the self-assured cops in their drag. The photographer invents a triadic structure of desire bringing together viewer (the spectator of the ad), viewed (the victims of police manhandling) and active victimizers (the police officers). Male spectators have the possibility of identifying with the victims, the victimizers, or both. Klein thus demonstrates how both an active and a passive dynamic can be associated with masculinity.

The second norm concerns the taboo associated with the phallic mystique. If it is possible to "see into" these undies, as the brand name C-IN2 promises, then all the toned bodies of athletes who formerly graced underwear ads are logically no longer necessary to compensate for the hidden male member. What we observe, however, in Klein's photographs is an even more hystericized hypermasculinity than that present in previous underwear advertising. This is particularly evident in the uniformed officers, one of whom has a belt covered with phallic substitutes. These replacements for the hidden penis all provide symbolic visual evidence that it *is* possible to "see into" this underwear. Sovell thus respected and rewrote the underwear rule book in this campaign and in so doing offered what the C-IN2 Web site refers to as "essential core products." It is a sign of the times and an intensification of previous sexploitation in men's underwear advertising that C-IN2 items look more hardcore than core.

In Europe, the French brand Hom has been participating in changing men's attitudes toward their bodies by its extensive use of transparent and elasticized materials. The function of these materials is to literalize the possibility implicit in the brand name C-IN2: "see into" men's underwear and thereby transgress the taboo associated with unveiling the penis. Since 2002, the *lingerie d'homme* range produced by Hom has been putting men's underwear on a par with women's underwear, notably by using the term *lingerie* instead of *sous-vêtement,* the usual word for underwear in French. The Hom Web site describes this collection as "An invitation to travel in the universe of seduction, sensuality, eroticism and fantasy." Concepts such as these are thought to be more "naturally" linked to female sexuality. Hom, however, promotes their appropriateness for males. Style names give a good indication of what Hom undergarments are imagined to procure for men. We find models such as Impulse, Sensual, Vertigo, Wild, Tattoo, Emotion, Extreme, Temptation, Torrid, Sensation, and Carnal. As well, there is the quasi-English "Sogood." Matching see-through and lacy embroidered T-shirts and underwear made of tulle polyamide, viscose, and Elasthane offer males similar pleasures in a body zone to those enjoyed by women. A visible sign of increased equality between the sexes in the matter and materials of underwear was the special area devoted to display forty-five manufacturers at the

2005 International Lingerie Salon held in Paris. Runway models showed off the world's latest designs in men's underwear to over twenty thousand visitors from the underwear profession.

Unlike the avant-garde twenty-first-century publicity of C-IN2 and Hom in which athletes were dispensed with, the Dolce & Gabbana 2006 and 2007 underwear campaigns marked a return to using sportsmen as models. Having recourse to athletes again in men's underwear advertising might suggest more undie trouble. And this is exactly what is apparent in the Dolce & Gabbana campaigns due to one all-important innovation. Rather than follow the traditional formula of featuring one sportsman in a single underwear ad, the Italian brand name invented an all-male group format showing men stripped off to their underwear together. In 2006, five prestigious Italian soccer players posed for Mariano Vivanco. We find Fabio Cannavaro, the captain of the Italian national team since 2005, two players who at the time played for Juventus (Manuele Blasi and Gianluca Zambrotta), and the remaining two from A.C. Milan (Gennaro Gattuso and Andrea Pirlo). The locker room and shower scene backgrounds of the publicity shots are described on the Dolce & Gabbana Web site as representing "the geometric and vivid environment of the Fifties." There is an obvious deification and emphasis on Antique statuary in the way the soccer players are described. The Web site likens them to "modern Greek gods" who display their "sculpturesque [sic] beauty." These Mediterranean gods are praised for the way in which they represent "contemporary man." This man is defined as someone who shows "care for himself and attention to his own body." By offering this definition, the Italian men's underwear campaign knew exactly how to formulate and represent metrosexuality.

What is especially interesting about these Italian soccer gods is the fact that they are not only displaying their curves and crotches to any interested spectator. They are exhibiting their bodies to each other. Paradoxically, whereas athletes had been employed as underwear models for three quarters of a century with the intent of destigmatizing interest in men's underwear and naked male bodies, when they are shown *en masse* in the same advertisement, the end result is that the accumulation of semi-naked males looks altogether queer. Like most menswear publicity commissioned by the designers Dolce and Gabbana, homoerotics is substantially present in the 2006 and 2007 underwear campaigns. The participation of national sports heroes (four of whom went on to participate in and win the 2006 World

Cup) in such sexually ambiguous advertising suggests that a significant change of thinking has taken place. The exact nature and implications of this change will now be examined.

What Do Undies Reveal?

Men's underwear advertising using athletes as models is especially
revealing about men and their bodies. It is possible to interpret
men's underwear ads in two ways: either as signs of perpetuating
traditional gender and sexual mythologies or as indications of resist-
ing such mythologies. Revised perceptions concerning expressions
of masculinity and how these are interpreted as signs of sexual orientation are particularly evident in men's underwear ads over the
last thirty years. Even if changed perceptions are much more noticeable since the turn of the century, they did not suddenly take place
overnight. As the case of Jim Palmer suggests, there were precursors
throughout the 1980s and 1990s. This investigation of athletes in
men's underwear publicity leads me to see the main changes in three
areas: seductive passivity, the phallic mystique, and fetishism.

The first change that can be highlighted is the positive portrayal
of seductive passivity in a masculine context. All men's underwear
ads are based on a construction of the model as a passive object of
the gaze, rather than an active agent of penetration. In this context,
Susan Bordo makes a worthwhile distinction between "face-off" ads
depicting a model and a spectator outstaring each other and those
ads which feature "languid leaners," whom she describes as more
"openly seductive" (Bordo 188). When advertisements show
briefed men with their eyes shut (such as the photograph of Tom
Hintnaus), this seductive passivity is even more obvious. In both
cases, however, the near nudity of the figures makes them seem disempowered, despite the exaggerated posturing of musculature. In
her study of the male nude, Melody Davis provides a similar interpretation concerning contemporary photography. She argues that
"if specularized, men will lose their potency and force [. . .] they
will become [. . .] mere objects, voids for the gaze" (Davis 67). This
is important because traditional gender mythology interprets such
objectifying and passivity as feminizing. In contrast, underwear ads
featuring hypermasculine sports heroes demonstrate the extent to
which the seductive passivity of males can be interpreted as a sign

of masculinity. Disempowerment, seduction, and passivity do not naturally pertain to females and female bodies.

Men's underwear advertising sustains the phallic mystique by covering genital bulges. At the same time, it strains against the mystique, especially by using tight-fitting or semitransparent materials. Speaking about American films of the 1990s, Peter Lehman is justified when he argues that "The penis in our culture either is hidden from sight, or its representation is carefully regulated" (494). Lehman further contends that "Silence about and invisibility of the penis contribute to a phallic mystique" (494). Encouraging such invisibility, the center of attention in all men's underwear iconography is the cotton pouch and by metonymic extension the penis. The tits and torsos, the panthers and poses, these are all secondary. What counts is the crotch. Muscled bodies in this context are phallic substitutes for what is always suggested, never shown, the hidden object of desire inside the brief. However, despite the bulges, all men's underwear posters and packaging (like pouched American body-builders from the 1950s) refrain from genital display. Melody Davis underlines the long history of covered male genitals when she claims that "the Western world since Christendom has determined that the penis should not be overtly displayed" (4). This convention lies behind French publicity for the Seven Deadly Sins jockstrap from the aussieBum collection. Next to a cricketer who is only wearing an aussieBum jockstrap, a helmet, gloves, and kneepads, we read: *Certaines choses se doivent de rester secrètes* (Certain things should remain secret). Obviously this claim is tongue-in-cheek, as demonstrated by the exposed behind of the cricketer.

If there was not now still such a mystique surrounding the male genitals, there would probably be a less hysterical attempt to compensate for the covering of men's private parts by excessive musculature in order to prove virility. Underwear ads typify this hysterical overcompensation. Depending on the eroticization, the phallic mystique is more or less transgressed. The undie revolution has helped perpetuate the aura of taboo surrounding the male member. Tantalizing representations of pouches and bulges on packaging and posters tease spectators of both sexes. Davis is surely justified in claiming that "the penis [. . .] is even more present if it is concealed or disguised" (5). Men's underwear ads demonstrate the pertinence of this statement. They powerfully suggest but refuse to show male genitals.

From a feminist point of view, the maintenance or disappearance of the mystique attached to the male genitals is important. Germaine Greer broaches the subject in her chapter on women's fear of men in *The Whole Woman* where she argues that "It is up to women to render the exposure of the male organ as trivial and meaningless as the [. . .] exposure of women's bodies already is" (357). For Greer, hiding the penis from public view helps support anxiety about penis size and gives too much importance to phallic power, the ultimate expression of which is rape. This is why she claims that "The most pressing need must be to demystify the penis" because "to perpetuate the mystique of the penis as a sacred object" (358) is in the worst interest of women. The undie revolution would seem to be unintentionally helping to fulfill this feminist objective.

Men's underwear fetishism is gradually entering mainstream culture, rather than remaining a subcultural interest. I offer this remark to develop Paul Jobling's brief use of a Freudian interpretation of fetishism in a 2005 discussion of men's underwear advertising (128–29). Klein and Weber were the first art photographers to exploit this aspect of men's underwear in their work. At its most basic, underwear is a piece of clothing designed to hold in testicles and to soak up viscous fluids. All other discourse on the subject, like this chapter, is potentially fetishistic. Some homosexual males realized the fetishistic appeal of underwear when they stopped buying Hanes and Jockeys. As soon as Calvin Klein, Gregory Sovell, or Gianni Versace started offering designer underwear, the first men interested in how their pouch looked and how other men judged their bulge were homosexual customers. A certain number of them even organized "underwear parties" so they could stand around checking out each other's packet. This form of gay fetishism is now becoming more common outside a homosexual context. Since 2003, for example, the Web site Freshpair.com organizes a National Underwear Day in New York every August. That is how mainstream fetishism has become since underwear design has become a matter of interest for a non-gay buying public. Athletes who pose in their briefs attract fetishists such as the thieves who stole the Hintnaus posters. Auctioneers of male underwear posters on the Internet are quick to realize the fetishistic potential of men's underwear. When trying to sell a photograph (especially a signed photograph of an underwear campaign by a celebrity model), to enhance their item, auctioneers sometimes add "possible gay interest?" What would be more apposite is "possible metrosexual fetishist interest?" Advertisements of male athletes wearing briefs have helped encourage generalized underwear fetishism. In *Fetish*, Valerie Steele quotes Freud's claim that "half of humanity must be classed among the clothes fetishists. All women, that is, are clothes fetishists" (187). In making this distinction, Freud means that males, unlike females, do not pay inordinate attention to their own clothes. He was wrong. The undie revolution provides proof that *all* men are potential clothes fetishists.

The revolution in men's underwear is a sign of wider cultural changes. The use of hypermasculine athletes in underwear advertising has had the desired or uncalculated effect of metrosexualizing the masses. This revolution has helped change perceptions of the male body and actively encouraged male eroticism. Athletes have been instrumental in disengaging men's interest in their own underwear from its former feminizing and homosexualizing connotations. Each athlete exposed in underwear has contributed toward making males look at themselves differently. Ubiquitous publicity of sportsmen standing or lying in their boxers or briefs invites all men to enjoy sartorial erotics, to learn seductiveness, and to take pleasure in attracting the gaze. Having said this, the important thing to remember about metrosexuality is its lack of watertight distinctions in terms of gender and sexuality. If we get rid of traditional gender and sexual parameters, attention given to underwear, clothes, and the body could then be seen as having nothing to do with gender or sexual orientation. Interest in the intimate parts of one's body and the bodies of others, even of the same sex, the desire to look beautiful, pride in erogenous zones, and a preoccupation with clothing which both hides and reveals the genitals: these are all normal human characteristics.

Valerie Steele begins the "Men's Underwear" section of *Fetish* with the claim that "Men's underwear has seldom carried the same erotic connotations as women's underwear, for the reason that men's *bodies* have not usually been interpreted primarily in sexual terms" (127). Athletes' advertising of men's underwear during the undie revolution works on exactly the opposite assumption. Men's briefs can be eroticized just like women's underwear. Advertising campaigns for men's underwear show that it *is* possible to interpret a man's body primarily in sexual terms. Millions of males of any sexual identity everywhere are now covering their nakedness in elaborate fetish items of clothing designed to enhance masculine erotic appeal.

6

Black Bodies

At the end of chapter 3, I drew attention to the significant number of black athletes analyzed in this book. Some of these athletes are influenced by mainstream, racially nonspecific dress styles which hold widespread appeal in the United States and abroad. Sportswear collections, New York fashion designers, and European couturiers cater to this demand. Former NBA players such as Michael Jordan, Magic Johnson, and the current NBA superstar Kevin Garnett are examples of black athletes who follow established American or Continental fashion houses. This is also the case for black athletes from other sports who have been mentioned in earlier chapters, notably Ozzie Smith. Leaving aside these cases, the first part of this chapter will focus on a noticeable number of black athletes, especially professional basketball players, who find mainstream fashion houses deficient and look instead to the pimp's traditional wardrobe as a source of sartorial inspiration.

A male who chooses to "pimp out" his body (adorn it with large tattoos, pimp-like clothes, and bejeweled accessories) shows a marked desire to be gazed at and admired as someone of wealth, power, and sensuous tastes. The "pimped out" look or appearance references a liking for mink coats, velvet suits, animal-print clothes, alligator shoes, tattoos, and chunky jewelry. It is worth recalling here that although the etymology of the word "pimp" is obscure, it is generally thought to be connected to the French *pimpant*, a word which means "alluring or seductive in outward appearance or dress." As the presence of "pimp" in "pimped out" suggests, at the origin of the pimped out appearance there is a flamboyant and hypermasculine pimp, a heterosexual male who controls, dominates (at times by violence), and lives off the earnings of female sex workers. The pimps in question, who provided the blueprint for the pimped out style, were for the most part African American pimps. Pimped out bodies today, therefore, have their roots in black culture.

Shane White and Graham White's study *Stylin'* provides a useful starting point to investigate how certain clothes, jewelry, and accoutrements can be considered expressions of what they call the "African American aesthetic" (23), defined as "the ways in which African Americans have clothed themselves, styled their hair, and communicated meaning through gesture, dance, and other forms of bodily display" (2). These examples of expressivity share a common focus on the body and highlight style, thus the title *Stylin'*. This study extends earlier observations made by cultural critics concerning the centrality of style in black culture. Already in 1989, bell hooks revealed that she was "particularly interested in the relationship between style as expressed in clothing and subversion, the way the dominated, exploited peoples use style to express resistance" (*Yearning* 217). In a similar vein, Shane White and Graham White demonstrate the importance of style in the African American aesthetic.

A word of caution needs to be offered here. In arguing for the existence of a single aesthetic common to African Americans, there is a danger of advocating essentialist logic based on ethnicity. It might be considered unwise to argue for the existence of an aesthetic which pertains to all African Americans, thus denying historical, cultural, and political contexts. Likewise, it can be ill-advised to subscribe to a monolithic interpretation of the "black body." In his essay "What Is This 'Black' in Black Popular Culture?" Stuart Hall discourages essentialism of this kind by claiming that "It is to the diversity, not the homogeneity, of black experience that we must now give our undivided creative attention" (30). Nevertheless, in the course of this same essay, Hall argues that within the black "repertoire" (a term he uses interchangeably with "aesthetic") "*style*—which mainstream cultural critics often believe to be the mere husk, the wrapping, the sugarcoating on the pill—has become *itself* the subject of what is going on" (27).

This chapter begins by examining the contribution of black athletes, especially basketball players, who have perpetuated the African American aesthetic by pimping out their bodies. They have done this by means of body modification and accessorizing. This analysis is based on the assumption that African American athletes have a preexisting cultural disposition to express style through a special attention given to hair, clothes, body accessories, and body modifications. Different sources of inspiration are available to express style. In *We Real Cool*, a study of black men and masculinity, bell hooks provides an indirect explanation to account for the fact that the pimped out style seems to be particularly attractive for some African American athletes. Hooks denounces patriarchal culture with vigor, criticizing the ways it restricts and confines males to reproducing gender rituals which are detrimental to men and women alike. According to hooks, it is black males who especially "endure the worst impositions of gendered masculine patriarchal identity" (xii). In chapter 2 of *We Real Cool*, "Gangsta Culture," hooks recognizes how sport can be an arena which encourages black men to either "assert patriarchal manhood," that is, reproduce the values of jock culture, or else forge an alternative masculinity which hooks characterizes as "humanist-based" (22).

My objective is to demonstrate the attraction of patriarchal manhood for some black athletes by showing how the pimped out style reproduces the traditional gender and sexual mythologies that make up patriarchy. The association between the pimped out appearance and black style is diminishing with the transracial incorporation of the pimped out appearance into mainstream fashion. The result of this mainstreaming is that the ideological basis of the pimped out look is likely to become dissociated from its links with conventional gender and sexual mythologies.

Examining how the black body has been represented in the past and how it has been "read" have a significant impact on interpreting contemporary black bodies exhibited in the pages of sports and fashion magazines as well as in advertising. Ronald L. Jackson begins *Scripting the Black Masculine Body* with the commonly argued observation that "Black bodies were inscribed with a set of meanings, which helped to perpetuate the scripter's racial ideology" (9). He insists on the importance of analyzing these inscribed meanings "for what they reveal about embedded racially xenophobic tendencies that are redistributed and recycled in mass-mediated cultural practices" (9). I am interested to find out what sort of racial ideology is redistributed and recycled by exposing and eroticizing the bodies of black athletes in advertising, in the sports press, and in fashion magazines.

In order to address such a problematic, this chapter examines how metrosexuality is contributing to the fetishizing of black skin and black bodies. In order to demonstrate this sort of fetishizing, I will consider two professional athletes who were active in the 1990s. One is Carl Lewis and the other Dennis Rodman. As an illustration of a more recent case of fetishized blackness, I will briefly examine a 2004 advertisement featuring the French Tae Kwon Do Olympic champion Pascal Gentil. I want to focus, as much as possible, on the intentions of fashion photographers and the perspectives of black athletes concerning representations which concentrate on what James Smalls terms "the sight, desire, threat, objectification, and commodification of the black body" (14).

Finally, this chapter examines the use of black bodies to promote sales of men's underwear. Choosing a black body to promote men's underwear is never neutral. Underwear advertisers are faced with a double-bind dilemma: ignore the black body and be accused of racism or feature the black body in advertising and be accused of encouraging racist stereotyping and supporting the fetishizing of blackness. Publicity which features a black body in underwear will be examined in and outside the United States from 1976 onward with the objective of making explicit this dilemma.

The African American Aesthetic

In *Stylin'*, Shane White and Graham White trace a propensity for an affirmative individual and collective sartorial style on the part of black Americans from the eighteenth century to the zoot suit of the early 1940s. A vast amount of historic material is examined concerning how the clothing of blacks before and after the end of slavery attracted comment from white travelers and from newspapers. *Stylin'* provides descriptions of urban centers where African Americans lived and paraded their clothes. All this material is examined in an attempt to "uncover the nature of black style" (3). The authors show that throughout the eighteenth century clothes served to signify status. Clothes designated whether one was black or white, free or enslaved. At this time, sumptuary laws were enacted in some states with the intention of demarcating ethnic and class distinctions. The South Carolina Negro Act of 1735 is one example of sumptuary legislation aimed at controlling slave clothing. In a chapter titled "Looking

Mighty Sprucy," the authors demonstrate the various techniques employed by black slaves in the American colonies to resist the obligation to dress simply and drably.

This sartorial resistance was a form of political, social, and racial empowerment. Descriptions of runaway slaves point to successful attempts by numerous African Americans to dress beyond their station. One such runaway was reported by a New York newspaper in 1794. John Jackson was described as "rather beauish" and last seen wearing a "dark blue coat, with a velvet collar and his [hair] powdered" (17). This chapter of *Stylin'* concludes that "travelers and other commentators often complained about slaves' propensity to dress 'above themselves,' to engage in forms of conspicuous display inappropriate to their lowly station in life" (31). In the eighteenth century, conspicuous display was therefore intimately linked to class and ethnicity as only whites were allowed to indulge in finery.

Two more chapters of *Stylin'*, "Dandies and Dandizettes" and "The Stroll," explore dandyism and *flânerie* in the period after slavery ended. These historical aspects of black style find a parallel with modern-day metrosexuality. In her *Travels in the United States*, the English noblewoman Lady Emmeline Stuart-Wortley noted having seen in New Haven in 1849 a "very curious specimen of a dandy," whom she dubbed "a sable Count d'Orsay" (an illustrious French dandy). She wrote in her travelogue that this African American's "toilette was the most elaborately *recherché* you can imagine" (White and White 92). In *The Cotton Kingdom*, the American landscape architect Frederick Law Olmsted mentioned coming across some blacks in Richmond, South Carolina in the early 1850s, whom he described as "dressed with foppish extravagance, and many in the latest style of fashion" (White and White 28). These fops were not alone in exhibiting lavish wardrobes. Sauntering down urban promenades became a favorite activity of African Americans in the nineteenth century. In 1832, a Swedish traveler visiting the Battery noted the popularity of Sunday walks with all classes, "particularly those of the sable cast, making a profuse exhibition of their finery" (White and White 94). This common practice inspires the authors of *Stylin'* to title another chapter "The Stroll," where they examine African American urban strolling. The authors take as examples Chicago and New York in the first half of the twentieth century. To demonstrate the continuity of the phenomenon, they quote a 1927 *New York Times* report on strolling in the "Black Belt" of Harlem.

Here African Americans, the reader is told, "run more to exaggerated styles and bright hues" (234).

Pimped Out Bodies

One manifestation of the African American aesthetic is the outlandishly dressed and highly sexualized pimp. Since the publication of Iceberg Slim's fictionalized autobiography *Pimp* in 1969, the pimp subculture, its trappings and philosophy have fascinated America. In the decade after this best seller was first published, blaxploitation films such as *Superfly* (1972) and *The Mack* (1973) popularized the pimp fantasy. Another film from the same period, *Willie Dynamite* (1973), features a New York pimp and hustler driving a Cadillac, spectacularly decked out in a lime green suit and a lavish fur coat. At the same time, his real-life counterpart became the subject of academic inquiry. In 1973, for example, Christina and Richard Milner published *Black Players: The Secret World of Black Pimps,* an investigation into the language, values, and the world view of black pimps in San Francisco during the early 1970s. This anthropological account of the underworld of pimps and sex workers provides an image of the pimp's wardrobe that we find reproduced in blaxploitation films. The Milners point out that the black player "may spend hours a day on his hair, clothes, and toilette" (8). The authors also mention "the pimp's love of theatricality" and "dressing up" (112). The word "front" is used to characterize the players' various props and costumes. This term refers to a pimp's "Flashy cars, expensive clothes, and dramatic personal style" (109). All these terms the Milners use to characterize real black pimps from the 1970s provide a blueprint for the contemporary pimped out style.

Academics, photographers, and fiction writers have all commented on the preponderance of African American pimps. The authors of *Black Players* reveal that in their fieldwork they only saw three white pimps and these exceptions imitated the style and speech patterns of black pimps. Likewise, fiction and photography also trace the pimp appearance to a highly expressive sartorial style favored by African Americans. In 2002, Rob Marriott's *Pimpnosis,* a fictional account of pimping, included contemporary photographs taken of real-life black pimps and their sex workers. Marriott's introduction to *Pimpnosis* provides a similar ethnographic frame for the stereotypical pimp front. He argues that "the flashy jewelry, the exaggerated clothes, and the outrageous accoutrements are all peculiar to the black imagination" (Funches 5).

It is helpful to understand why the pimp has been, and continues to be, a major distinctive representation in American culture. Eithne Quinn addresses this question in her discussions of blaxploitation films and gangsta rap. Class and style politics are for her the central issues. Quinn argues that "The pimp is a ghettocentric icon of upward mobility for black working-class males, spectacularly refusing, through heightened style politics, the subservient typecasting that has historically been imposed on them" (122). This interpretation brings together class, ethnicity, and style in helping to account for the popularity of pimps and the pimp lifestyle as fantasies over the last thirty-five years.

However, another explanation centering on black sexuality also needs to be taken into account. Patricia Hill Collins's work on gender and racism identifies another aspect of the African American aesthetic that is revealing for what it tells us about why the pimp should be held in such high esteem as a cultural type. In *Black Sexual Politics*, Collins argues that "Historically, Western science, medicine, law, and popular culture reduced an African-derived aesthetic concerning the use of the body, sensuality, expressiveness, and spirituality to an ideology about *Black sexuality*" (98). A similar viewpoint was expressed by bell hooks a year earlier in "It's a Dick Thing: Beyond Sexual Acting Out," chapter 5 of *We Real Cool*. In this chapter, hooks denounces a generalized sexual acting out by black American males which reduces relations between men and women to what she calls a "dick thing." For her, the "dick thing," which insists on black males and the black body as always already hypersexual, is a "white racist sexist pornographic sexual fantas[y]" (67). This comment is useful as it allows us to see how the black pimp fantasy is based on and sustains the hypermasculine and hypersexual stereotypes that have attached themselves to black American males.

NBA Tattoos and Bling-bling

Some black athletes are highly proficient at performing pimped out dick thing masculinity. Whereas scholarship has effectively shown how numerous gangsta rap artists have been at the forefront of promoting the pimped out appearance, the place occupied by athletes in this lineage has not yet been adequately analyzed. Basketball is the professional sport which has always included the greatest number of black pimped out athletes. One reason why basketball attracts black players especially is addressed in Todd Boyd's *Young, Black, Rich and Famous*, a study of the NBA and hip-hop culture. Boyd argues that "the far-flung power of the game" is due to the fact that basketball is "an opportunity for social and economic mobility" (36). This sport is perceived as the one in which a young black American has the best opportunity of becoming rich and famous. The extremely high percentage of black players in the NBA (in 2007 around 75 percent) explains why basketball is a propitious arena for pimped out males. Basketball, like the pimped out look, epitomizes wealth and upward social mobility.

Basketball also epitomizes hypersexuality and hypermasculinity. Dennis Rodman attests to this in his first autobiography, *Bad as I Wanna Be*. Here Rodman provides a revealing account of how basketball is closely linked to jock culture's gender and sexual myths. At the beginning of chapter 8, Rodman states that "Fifty percent of life in the NBA is sex. The other fifty percent is money" (Rodman and Keown 179). Concerning the sexual side, Rodman relates how droves of women groupies follow players after games and hang around their hotels swapping stories. It would seem that a basketball player, more than any other professional athlete, has an immediate entourage of ready and willing sexual partners. Even the uniform has acquired a fetishistic value in attracting potential bed partners. Rodman succinctly refers to this commodity as "the ticket to whoreville and fuckville and slutville" (184). According to Rodman, an NBA player is considered by women (perhaps one could add by a sports-adoring society at large) as "the ultimate sex object" (179). The pimped out appearance adopted by certain NBA players reinforces this image of men who have innumerable women at their beck and call.

Stuart Hall draws attention to the black body as a site of style politics by arguing that "These cultures have used the body—as if it was, and it often was, the only cultural capital we had. We have worked on ourselves as the canvases of representation" (29). This observation rings especially true if we examine the prevalence of tattooing and one particular body accessory, bling-bling, in the NBA. These two signs of the pimped out body have captured the attention of journalists, cultural critics, and sports fans in and outside America. Since the mid-1990s when Dennis Rodman first popularized tattooing, this practice has become more generalized as a trend among NBA athletes. By 2003, Rodman lamented the banality of this type of body modification, telling the *New York Times* that "Even all the boring white guys got tattoos now" (Rodrick 36). In 1998, 35 percent of NBA players sported tats, compared with 4 percent of the general population, whereas in 2005 well over half were decorated. Andrew Gottlieb's illustrated book of NBA tattoos, *In the Paint,* provides photographs and analyzes the tattoos of twenty-four players. Only five of these athletes are nonblack.

One of the fears expressed by bell hooks in her study of black masculinity is that black males "are socialized from birth to embrace the notion that their manhood will be determined by whether or not they can dominate and control others" (*Cool* 57). Many tattoos reproduced in Gottlieb's book on the NBA provide evidence of this socialization. If we look at the most well-known case of a tattooed NBA player, Allen Iverson, we find that his twenty-odd tattoos fall into three categories: descriptions of himself or qualities he prizes, groups with whom he identifies, and the names or initials of close family members. Of these, the first category is the largest, suggesting that his body decorations are mainly an attempt to express who and what he is by means of words and pictures inscribed on his flesh. Self-identifying pictures include a bulldog, a soldier's head, and a panther. Two words appear in Chinese, "belief" and "loyalty." Three nicknames are inscribed: "Jewelz," "VA's Finest," and "The Answer." He also has a series of mottos he supposedly lives by: "Hold My Own," "Fear No One," and "Only the Strong Survive." Biographer Larry Platt believes that Iverson "really got hooked on expressing himself, on the notion that he could carve into his skin announcements of who he was. You want to know who I am, he'd say, 'Just read my body'" (164). These inscriptions, it could be argued, turn Iverson into a living endorsement of patriarchal masculinity, equating manhood with power, violence, strength, and domination over others. Similar ideas are expressed by three of Shaquille O'Neal's tattoos: a Superman logo, "Man of Steel," and "Against the Law." This jock culture logic which preaches the survival of the fittest and most powerful males is in direct opposition to metrosexuality, the motto of which might be "Only the Beautiful Deserve to Survive."

Bling-bling, or "bling" for short, another body decoration enamored by ballplayers, is also sign of power. Bling is the generic term borrowed from rap culture to refer to expensive and flashy body jewelry. The proliferation of bling on male bodies moved *New York Times* writer Ruth La Ferla in early 2004 to use this headline: "Are Diamonds Now a Man's Best Friend?" Another journalist coined the term "conspicuous jock consumption" (Hruby C1) to describe the buying of lavish custom-made jewelry that adorns the bodies of many NBA athletes. In his foreword to *Bling Bling,* an illustrated history of hip-hop jewelry, the singer Ludacris clearly identifies bling as an African American cultural practice. He claims that "Being Black, coming from a background of struggle, all of that has a lot to do with the bling mentality. Our whole culture has it. We always feel like we have to prove something and we have to be real flashy in order to show what we have achieved. That's just the nigga mentality" (Oh ix). In this statement Ludacris sees bling as a symbol of social and economic empowerment.

Ear jewelry is the most common example of basketball bling. The *Encyclopedia of Clothing and Fashion,* published in 2004, offers four large-format informative pages under the entry "Earrings." Only eight lines are about men's earrings. One might be tempted to conclude that ear jewelry has been almost exclusively a feminine and feminizing gender ritual for the last four and a half thousand years. Susan Ward, the author of this entry on earrings, singles out Ancient Egypt as a site where men and women wore earrings. She then jumps to the late sixteenth century to describe "fashionable gentlemen" (392), who were known to adorn themselves with a pear-shaped pearl pendant in one ear. Portraits of Shakespeare and Sir Walter Raleigh provide evidence of this practice. We finally make a leap of four centuries. Ward claims that until the 1970s "earrings had continued to be worn by sailors, by some homosexual men, and by members of groups such as motorcycle gangs" (394). Curiously, the reader is not told that hip-hop culture has made ear jewelry extremely popular among young urban males in many countries. Of more interest to the discussion here is the fact that this fashion has been considerably encouraged by athletes' taste for earrings and diamond ear studs. Basketball players, especially, spend a fortune buying such accoutrements, not for their girlfriends, but for themselves.

To encourage conspicuous jewelry consumption by males, Chris Aire's company "2 Awesome International" has featured famous clients from the sports world on its Web site. Here LeBron James once wore a "diamond flooded timepiece" and Allen Iverson displayed a diamond bracelet and timepiece. Both were out-blinged by another satisfied customer, rap singer 50 Cent in his red gold timepiece and platinum jewels. Aire has been selling his rocks to NBA stars since 1998 when he passed Damon Stoudamire a diamond-encrusted Rolex and a necklace. Larry Hughes, who joined the Cleveland Cavaliers in 2005 for an estimated $70 million, appeared in the 2002 catalog for Aire's company. He modeled $22,000 diamond rings and a $180,000 timepiece. A $115,000 rope pendant beautified his neck and his wrist was adorned with a 34 carat $150,000 bracelet. Hughes not only modeled, he bought all this bling. He was one of three NBA players and one NFL player who wore Chris Aire jewelry at the Olympus Fashion Week in New York in 2005. Aire offered a plausible explanation for this bejeweled splendor in the *Washington Times* when he opined, "You have people who are fashion conscious. They like the nice things in life. And money is really no object" (Hruby C1).

This disregard for cost and absolute regard for conspicuous accessories signifying social and economic status gives a good idea of the present pimped out mindset of many NBA players. In March 1998, *Sports Illustrated* carried a piece on Allen Iverson, described elsewhere by Todd Boyd as "the epitome of young, Black, rich and famous" (Boyd 7). Rick Reilly's article recounts an ordinary day in the life of a pimped out jewel addict. Reilly reports the opening of seven envelopes by "Jewelz," as Iverson is known in the hip-hop world. In the first envelope Jewelz finds "a brilliant gold watch dripping with diamonds, huge steroid-fed diamonds" and a timepiece worth $80,000. Inside the second envelope he discovers "a gorgeous gold bracelet lousy with diamonds, a diamond-palooza, 120 carats." The third envelope, we are told, contains two diamond earrings "big enough to make Elizabeth Taylor punch a hole in her vanity." The list goes on. Iverson's defensive reaction, in front of all these pimped out manacles, is revealing. He pleads with the reporter that "People see someone with a lot of jewelry on, they go, 'He's a drug dealer, he a pimp, he doin' somethin' illegal.' But they don't have to look at me like that." Rather than avowing allegiance with criminals, Iverson comes up with an almost Freudian explanation for his diamond addiction. He reveals that "When I was little, my mom and I used to sit in the dark and talk about jewelry—all the cool jewelry we were gonna have someday" (91). (This description of mom and son discussing their tastes in precious stones could almost be lifted from a Liberace biography). Interestingly, Iverson links a passion for bling

asculinity, sexual confidence, and dressing in contrast to
r social station are vital elements making up pimped out
lity. The spread of metrosexuality will probably help the
t look become more racially indistinct with time. This
ssipate the "dick thing" ideology at the historic basis of
out appearance.

Fetishizing Black Bodies

ng of race has a history of engaging researchers in the
tcolonial studies and photography. We can trace this
st back to Homi Bhabha, who in 1983 adapted Freudian
gued that "Skin, as the key signifier of cultural and ra-
e [. . .] is the most visible of fetishes" (78). A decade
postcolonial writer, Anne McClintock, further opened
on race and fetishism in *Imperial Leather,* her study of
nd sexuality in colonialism. There she called for "a re-
gation that would open fetishism to a more complex
istory in which racial and class hierarchies would play
role as sexuality" (184).
uch investigations had already taken place in the late
bena Mercer published "Imagining the Black Man's
d "Skin Head Sex Thing: Racial Difference and the
aginary" (1989). In these texts that were later re-
ome to the Jungle, Mercer developed and refined a cri-
n the white American photographer Robert Mapple-
for his many eroticized photographs of African
he earlier essay, Mercer interpreted Mapplethorpe's
he black body in terms of a colonial fantasy, suggest-
mage thus nourishes the racialized and sexualized
ppriating the Other's body as virgin territory to be
possessed by an all-powerful desire" (177). By 1989,
h less adamant in his language and admitted that it
o decide if Mapplethorpe reinforced or undermined
t black sexuality.
ns of black athletes in advertising, in the sports
ashion press invite us to think about how the desir-
d-at-ness of black bodies and black skin encourage
A good illustration of this phenomenon is Annie

with self-advancement through crime and clearly identifies, even if
he rejects, its association with hustling.

Bling such as Iverson's jewels has become so popular among
NBA players that in October 2005 Commissioner David Stern im-
plemented a new dress code based on a general policy of "business
casual" to apply when players are engaged in team or league business. Half the list of banned items reads like the contents of a hip-
hop accessory shop: sleeveless shirts, shorts, T-shirts, throwback jerseys, headgear, chains, pendants, or medallions worn over clothes.
Sunglasses are banned indoors and headphones are only allowed
on the team bus, the plane, or in the team locker room. This new
dress code provoked positive endorsement from Magic Johnson,
but others were forthright in denouncing it as a racist cramping of
style. Dennis Rodman had already made his thoughts clear concerning such censure in his 1997 autobiography. There he revealed
one of his more unusual fantasies: "I'd like to take NBA commissioner David Stern as my prisoner, strip off all his clothes, rub lipstick and makeup all over him, dress up like Frank [Sinatra] and
sing to him . . . 'I did it my way'" (Rodman and Silver 26). So many
other black NBA players have also been doing it their way in mat-
ters of sartorial style that this collective expressivity finally provoked the 2005 dress code, the object of which was to de-pimp the
NBA and take away its gangsta image, partly reinforced by its perceived associations with hip-hop culture.

Man in the Middle, the autobiography published in 2007 by former NBA player John Amaechi, provides a vivid picture of contemporary pimped out, "dick thing" masculinity:

> The pro locker room was the most flamboyant place I'd ever been
> this side of a swanky club full of martini-drinking gay men. [. . .]
> The guys flaunted their perfect bodies. They bragged of their sexual
> exploits. They checked out each other's cocks. They primped in front
> of the mirror, applying cologne and hair gel by the bucketful. [. . .]
> They tried on each other's $10,000 suits and shoes, admired each
> other's diamond studded rings and necklaces. [. . .] As I surveyed
> the room, I couldn't help chuckling to myself: And I'm the gay one.
> Hah! (140)

The "flamboyance" of NBA locker rooms, as described by Amaechi,
could easily go by another name, metrosexuality. The way he reads
pimped out metrosexuality as "gayness" depends on the underlying

camp, or even queer dimension of a gaggle of heterosexual males, bent on looking "real cool" together.

Mainstream and Transracial Pimped Out Bodies

The mainstreaming of the pimped out appearance may help to de-hinge this style from its black roots. Designers such as Versace, Cavalli, Dolce, and Gabbana have blithely and conspicuously been sending white male models down the catwalk in furs, leopard-skin designs, and snakeskin patterns since the 1990s. One of the most influential stylists participating in this transracial mainstreaming is hip-hop impresario and singer Sean "Diddy" Combs. Combs's Sean John 2000 Fall Collection, for example, featured white and black models wearing long fur coats, fur trousers, rhinestone-studded jeans, diamonds galore, and brightly colored leather coats. His collections are bringing the pimped out style to the center of the New York fashion world. When Combs opened a Sean John store on Fifth Avenue in August 2004, it was a sign that the pimped out look could be turned into high fashion. He won the prestigious Council of Fashion Designers award in 2004 for the "Men's Wear Designer of the Year."

Since the turn of the century, Combs has been cultivating what is known as the "ghetto fabulous" style. Used in the latter half of the 1990s, ghetto fabulous refers to an exaggerated taste for designer clothes and accessories, especially by nouveaux riches African Americans. Combs attributed to himself the launching of the trend when he once stated, "I'm the nigger who started it: I'm the one driving around in the Rolls Royce with his hat turned, goin' down Fifth Avenue with the system booming in the back. Walkin' into Gucci, shuttin' it down, buying everything at the motherfuckin' same time!" (Kamp 142). Combs's silver Bentley, Versace furs, tattoos, and diamond ear studs give a good idea of the style and recall typical pimp iconography. In April 2005, Miami Heat All-Star NBA player Dwyane Wade agreed to a one-year modeling contract with the label Sean John, thus reinforcing ties between the sports world and hip-hop high fashion. A year later, *GQ* responded favorably by naming Wade the best-dressed player in the NBA.

A significant indication of the incorporation of the pimped out style into mainstream fashion and a reminder of its close association

with the African American aesthetic cember 2005 featuring 50 Cent, the mo singer pushing pimp ideology in his tattooed model stands defiant on the Klein shirt, the sleeves of which hav Black Label tie is thrown over his sho ering his half-unbuttoned shirt fro New York fashion are accessorized b streetwear company that 50 Cent h issue of *GQ*, 50 Cent models more items, but the most striking image aire wearing a luxurious Alixandr play of pimped out excess and pr *GQ* demonstrates to what extent creditation in New York, the hub dustry and the center of the comn

Soccer celebrity David Beckh pean example of an athlete who peal of the pimped out appeara demonstrates the reappropriatic to black expressive style. This multiple tattoos, together with ostentatious body jewelry. This from various ethnic backgroun his appropriation of a parti Britain's Channel 4 produced *ham.* A year later, Beckham su "Sporting Personality of the Awards. The television doc player's sartorial expressivi that was being popularizec United States. The names of in honor of rap singer Snc only comforted the elision. gram was meant to be tong ers were offended by the p and metrosexual idol coul *Beckham* is not without ser ing African American exj elements associated with

Hyperr one's form metrosexua pimped ou may help d the pimped

The fetishizi fields of pos critical intere theory and a cial differenc later, another up the debate race, gender, newed invest and variable h as formative a

However, s 1980s when K Sex" (1986) an Homoerotic In printed in *Wel* tique centered thorpe, known Americans. In fascination for ing that "each fantasy of appr penetrated and Mercer was mu was impossible racist myths abo

Representati press, and in the ability and looke racial fetishism.

Leibovitz's photograph of track Olympic champion Carl Lewis which was commissioned by the Pirelli tire company in 1994. This image is based on shoe fetishism and bondage. Lewis wore a black one-piece runner's outfit and adopted a crouched pose with his hands on the ground as if he were about to start a sprint. His jutting buttocks and long legs are the focus of the shot as well as the now famous red stiletto heels. It is the shoes, of course, which mark the originality of the photograph and give it a transvestic and fetishistic thrill. "The shoe or slipper," Freud wrote in a 1910 footnote to his essay on sexual aberrations, "is a corresponding symbol of the *female* genitals" (67). This may be the case, but the pointy heels of the women's shoes that Lewis agreed to wear for the publicity shot are typically phallic. They provide an effective image of the "power" referred to in the accompanying slogan, "Power Is Nothing Without Control." When Valerie Steele quotes from the 1962 magazine *High Heels* in her book *Fetish*, she offers an interesting insight into the phallic symbolism of Lewis's red stilettos. In this fetishist magazine, the high-heeled shoe is celebrated as a weapon. It is described as a "symbol of aggression. It signifies power. It indicates domination" (101). Shoes also bind the feet, which is why they are also typical bondage accessories. Lewis's tight red shoes therefore perfectly put across the idea of "control" contained in the Pirelli slogan.

The Pirelli advertisement is a remarkable instance of fetishizing black body parts. The choice of Lewis as model depends on an essentialist stereotype which promulgates the idea that black athletes benefit from a "natural" proficiency in sports. Athletic proficiency, meant to suggest powerful Pirelli tires, is reinforced by means of fetishizing blackness. This idea lies at the basis of Jon Entine's study, *Taboo: Why Black Athletes Dominate Sports and Why We're Afraid to Talk about It*. Entine quotes examples of internalized racially essentialist stereotyping by Lewis himself and O.J. Simpson. In 1988, Lewis reportedly said that "Blacks—physically in many cases—are made better. Does anyone really question that?" (Entine 4). Of more interest is an observation by O.J. Simpson, especially for what it implies about fetishizing blackness. In 1977, Simpson claimed that "We are built a little differently, built for speed—skinny calves, long legs, high asses are all characteristics of blacks" (Entine 246). Interestingly, Leibovitz's Pirelli photograph foregrounds exactly these same three features with the result that it reproduces the racially essentialist ideas of Lewis and Simpson. Exactly the same kind of fetishizing is visible in the 2001 and 2002 French advertisements for the Sloggi brand of men's underwear. A black sprinter is featured in the same crouching pose wearing body-hugging Lycra shorts. As in the Pirelli publicity, a black athlete is more or less reduced to calves, legs, and ass.

Lewis is not just any black body. For an athlete often suspected of a nonnormative sexual orientation, the pose adopted by Lewis was particularly daring. This is corroborated by the fact that the advertisement was only used in Europe and not in the United States where the photo session took place. In April 1994, Robert Fachet claimed in the *Washington Post* that the pose was "too controversial" to be displayed on American billboards. The contentious nature of the Pirelli photograph can be imputed to the transvestic stilettos, implying feminized phallic endowment and the upraised buttocks with their suggestion of an invitation to sexual penetration.

It is intriguing to wonder how Lewis perceived the tire advertisement and what were the photographer's intentions. According to the *Atlanta Journal-Constitution,* the athlete reacted positively. Lewis is reported to have offered two reasons why he agreed to do this particular commercial for Pirelli. They paid him a six-figure sum for it and he liked working with the photographer. He saw the Italian manufacturer's endorsement as a sign of his continued popularity and said he thought the ad was "Fine, just as long as it's not derogatory [. . .] They wanted to get the most shock value" (Fish F4). If shock value was obtained by having his body linked to crossdressing, sexual passivity, and fetishistic bondage, then Lewis seems to have been unconcerned about such associations. "What's the big deal?" he told the *Observer* (Mackay 10). An American media report quoted the general point of view of Leibovitz and others speaking to Lewis's manager. This reaction gives an admittedly partial and possibly untrustworthy access to the photographer's intention behind the Pirelli scenario. Leibovitz, along with other people, said that the photograph was not about "sexuality or anything" (Fish F4). Such an assurance disguises the fact that for cultural critics, such as bell hooks, the Pirelli photograph is a "big deal" because it perpetuates racial fetishizing by purveying the derogatory idea that black sexuality is linked with deviance.

In *Black Sexual Politics,* Patricia Hill Collins discusses what she terms a "primitivist discourse" (100), defined as creating a category of "beast" and interpreting the sexuality of beasts as "wild." Collins explains more fully what she means by this discourse when she points out that "Linking African people and animals was crucial to Western views of Black promiscuity. Genital sexual intercourse or, more colloquially, the act of 'fucking,' characterized animal sexuality" (100). A similar point of view is expressed by bell hooks in *We Real Cool* where she presents the following critique:

> At a time when black males are losing ground on all fronts [. . .] rather than creating a politics of resistance, many black males are simply acquiescing, playing the role of sexual minstrel. Exploiting mainstream racialized sexist stereotypes they go along to get along, feeling no rage that they must play the part of [. . .] hypersexual stud to gain visibility. (80)

Using these observations by Collins and hooks as a basis, I would like to analyze depictions of primitivism and hypersexuality in photographs of Rodman which have appeared in the sports press and men's fashion magazines, and compare these to statements from Rodman's autobiographies in order to show a consistent picture of fetishizing a black body. The May 1995 cover of *Sports Illustrated* provides a spectacular portrayal of such fetishism which is unusual for a mainstream sports magazine. For the occasion, Rodman dyed his hair orange-red and wore a skin-tight pair of black spandex shorts, a halter top with a zip-up front and over-the-shoulder braces. Accessories included three large earrings, a nose ring, and an imposing rhinestone dog collar. The "Rare Bird," as he is called, is sitting on a leopard-patterned chair, the legs of which reproduce the shape of a twining snake. Michael Silver's article "Rodman Unchained" contains five photographs of the athlete reclining on a red leather divan and wearing a body-hugging black sleeveless latex top with zips. The sports reader is offered a curiously high concentration of fetish colors, materials, and accessories. In the first double-page shot, Rodman's eyes are screwed up as if he were in pain. One end of a chain is attached to an earring and the other end to a ring implanted in his navel. Even if Rodman adopts more relaxed poses in the photo shoot, this combination of leather, chains, and pierced body parts constitutes a catalog of fetishes. All the postures are sexually inviting, as the pun in the title suggests. "Unchained" in the context can refer to the taking off of S/M accoutrements or imply that Rodman is sexually hyperactive.

The beginning of chapter 5 of Rodman's autobiography *Walk on the Wild Side* is a useful reference point to compare with the *Sports*

Illustrated title "Unchained." Using the image of the tiger to make explicit his fantasies, Rodman confides, "I have this fantasy that I can live my life like a tiger in the jungle—eating whatever I want, fucking whenever I want [. . .] and roaming around butt-naked, wild and free" (Rodman and Silver 60). These fantasies are perfectly captured by another title and a main photograph used in *GQ*'s (U.S.) coverage of Rodman in January 1995. Scott Raab's piece on Rodman titled "Wild Thing" has facing the title a full-page shot of a butt-naked man walking in long grass. The animal skins that Rodman wears, or sits on, function as fetish symbols of deviant black male sexuality. If the image of the tiger symbolizes wildness in the autobiography, it is the leopard image which continues to be used in photographs in order to convey Rodman's modern primitive persona. Scott Raab, the *GQ* journalist who interviewed Rodman in 1995, returned to his subject two years later with a piece titled "Dennis Rodman, in the Pink" in which four photographs feature the player in a pair of pink swimming trunks. More significantly for my argument, Rodman is also wearing a long-flowing leopard robe, which provides yet again another fetish image symbolizing wild erotic fantasies and, if we are to believe the autobiographies, a hyperactive sex life.

In 1986, Kobena Mercer argued that "black men are confined and defined in their very *being* as sexual and nothing but sexual, hence hypersexual" (174). This general assertion is particularly pertinent in the case of Rodman. In 2001, Mélisse Lafrance and Geneviève Rail supported this critical point of view by arguing that "representations of Rodman's aggressive, hyper-masculine sexuality are always already mediated by his blackness" (41). The "Got Milk?" advertising campaign which has been running in the United States since 1993 can be taken as a case in point to support this hypothesis. Many celebrities from the cinema, television, sports, and the music industry have lent their names to advertise milk, all wearing the characteristic milk mustache. Whereas white athletes who have participated in the campaign tend to be photographed fully clothed (this is the case for Andy Roddick, John Elway, and Cal Ripken Jr.), Dennis Rodman's "Got Milk?" poster features a head and a naked torso. The beginnings of a pubic trail and the upraised arms thrown behind the head imitate an eroticized pin-up pose. With his upper lip suggestively covered in a white liquid, Rodman looks lasciviously at the spectator. An even more provocative pose was adopted by rap singer Nelly for his milk poster. Another head and naked torso, here bedecked by bling and harboring imitation tattoos ("9 essential nutrients," "what active babies need," and "got milk?") confronts the viewer. The thumb pulling down the top of his trousers and the slightly parted lips entice the viewer not only to get milk, but also to get excited. The "Got Milk?" posters of Rodman and Nelly, like Leibovitz's photograph of Carl Lewis, reproduce the fantasy of black bodies as hypersexualized representations of racial otherness.

In his autobiographical writings, Rodman both supports and rejects the fetishizing of blackness. His fantasy of living like a tiger in the jungle, photographers' depiction of him with leopard skins, and his endorsement of "wild, uninhibited, outrageous sex" (Rodman and Silver 74) tend to reinforce a primitivist self-identification that is especially evident in the athlete's fetishizing of the "dick thing." In *Walk on the Wild Side*, Rodman takes pleasure in describing his penis as a "giant" (89), a "monster" (140), and a "big black dong" (240). Photographs used to illustrate chapter 6 of the autobiography show Rodman's naked body painted in animal stripes. One of these depicts the player snarling on all fours, near which we find the text "I like it when people get kinky" (86).

Despite such reinforcement of racial fetishizing, Rodman has openly and systematically refused to be seen as a representative "black player." In his earlier autobiography, *Bad as I Wanna Be*, Rodman describes himself as "somebody who doesn't see skin color" (Rodman and Keown 166) and spurns any idea that he is a spokesman for all African Americans. Instead, he asserts, "I'm color neutral. I'm black, but my friends joke about me being a 'white' black man" (166). Rodman's rule of thumb expressed in his first autobiography is: "*Fuck the race and the people, I'm going to be honest with myself*" (166). However, one result of Rodman's honesty about his sexual proficiency and sexual curiosity is that it encourages the sort of racial fetishism that has been denounced for perpetuating offensive and derogatory stereotyping of African American males. He is complicit with photographers' portrayals of him as a modern primitive. Ronald L. Jackson addresses this complicity by arguing that some "Blacks become complicit with negative inscriptions of their bodies when they uncritically adopt structures designed to demean or essentialize blackness" (110). Despite Rodman's "fuck the race" standpoint, representations of the player in the late 1990s, either autobiographical or in the sports and fashion press, all support what Lafrance and Rail describe as the "dominant culture's desire to make contact with the Other (and to live out its fantasies of savagery, hypersexuality and deviance through the consumption of black sporting bodies)" (47).

The fetishizing and the consumption of black sporting bodies are not limited to African American athletes. One non-American example is publicity using Olympic medalist Pascal Gentil, a French Tae Kwon Do champion originally from the Caribbean island of Martinique. In the winter 2004–2005 issue of the French magazine *C&G* (*Concept & Graphisme*), four black and white full-page shots taken by Moroccan photographer Karim Ramzi featured Gentil in an advertisement for luxury watches. Sixteen more photographs from the sequence are visible on the official Web site of the athlete. In each of the four magazine shots, Gentil is naked (except in the first photo where there is a glimpse of white swathing his waist near the frame; otherwise his torso is completely naked). He wears from one to eight luxury watches at the same time. This series of photographs is an excellent illustration of Bhabha's observation that skin is the most visible of fetishes. In the article accompanying the photo spread, it takes Catherine Masseret two lines before she focuses on the athlete's ebony body, which she describes as sculpted to perfection. This compliment would seem to typify what Kobena Mercer means when he speaks of the "sexual idealization of the racial Other" (178). Two shots in the *C&G* advertisement further demonstrate the fetishizing of black skin. In one, Gentil is standing back to the camera with his fingers sprawled and hands resting on his buttocks. He is naked except for two rings on a finger and five watches on his wrists. In another pose, he is sitting (only arms, the top of one leg, and a truncated torso are visible) with seven watches extending up his forearms. The top of the photo is cropped so that the viewer does not see beyond his lips. Here Gentil is reduced to black skin and an anonymous, almost headless fetishized stump of luxury consumption.

In his introduction to *The Homoerotic Photography of Carl Van Vechten,* James Smalls insists on the importance of viewer subjectivity and the unstable relationship between spectator and image when gauging racial fetishism in photography. He adroitly points out that "meaning does not reside with the photograph itself, but is created by the onlooker who brings to the image his or her own racial, sexual, aesthetic and cultural 'baggage'" (16). Other factors to be taken into account are the sex, sexual orientation, and racial background of the photographer. Thus the heterosexualized white "colonial fantasy" which might be seen to impact on Leibovitz's photograph of Carl Lewis is vastly modified in Ramzi's photographs of Pascal Gentil where the initial gaze is not that of the "colonizer," since the photographer is male and of Moroccan Berber background.

Deciding whether there is intentional or unconscious fetishism of blackness and working out to what extent black models are manipulated or complicit in representations of the commoditized black body is a difficult, if necessary enterprise. From the illustrations discussed here, it would seem that it is not uncommon for black athletes to be complicit in recycling racist ideology concerning blackness. Since metrosexuality encourages the exhibition of bodies, especially denuded bodies, it participates in purveying such stereotyping. This is particularly evident in the advertising of men's underwear.

Black Bodies in Briefs

Chapter 5 demonstrated that the bodies of male athletes featured in underwear advertising are for the most part white bodies. The imperative of "all-American" models for men's underwear advertising seems to justify the larger number of white athletes chosen by underwear companies to work for them. Jockey, however, in their 1976 and 1978 campaigns did make a substantial effort to include African Americans. Present were NBA players Jo Jo White, Jamaal Wilkes, Jim McMillian, and Marques Johnson. Jockey also picked left-fielder Lou Brock as well as running backs Terry Metcalf and Lydell Mitchell. Since this heyday of racial diversity the bodies of black athletes have been much less present in men's underwear publicity.

Michael Jordan's twenty-year endorsement of the mainstream label Hanes is an interesting case to consider for the way it both draws attention to and hides the black body. Unlike the denuded publicity of white sports stars shown in their briefs, Jordan's body is not always revealed in just underwear. The 1989 Hanes campaign featured Jordan in bright red briefs. However, the 2002 television ads "As Long as They're Hanes" and "Boxers or Briefs?" portray the retired athlete in a T-shirt with sweatpants in the first ad, or wearing another T-shirt and trousers with a suit jacket thrown over his shoulders in the second. This hesitancy to reveal Jordan in his underwear exemplifies what Ronald L. Jackson terms "corporeal elision" (60).

Jackson uses Jordan's "Boxers or Briefs?" ad to demonstrate how this elision works in reverse. In this clip, two white women sitting on a park bench giggle in surprise when they see a fully dressed Jordan pass by. He addresses them by refusing to specify if he is hiding boxers or briefs underneath: "Don't even ask. They're Hanes." Despite the fact that Jordan is not displaying his crotch, Jackson is justified in reading this particular Hanes ad (as well as others by the same company which feature a black male and a white male) as reviving the "age-old myth about White and Black male phallic comparison" (61). Showing Jordan in his briefs, especially red ones, makes this comparison potentially even more blatant. Still, as Jackson points out, covering the black body may be more effective than revealing it. Elision is thus reversed by forcing television viewers to imagine black penis size.

An obvious reason to help explain the scarcity of men's underwear advertisements using the bodies of African American athletes is the prevalence of what Jackson calls the "'Black Masculine Body as Sexual' stereotype" (79). In her 1994 essay, "Feminism Inside: Toward a Black Body Politic," bell hooks makes explicit the racist nature of this sexual stereotype when she argues that "the black body continues to be perceived as the embodiment of bestial, violent, penis-as-weapon hypermasculine assertion" (131). Hiring a black male to pose in underwear may appear to revive such negative stereotyping and thus account for the reluctance of underwear companies to feature naked black bodies in their publicity, or the preference to show Michael Jordan fully clothed.

Nevertheless, there are signs in the United States that advertisers of men's underwear are willing to use black models, thus braving the taboo linked to eroticizing the black body to sell this item of clothing. Tyson Beckford, the American supermodel and actor of Jamaican and Chinese origin, modeled Ralph Lauren underwear from the mid-1990s onward. In mid-2005, the comedian Damon Wayans joined the team of Hanes models. A year later, the "Comfort Soft Waistband" television ad for Hanes featured a black professional dodgeball player. Late 2007, as part of the celebrations marking Calvin Klein's twenty-five years in the men's underwear industry, the American model and actor Djimon Hounsou originally from Benin was chosen to launch Calvin Klein Steel underwear. All this publicity may be seen to justify bell hook's suggestion that "Whites see the black body to confirm that it is the exotic supersexed flesh of their fantasies" (*Cool* 79).

A sign that the black body of an athlete is still being inscribed as always already supersexed can be found in men's underwear ads for the European brand Sloggi. Since 2005, the ex-tennis champion Yannick Noah of Cameroonian and French origin has featured in publicity shots alone, in the company of scantily clad white women, and, for the 2006 campaign, in between two white males dressed in full military uniforms. One 2005 publicity shot shows Noah in boxers smiling at the camera, while a long-haired brunette wearing a string and visibly nothing else grips Noah's shoulder. The white female model has her back turned to the camera thus showing her mostly uncovered buttocks. Ronald L. Jackson helps elucidate the potential impact of this image when he discusses the stock figure of the "buck" or the "brute," defined as a "dark-skinned muscular, athletically built character" (41). He is a "sexually pernicious beast" (41), who demonstrates his brutishness by raping white women. If this Sloggi advertisement were used in the United States, it is possible that it might be decoded in the context of such antimiscegenation fears that bolstered the racist stock figure Jackson analyses. In the context of advertising a commodity such as men's underwear, another problem arises. In *We Real Cool,* bell hooks provides a critique of an economy of desire which seems to privilege, but in reality discriminates against a black body. Hooks argues that "'hypermasculine black male sexuality' is feminized and tamed by a process of commodification that denies its agency and makes it serve the desire of others, especially white sexual lust" (79).

Examining the history of the pimped out body and analyzing denuded representations of black athletes lead to the conclusion that metrosexuality *can* be instrumental in redistributing and recycling a racist ideology. When white bodies are exhibited as objects of desire and the gaze (this is the subject of the next chapter), they are not systematically inscribed in the same way as black bodies. Because black bodies have historically tended to be read as representing deviance, exposing the black body to a predominantly white gaze and eroticizing the black body can evoke or encourage a "dick thing" sexual fantasy according to which black skin and black bodies are always already hypermasculine and hypersexual. This fantasy can inhabit the bearer of the gaze, or even be actively endorsed by the black subject who wishes to have his social and sexual prestige enhanced. Skin, bodies, clothes, and corporeal accoutrements can all be fetishized and endowed with an erotic significance. But when black skin and black bodies are commoditized, this objectification always runs the risk of purveying a racist and sexist ideology.

7

Sporno Stars

In his 1996 study, *The Erotic in Sports*, Allen Guttmann begins with the observation that "the topic of eros and sports is obviously, for many [. . .] a taboo" (4). He addresses the subject of his monograph after noticing "the more or less unproblematic recognition of athletic eroticism by the pagan cultures of classical antiquity" which "stands in sharp contrast to the hostile comments, the 'erasure,' and the confused obfuscation that have characterized most modern discussions of the subject" (6). This chapter extends the research of Guttmann by demonstrating how metrosexuality is contributing toward making sports erotics normal again. The passivity, the desirability, and the looked-at-ness of male bodies, provide a template for a new masculinity, the full repercussions of which will be examined in the final chapter.

This chapter begins by providing historical background which is necessary to understand how contemporary representations of denuded athletes are at times inspired by and imitate two previous key moments in the history of male sports nudity. One key moment is perceptible in ancient Greece athletics and the other in twentieth-century American physique photography. In ancient Greece, all young males trained naked in order to become soldier-warriors. Early twentieth-century postcard representations of the male nude were mostly of bodybuilders happy to flex their muscles. The males who posed for mid-century male physique magazines were a heterogeneous group. *Physique*, Winston Leyland's study of one particular muscle magazine, informs us that "Some were dedicated bodybuilders" and others were "lean sun-worshippers, servicemen, movie star hopefuls, drifters and an assortment of boy-next-door types" (1). The ostensible reason motivating this varied lot of men was the hope of catching the eye of a Hollywood director. Since the beginning of the twenty-first century, some of the highest paid and most proficient athletes in the world have been showing off their bodies, in contrast to the largely anonymous military athletes and unknown bodybuilders who posed in the past. Professional athletes can earn a lot of money for themselves or for a charity if they exhibit their flesh outside a sports context.

The sex and sexual orientation of spectators who look at nude athletes have partly altered. In ancient Greece, women were barred from watching male athletes train or perform. This means that male sports nudity was a homosocial and sometimes homoerotic activity from which the female gaze was excluded. Likewise, muscle magazines were destined for all-male viewers who were erotically aroused by the bodies of other men. It is only when we come to contemporary representations of denuded athletes that we notice a revolutionary change. For the first time, women as well as men are assumed to be interested spectators. Except for gay magazines, the intended male audience includes heterosexual males. This makes for an intriguing situation. One might have thought that only women and gay men were interested in the denuded bodies of athletes. Increasingly, though, this pleasure is being forced onto the attention of heterosexual males.

The principal concept that I will be using to analyze sports nudity is "spornography," a term Mark Simpson coined in a July 2006 article published by the American gay magazine *Out*. The word "sporn" already existed to designate unwanted spam of a sexual nature. In contrast, spornography is in high demand. The neologism joins together "sport" and "pornography" to refer to the sex-object status of athletes, an attribute which is turning an increasing number of professional athletes into "sporno" stars. The word sporno is already enjoying some currency, as attested by queerbeacon.net, a Web site dedicated to how homosexuality is treated in films. The site offers a sporno gallery of over four hundred photos showing off athletic nudity. It needs to be pointed out that despite the presence of the word "porn" in "sporno," I will not be entering into any discussion about pornography. I am using spornography simply as a convenient shorthand formula to refer to the erotic desirability of an athlete's body. Whether images of denuded athletes are perceived of as pornography is beyond the scope of this analysis. Spornography is a form of eroticism which exhibits the body of a sportsman as an object of desire.

The ease with which an increasing number of professional athletes from different countries are now comfortable about revealing their bodies is an exciting new trend in sports sex. Despite the Greek example of collective athletic nudity, since antiquity, male athletes have been discouraged from exhibitionism both in and away from the prescribed space where they perform their sport. A useful case to recall is the Harvard-educated soccer goalkeeper Shep Messing, who in 1974, two years after participating in the Munich Olympics, was paid $5000 to do a nude photo spread in the New York women's magazine *Viva*. After publication of this daring pose, the player was immediately released from his contract with the New York Cosmos team and fired for violating a morals clause. Contrasting with this negative perception of athletes showing off their bodies dating from the mid-1970s, spornography is becoming increasingly accepted. Gymnasia, sculptures, pottery, postcards, and physique magazines have given way to a number of new formats that will be analyzed in turn: gay magazines, sports photo albums, calendars, commercial catalogs, and fashion photography. These are the main nonsports arenas where professional athletes are revealing their bodies in the twenty-first century.

Sports Nudity

One of the exceptional facets of ancient Greece is the fact that athletes trained and competed naked. Nudity in male athletics was culturally accepted and considered as the norm. Etymologically, "gymnasium" means "place to be naked." Greek athletic nudity was particularly famous in a Spartan festival known as "Gymnopaedia," meaning "naked playfulness." During this festival, ancient equivalents of football, boxing, and wrestling were performed by naked males. Male nudity was also a characteristic of the ancient Olympics and was more generally visible in *kouroi*, sculptures of male youths common in the second half of the seventh century and sixth century B.C. One consequence of athletic nudity is the increased ability to appreciate the beauty of male bodies. Another is the arousal of sexual desire. In his study of Eros and ancient athletics, Thomas Scanlon reminds us that "The custom of athletic nudity [. . .] was an inherent part of the social nexus that fostered the association of athletics, male beauty, and sexuality" (206–7). He underlines the idea that the body of a young athlete in ancient Greece even constituted an ideal physical type. This idealization is corroborated by the widespread use of the word *kalos* (beautiful) which was inscribed next to naked athletic figures on vase paintings.

Adaptations of this Greek cultural norm can be detected at various times since antiquity in different cultures and places. Such an adaptation took place notably from the end of the nineteenth century until the 1960s when bodybuilding postcards, mail-order photographs, physique magazines, and later on movies, relegitimated nude (and sometimes pouched) representations of the male athletic body. In Germany, France, Britain, and the United States, such "beefcake" as it became known, circulated widely until legislation allowed the merchandizing and commercial exploitation of more explicit representations of male nudity. American beefcake finds its origin in New York. Italian immigrant Tony Sansone (1905–1987) was America's "first male physique icon" according to the subtitle of John Massey's biography *American Adonis*. In 1929, Sansone met New York photographer Edwin Townsend, who had worked for *Harper's Bazaar* and *Vogue*. Struck by the physical beauty, grace, and musculature of Sansone, Townsend published several booklets featuring nude photographs of the American Adonis. At times adopting poses reminiscent of Greek statuary, Sansone provided an aesthetic model for future bodybuilder photography in America.

Interest in the male physique was particularly noticeable in Los Angeles during the 1950s and 1960s. The Athletic Model Guild (AMG), set up in 1945 by Bob Mizer, was the first male model photographic studio in the United States. For nearly four decades, Mizer published *Physique Pictorial*, a quarterly which featured nude photographs of over six thousand amateur models. During this time, Bob Mizer provided America with a plenitude of near-naked or completely naked male bodies. Since it was illegal in the early years to send frontal nudity through the post, models just wore a posing pouch. *Physique Pictorial* was an instant success, selling up to forty thousand copies per issue in the late 1950s. This publication, in the somewhat inflated words of muscle magazine specialist F. Valentine Hooven, "celebrated the male body with a directness that had not been seen since the collapse of the Roman Empire" (50). From 1956 until 1966, Bruce of Los Angeles brought out a similar magazine, *The*

Male Figure. He was also behind a mail-distribution service of physique photography bought by art students, bodybuilders, and a growing homosexual market. The latter he satisfied with trunks of male nude photographs he sold from hotel rooms across the country. This physique iconography was modeled by males who posed for male photographers. It was then sold to an all-male readership. This explains why Thomas Waugh argues that the postwar physique culture of photographs, magazines, and films "is one of the great achievements of gay culture" (176). "The whole operation," he continues, "was predicated on bodybuilding as a channel—and at the same time a camouflage—for the sexualized male body" (176). Male physique magazines were supposedly destined for a readership officially identified as students of art or "muscle enthusiasts" (this euphemism was generally understood to mean men attracted to other men). In fact, as Waugh convincingly demonstrates, it was an open secret that a large part of the beef was served up by homosexual photographers for a mostly closeted homosexual public. In stark contrast with this closeted atmosphere, the gay gaze is now being openly solicited by certain athletes.

The Gay Gaze

The gay gaze can be sought after on purpose or unintentionally by athletes. Australia and Brazil are two countries where the gay gaze is being intentionally solicited. One significant innovation in sports sex is for a professional sportsman to pose nude for a gay publication. This is what the Australian rugby player Ian Roberts did in 1995 after his homosexual outing. Since then, Roberts has been the object of numerous photo spreads in the Australian gay press. Such media exposure presupposes that a professional athlete is courageous enough to publicly identify as homosexual (chapter 1 underlined the rarity of this event). It also demonstrates a wish to further flout jock culture's conventions by deliberately stimulating homoerotic desire in other men. After posing nude for the Australian men's interest fashion publication *(NOT ONLY) blue* in February 1995, Roberts returned to the same magazine in February 2001, once he had retired from professional sport. That month he did a number of fashion poses including one double-page spread where he is shown with a phallic snake slithering over his shoulder and arms. Even if one shot shows the former rugby player provocatively pulling down on a pair of red spandex shorts, there is no full frontal nudity. For this we have to go to the hothouse of sporno homo-sex, Brazil.

The most sexually explicit spornography has been appearing since 1999 in the Brazilian gay publication *G Magazine*. Naked torsos, bare bottoms, and a host of full frontal shots have become staple fare from some of the country's soccer players. Typifying this new variety of sports erotics, in February 1999 Claudinei Alexandre Pires (known as "Dinei") was billed on the cover as showing it all. He was not the first soccer player in Brazil to do so, as Marcos Andre Batista Santos (known as "Vampeta") had already been given cover status in January 1999. Their example was followed by Bruno Carvalho in July 2002, Túlio Costa (known as "Maravilha") in December 2003, Alexandre Gaúcho in February 2005, and Fabiano Borges in August 2005. By posing fully naked with exposed genitals for a gay magazine, these sportsmen demonstrate an inhibition about soliciting same-sex desire that would be anathema in the United States. As we will see, some athletes have inadvertently provoked adulation from gay fans, but there is a difference when sportsmen go out of their way to deliberately pose in photo spreads for gay spectators. In Brazil, no special public shame would seem to be attached to this sort of exhibitionism on the part of athletes.

Dwayne Johnson, otherwise known as "The Rock," is an exceptional example in the United States of a retired figure from the sports world who has posed for the gay press. His elaborately tattooed torso has helped turn the former football player and wrestler of African American and Samoan background into a movie star and a sex symbol. *Details* carried an article and photo spread of The Rock in early 2005 to coincide with the release of the film *Be Cool* (Brown 124–29). Perhaps surprisingly for an ex-athlete, he plays the role of a gay bodyguard. Unlike some of his tattooed athletic brethren, The Rock is not a victim of jock culture's one-track interpretation of gender and sexual mythologies. Identifying as heterosexual, the star does not have a problem donning drag for *Saturday Night Live* or gracing the cover of the gay magazine *Out* in March 2005 where he was provocatively billed as "The Rock Goes Gay: The action star on playing queer in his kick-ass new movie." Close-up shots of The Rock's naked torso in *Details* (including one in which his eyes are shut) insist on the actor's sex appeal. He models clothes and accessories (Levi's jeans and a Gucci necklace in *Details*, Armani Exchange and Dolce & Gabbana fashion items offset by necklaces, chains, bracelets, and watches in *Out*).

In an October 2003 *GQ* (U.S.) article devoted to The Rock, Andrew Corsello comments that The Rock's overall air "conveys an openness and vulnerability" (264). The Rock seems to share the journalist's point of view by claiming: "I do think that in addition to the cockiness and the humor, vulnerability has always been part of my appeal" (264). Vulnerability prevents professional athletes in the United States from exposing themselves in the gay press. When an athlete's body is looked at by gay spectators, this makes the athlete the potential object of criticism by homophobic fans. The Rock's desire to allow his body to be looked at and desired by readers and film viewers of any sex and sexual orientation depends on an openness of mind that is not shared by many professional athletes in the United States.

In contrast to this intentional inviting of the gay gaze, many professional athletes involuntarily attract the attention of gay fans. One representative example is the Portuguese soccer star Cristiano Ronaldo who plays for Manchester United. Ronaldo typifies what can happen when an athlete, imitating his ancient Greek forebears, shows nudity in a sports context. He is also a good illustration of how television and the Internet play important roles in bringing out into the open the previously closeted admiration of male athletes by homosexual males. In soccer, revealing the torso is not permissible except at the end of a match when jerseys are sometimes exchanged between players of opposing teams. Ronaldo memorably displayed his naked torso during the Euro 2004 soccer championship by taking off his jersey after scoring the first goal for Portugal in the semifinal against the Netherlands. He paraded half-naked around the stadium ostensibly to his intense pleasure and that of some spectators. For this act of unauthorized exhibitionism, the player was shown a yellow card by the referee for conduct ill-becoming a sportsman. This striptease also provoked an uncalculated result. After millions of fans were entertained by the resplendently naked torso, Ronaldo was later voted the country's sexiest player by a Portuguese gay Web site. This popularity with gay fans was confirmed during the 2006 World Cup when a Dutch gay magazine readers' poll voted him the most attractive and sexiest player in the whole competition.

Having shown what there was to offer under his kit, it is not surprising that Ronaldo's first commercial sponsorship and fashion magazine coverage was secured soon after the Euro 2004 striptease. The association with Pepe Jeans predictably concentrated on the athlete's beefcake potential. In January 2005, *Vogue Sport* (Italy) honored the soccer star with a cover shot, a short article, a double-page advertisement, and photographs taken by Steven Klein. The cover of the magazine dubbed Ronaldo "THE HOTTEST NEW GUY" and, in Italian, scattered compliments throughout the article such as "Beckham's heir," "new fashion icon," and "face of a macho Latin" (Maggio 236). The *Vogue Sport* cover shows Ronaldo sitting on the back of a truck, wearing only jeans and boots. In this photograph, the front of his jeans is undone and the viewer catches a glimpse of white underwear. Ronaldo's hand is resting near his crotch. This image is further eroticized by the inclusion of multiple accessories: ear studs, two pendant chains, two silver rings, a leather wristband, and a bracelet. The *Vogue Sport* title left begging an unanswered question. Hot for whom? Obviously women and men find Ronaldo attractive. Since the Pepe Jeans contract, other fashion magazines and sponsors have become interested in Ronaldo's sex appeal. In April 2005, the cover of the Portuguese version of *GQ* exposed one of Ronaldo's nipples. It was made tantalizingly visible next to a string of necklaces (Rodrigues). Nipples were hidden but easily discernible in two endorsement deals. Ronaldo wore a skin-tight sports kit for a 2005 Nike Pro campaign and a skin-tight jersey for a 2006 Coca-Cola promotion.

An athlete's status as an object of erotic desire is helped by referencing the model of Greek athletic perfection. This is why *Vogue* celebrated Ronaldo as the "new Apollo" (Maggio 234). One of the photographs accompanying the single-page article, where Ronaldo is wearing white canvas Pepe Jeans pants, shows a stunning, fully lighted and naked torso, the whiteness of which recalls the marble of Greek *kouroi*. The slight frown, smooth pink nipples, and muscle lines descending into the groin provide evidence of what Serge Maggio terms *"bellezza adolescenziale"* (236), adolescent beauty. Klein's flattering portrait turns the divine ephebe into a bejeweled modern-day *kouros* with undeniable appeal.

The British edition of *GQ* took an interest in Ronaldo in September 2005 as part of a "Football Style Special" issue. Two other Premiership players were interviewed, a British goalkeeper and a Dutch left wing, who posed for the camera wearing Hermès, Prada, Louis Vuitton, and other fashion labels. However, the star of the photo shoot is obviously the boy from Madeira. Posing in layback urban wear, including a Prada grey jacket and a DSquared2 pair of tan leather trousers, Ronaldo opens the photo spread in a hooded top. In this close-up shot, the star looks right into the camera with a brooding stare. The slight sparkle from the ear diamonds, together with the black hood resembling long black hair from a distance, provide Ronaldo with an androgynous appeal.

In the absence of commentary on the part of Ronaldo concerning his sex symbol status for both sexes, one can only wonder to what extent he knows about, endorses, or refuses this adulation. All athletes are potential objects of the gay gaze. This fact incites a minority of professional athletes to exploit the gay press as an avenue of exhibitionism. Many, like Ronaldo, either are unaware of the fact that they are looked at by a gay public or they are not concerned enough to allow this to stop them from showing some nudity for the camera. Another minority openly accepts the gay gaze and feels flattered as a consequence. This small group of athletes will be examined in the next chapter when we look more closely at Ian Thorpe and David Beckham.

Soccer Photo Albums

Homoerotics is not the central focus, but it is certainly not excluded from *Calcio*, a photo album published in 2003. This album, as well as its successors, *A.C. Milan Dressed by Dolce & Gabbana* (2005) and *Milan* (2006), offers scores of athletes, dressed, undressing, or half-naked. *Calcio* features over forty soccer players from Italian teams wearing Dolce & Gabbana designs. Interviewed by Peter Howarth when *Calcio* first appeared, Domenico Dolce stated that "Fashion was really getting too removed from real life [. . .] So we looked for new references and footballers are perfect. They are real men [. . .] Now they are wealthy, beautiful, healthy, and women love them [. . .] and men love them too" (Howarth, "Beautiful Game" 15). Dolce understood that a large part of the interest in using sportsmen's bodies to model clothes is that both sexes will be inclined to look. Howarth's article was reproduced a week later in a Canadian newspaper, but curiously the afterthought "and men love them too" was excised ("European Designers" B12). This evident truth seems to have worried one Canadian newspaper editor. Suggesting that men "love sportsmen," as

Dolce does, is of course ambiguous. Are heterosexual males only permitted to be keenly interested in athletic proficiency, leaving women and homosexual men to see sportsmen as potential sex objects? Spornography repeatedly shows how it is difficult to unravel the two sorts of appeal. Dolce and Gabbana realize that there is a necessary carryover between athletic prowess and aesthetic appeal. In excising "and men love them too," the censor was trying to deprive spornography of its homoerotic component and appease straight readers by pretending that it does not exist. It sounds like an attempt to save the heterosexual reputations of males who are *too* interested in sportsmen. Being interested in sportsmen and loving sportsmen, in whatever form, are aspects of the same continuum.

Cultural critic Michael Bronski penned a useful term to describe the three Dolce & Gabbana photo albums when he used the formula "blatant male pulchritude" in another context. The photographer of these albums, Mariano Vivanco, has been instrumental in putting Italian male pulchritude at the forefront of European spornography. Christian Vieri appears in *Calcio* wearing a sweater and white bum-hugging boxer briefs. There is a five-part reverse striptease in which Vieri gradually puts on a pair of trousers over boxer briefs. There are seven photos of Fabio Cannavaro, including a fetishistic shot of just his bare feet. Another photo of Cannavaro shows a glimpse of groin next to the brand name of some Dolce & Gabbana white underwear. A further image reveals a naked torso from behind, thus allowing the viewer to clearly see the soccer player's Chinese and Gothic script tattoos. The photo of Francesco Coco in the shower wearing drenched white Dolce & Gabbana underwear catches the entire spirit of *Calcio*. One titillating shot of Coco in a change room shows the player nonchalantly taking off a sock, one leg raised to the chin, thus covering the intercrural area. *A.C. Milan Dressed by Dolce & Gabbana* shows the Milanese soccer team off the field. Naked torsos, jeans lowered to reveal swimwear, and glimpses of white underwear are three methods used to catch the attention of readers. Four shots of midfielder Massimo Ambrosini combine all three strategies simultaneously, while adding another, a hand poised over the crotch. *Milan,* the most recent volume in the series, presents another one hundred and forty shots of seminude athletes. In the single page of text in *Calcio*, the designers speak of the soccer players as "the new spokesmen for a fresh kind of beauty. A beauty that's healthy, wholesome and clean" (*Calcio* 140). This may ring hollow as an accolade, but at least the photo albums are providing a host of Italian sportsmen an international audience who can now decide who deserves being put into online sporno galleries.

One athlete featured in *Calcio,* soccer player Hidetoshi Nakata, has been dubbed the "Asian Becks." Nakata attracted media coverage in Europe, Asia, and the United States before retiring from professional soccer in 2006. *GQ* (U.S.), for example, ran a photo shoot in July 2004, highlighting the question, "Is there a better-dressed athlete in the world than renegade Japanese soccer sensation Hidetoshi Nakata?" ("Mix It Up" 128). This mix and match photo sequence was inspired by labels as different as Armani, Burberry, Versace, Calvin Klein, and Comme des Garçons. Four portraits of the player are included in the photo album. Nakata is shown provocatively sprawled back on top of a fur rug, wearing a tank top, Dolce & Gabbana jeans, a wide leather belt, and multiple necklaces. Another shot reveals a naked washboard torso, a Beckhamesque rosary necklace, and tatty jeans, lowered just so that we can catch the waistband of the designers' underwear. More so than in the magazine coverage of Nakata, there is an attempt here to exploit the spornographic potential of the soccer player's body. Nakata has been categorized in the media as belonging to the select club of rich, handsome athletes who attract the label metrosexual. In September 2004, the French magazine *Préférences Mag* included a two-page portrait of the player who was dubbed *"le bel enfant de la balle"* (Baraquin 20), the good-looking soccer kid. The introductory paragraph of the *Préférences* article insists on the soccer player's hair and clothes extravagances. His pimping out, shown by his taste for flamboyant fashion, flashy cars, and bling jewelry, could also have been mentioned.

It therefore came as no surprise to learn that in 2005 Nakata was the main celebrity present at the launch of *We Men,* Taiwan's first magazine targeted at metrosexual males. He figures on the cover of the first issue, pulling down his black trousers with a thumb to reveal naked buttocks. Nakata is decked out in an array of luxury accessories: a Dior Homme scarf, a necklace, and a bracelet matched with a Dior watch. The Table of Contents page includes a shot of Nakata wearing a Dolce & Gabbana black shirt offset by accessories, three Chrome Hearts necklaces neatly nestled between his pectorals. The article includes a double-page spread where the athlete adopts a playboy pose by reclining on a leather couch in the hands of two bikinied and feathered models. In this pose, the gaping Dolce

& Gabbana white shirt teamed with ripped and studded Dolce & Gabbana blue jeans suggestively highlight sports erotics.

Sports Calendars

The sports calendar is an obvious format for turning athletes into sporno stars. Calendars featuring sportsmen have been available in the United States for decades, but they typify a premetrosexual approach to displaying monthly muscle. Professional American athletes refrain from being photographed nude. NBA and NFL calendars, for example, are full of clothed action shots. Some nudity has been visible in the mainstream magazine *Sports Illustrated*, an unlikely publication to display sports nudity since it is targeted at a mass readership made up mostly of heterosexual males. Baseball heroes have been breaking new ground by posing semi-naked in *Sports Illustrated* since February 1997 when, unusually, five shortstops posed together shirtless, all wearing necklaces with cheeky grins. Derek Jeter, Alex Rodriguez, Alex Gonzalez, Rey Ordonez, and Edgar Renteria could be taken for South Beach boys. In December 1998, Sammy Sosa and Mark McGwire appeared wearing togas on a *Sports Illustrated* cover and in March 2001 an imposing and shirtless Nomar Garciaparra brought another imposing bare chest to the sports sections of newsstands worldwide.

Contrasting with this reticence in the United States to display nude representations of athletes, sports calendars in Australia and France offer an annual supply of partially or fully naked athletes. Calendar spornography was pioneered in Australia where shirtless shots of prime Australian beef have been on sale since 1993 in the "Men for All Seasons" calendars featuring professional Football League players. Professional rugby players have also provided a steady source of spornography. A competition called the "Sexiest Man in League" has been running in Australia since 1996. Sponsored by Adidas Active Skincare since 2004, this competition presents an annual sporno star whose sexiness and stylishness attract the attention of the country. Avoiding full frontal nudity, Australian professional rugby players appeared in the League of Their Own 2006 calendar, the Naked Rugby League 2007 calendar, and the 2008 Naked for a Cause calendar.

French rugby calendars featuring the team *Stade Français* clearly reference athletes from antiquity and American male physique photography. Evoking an obvious parallel with antiquity provides an added justification for spornography. Each French rugby calendar has the same title, *Dievx dv stade,* stadium gods. Using the letter "v" instead of "u," as the dictionary requires, is an attempt to render typographically a Latin frame of reference for these contemporary divinities, made to recall their antique forebears. For example, the beginnings of American male physique photography, classical statues from antiquity illustrate a similar source of inspiration. Many photographers reproduce an imagined Greek or Roman context by means of props: animal skins, fig leaves, leather sandals, and spears. "The Dying Gladiator," one of Sarony's 1893 portraits of Eugen Sandow, shows the strongman lying on a leopard skin, holding a sword and shield (Chapman 15). Bob Mizer and Bruce of Los Angeles frequently used Greek columns as stage props for their athletes. A photograph of model Miles Conley in *Physique Pictorial* shows the tattooed and pouched bodybuilder lying down and looking downward at his reflection like Narcissus. Behind him, there is a painted backdrop featuring the ruins of a Greek temple. One of the early male physique magazines was called *Grecian Guild Pictorial;* others went by the name of *Adonis* and *American Apollo.* Antiquity also provides a series of metaphors (as strong as Hercules, as beautiful as Apollo or Adonis) that helps transform muscled mortals into Olympian deities.

The 2004 Stadium Gods calendar, photographed by François Rousseau, propelled the mostly naked French rugby team into spornographic celebrity. This was helped by capturing the event in a book and on a DVD. Thirty black and white shots of the *Stade Français* rugby team, together with athletes from other sports, were fingered, admired, and adulated in and outside France. All 100,000 copies sold out, turning this particular calendar into a collector's item. This was followed by *Dievx dv stade: Le livre,* a coffee-table book of Rousseau's photographs, prefaced by Madonna. An American version of this album, published in late 2005 and retitled *Locker Room Nudes,* suggested that there was once again an American market for spornography after its furtive version in the 1950s and 1960s. Cashing in on modern technology, a 100-minute DVD documentary of the photographic session satisfies heterosexual and homosexual voyeurism even further. Using fantasies of locker room frolics, bathroom and shower scenes as well as gymnasium backdrops, Rousseau revitalized ancient Greek athletics and mid-century Los Angeles beefcake.

If American athletes seem unwilling to copy the example of some Australian and French sportsmen, American firefighters have no qualms displaying their naked torsos for calendar fodder. Firefighter calendars are the closest thing to Australian and French calendar spornography, especially the New York Fire Department's "Calendar of Heroes." Half-naked shots of musclemen in uniform provide a stunning spectacle of fetishized masculinity. The cover of the 2006 DVD *The Making Of: Firefighter Fundraising Calendar* features a titillating bare-chested Titan of a firefighter who carries a remarkably heavy chain over his shoulder. Such an S/M accoutrement attaches this fantasy figure to the tradition of Bob Mizer's mid-twentieth-century Athletic Model Guild photographs in which ropes and chains were commonly used to evoke sexual restraint. Resistance to the spectacularization of male nudity is thus dependent on professions in the United States.

A&F Catalogs

The erotic titillation of the French Stadium calendars has a widespread American version in the form of commercial advertising. Abercrombie & Fitch catalogs, full of boy-next-door muscle hunks, are reminiscent of Australian, European, and Brazilian sports erotics. Founded at the end of the nineteenth century, the clothing retailer Abercrombie & Fitch (A&F) acquired a reputation for catering to the sartorial needs of rugged, outdoor types such as Theodore Roosevelt and Ernest Hemingway. The company underwent a transformation in the 1990s, when creative director Sam Shahid (who previously worked for Calvin Klein) took over advertising operations. At the end of 1997, Shahid employed photographer Bruce Weber to produce a store quarterly catalog. This magazine has attracted a wide readership due essentially to its provocative soft-porn poses. The Christmas 2003 catalog, supposedly endorsing group sex, fell foul of family associations and publication temporarily ceased. By fall 2004, however, the A&F institution was back under a new name, *A&F Magazine*.

Two ingredients make up A&F mythology, collegiate sports and the commercial commoditization of half-naked male bodies. Weber constantly uses different sports in the catalogs as a pretext to portray divested shots mostly of male bodies. It is obvious that this epic series of quarterlies which embodies the frat fantasy is mainly a glorification of youth, virility, and masculine erotics. The use of sports by A&F has been obsessive as a means to peddle drab clothing. Television clips selling the brand center on square-jawed, all-American jocks who spend their time kayaking, skimboarding, freeflying, skeleton racing, bobsled racing, sailing, snowboarding, surfing, wakeboarding, or just simply playing football. As well as underlining the centrality of sports in American culture, these catalogs also allow Weber to revive mid-century male physique photography and adapt it in order to explore a form of spornography similar to that present outside the United States. The major difference is that spornography elsewhere concerns professional athletes. The A&F catalogs are based on male models who simply act out jock fantasies.

In a chapter entitled "Why I Hate Abercrombie & Fitch" from a book of the same title, Dwight A. McBride convincingly shows how A&F marketing strategies fundamentally discriminate on the basis of race, color, and national origin. The author carried out fieldwork among former employees of the clothing company, examined past catalogs, and analyzed their guidelines for brand representatives. The A&F lifestyle, characterized by McBride as "young, white, natural, all-American, [and] upper-class" (86), depends on promoting an all-white policy for its advertising and front shop staff. This policy led to a lawsuit which was filed against the company in 2003 for alleged discrimination against Latinos, Asian Americans, and African Americans.

McBride's reading of Abercrombie & Fitch's elision of all-American with whiteness raises questions about previous representations of the naked male body discussed in this chapter. If the American clothing company excludes ethnic minorities from its spornographic catalogs, does this concentration on white bodies constitute a defining characteristic of spornography in general? If we go back to Athletic Model Guild physique photography from the 1950s to the 1970s we find predominantly white bodies, although ethnic variations certainly do exist throughout the thousands of shots contained in the many editions of *Physique Pictorial*. The photographs of players from Italian soccer teams in the Dolce & Gabbana photo albums also reflect a noticeable ethnic homogeneity. Of the forty-five players represented in *Calcio* very few are of non-Italian origin: two are from Brazil, another two from Portugal, one player is Algerian, and another is

Japanese. *Calcio* could purvey the idea that sporno stars are nearly exclusively white. However, this whiteness corresponds to the ethnic composition of professional Italian soccer teams. It does not reveal a desire to exclude nonwhite bodies. Likewise, the French rugby calendars correspond to a reality in French rugby. Few males of ethnic minorities play this sport. The 2005 rugby calendar, for example, features only one black player, a track athlete invited to participate in the calendar exhibitionism. It is only when American firefighter calendars are considered, that is, when a nonsports context is operating, that ethnic diversity becomes the rule and not the exception in representations of denuded male bodies. And, of course, this is not spornography. Boxing, however, as the next section demonstrates, is conducive to exhibiting a range of ethnicities.

Fetishizing the Exotic

The denuded bodies of boxers and their silky attire are particularly effective in attracting the gaze. Wearing boxing trunks leaves heads, torsos, and lower thighs naked in the tradition of Greek athletics. Such exposure of flesh clearly encourages the potential sex-object status of young males. To demonstrate how boxers are at the forefront of spornography, I will examine "Prince" Naseem Hamed, a boxer of Yemeni origin. He became Britain's most famous boxer in the final decade of the twentieth century. My second example is another British boxer, Amir Khan, of Pakistani origin. He rose to celebrity after a silver-medal Olympic victory in 2004. Finally, I will turn to Brahim Asloum, the French flyweight boxer of Algerian Kabyle origin who received worldwide recognition after winning gold at the Sydney 2000 Olympics. Soon afterward, Asloum turned professional and remained unbeaten until a Paris match in December 2005 when he lost to a Venezuelan opponent.

Each of these athletes demonstrates various metrosexual lifestyle choices, has modeled in the fashion press, or participated in advertising commodities. However, what I find especially interesting about these young Muslim boxers is the fact that they have each become fetishized as the exotic Other. Even if Hamed and Khan were both born in Britain and Asloum in France, their family backgrounds are non-European. This means that their bodies are gazed on and gloated over in a special way. Thomas Waugh addresses this problematic when he affirms that "All northern sexuality, homo or hetero, is quickened by the dream of Elsewhere and the Other, the Exotic and most often the Oriental" (49). Hamed's otherness is perceptible in his Orientalizing. By this I mean that he is associated with a fantasized East situated in Asia or Arabia. Khan's exoticized otherness presents a case of skin fetishizing. Asloum's North African Muslim background has inspired the fashion press to offer a sexual fantasy based on a religious theme.

The investigation of Naseem Hamed's shorts which follows reveals the silky and sexy underside of British boxing. Fashion publications such as *GQ* and *Esquire* were quick to pick up on Prince Naseem (affectionately known as "Naz") as an item of interest after he won the WBO World Featherweight Championship in 1995. He triumphed again at Madison Square Garden in 1997, suffered his first defeat in 2001, and has not fought professionally since 2002. Asked once what he intended to do with his earnings, Hamed stated, "I'm interested in doing a lot of shopping, spending plenty of money on the right clothes" (Evans 97). The biographer who picked up this comment helps provide more metrosexual credentials for Hamed, including one where the boxer speaks of his "passion for shopping in London or New York" (Evans 190). The *Sun* newspaper did a fashion spread on the prince in 1995. An endorsement contract with the Joe Bloggs clothing brand offered the boxer the possibility of designing his own range of clothes. Hamed's designing skills seem to have impressed the managing director of Joe Bloggs, who affirmed that the boxer had "real talent and could make a living as a designer" (Evans 186). Despite these purported tailoring talents, Hamed's main skills lay elsewhere. His flamboyant antics, such as somersaulting into the boxing ring and the camp theatrics of his arrivals before a match, were noticeably aided by leopard-skin trunks which became a major distinguishing trademark.

Leopard skins and the feline in general have a tradition of being associated with male and female sexuality. The New York 2005 exhibition "Wild: Fashion Untamed" highlighted the extent to which clothes made of imitation leopard skin have become objects of fascination, especially in women's clothes. In the catalog accompanying the exhibition, Shannon Bell-Price and Elyssa Da Cruz point out that "At the dawn of the twenty-first century, fashion continues to clothe its clients in the patterns of the solitary leopard, the fearsome tigress, and the exotic zebra" (117). The authors draw attention to the use of the feline in sartorial designs to insist on women as "coquettish and overtly sexualized" (117). While it is undeniable that leopard-skin clothes evoke ferocious female sexuality, it must not be forgotten that animal markings also act as a sign of overt male sexuality. In Greek mythology Dionysus, the god of wine and orgiastic delights, was often portrayed wearing a leopard skin or accompanied by leopards. Both he and his female followers, the Bacchantes, were associated with drunkenness and licentiousness.

The choice of leopard-skin shorts as a trademark reveals the commercial strategy of selling Prince Naseem as an exotic product. Commoditizing the Hamed package depended largely on taking advantage of the non-British origin of his family. The boxer made several trips to Yemen and was treated royally by the régime, eager to promote one of its sons as a role model. The staging of his entrances into the ring provided an excellent chance to insist on Hamed's foreign background. For a fight in Sheffield in 1994, Hamed appeared wearing an orange turban, a headdress of Asian origin which has links with Arab culture. Newcastle in 1996 witnessed the prince who, according to a biographer, "arrived on a giant, gold-colored throne carried by his six Nubian minders, accompanied by two near-naked ladies scattering petals to the crowd" (Evans 201). In this carefully controlled *mise-en-scène*, the enthroned leopard boy assumed the role of a king surrounded by his entourage of courtesans. This theatrical spectacle fetishizes ethnicity by referencing the myth of Oriental splendor and sensuality.

A photograph published in a men's magazine and a publicity stunt for a chocolate bar both provide evidence of fetishizing the boxer's body and investing it with sex appeal. Another two courtesans were chosen to sit on either side of the "Asian Bull" (as Hamed was called) in November 1994 when he appeared on the cover of *Loaded*. To introduce Bill Borrows's "Little Ali" (a pseudonym with Arabic resonance), there is a photograph of the twenty-year-old sitting in a limousine, befriended by two alluring models. Apart from socks and sneakers, he is wearing his leopard-skin boxing shorts in close proximity to the hands of his female admirers. Obviously the sex kitten in this photo is the boy showing his hairy thighs, not the hired babes next to him. Realizing that he had been an unwilling agent in titillating readers, the boxer later commented: "That is the first and last time I will do anything like that. I can see how people might easily get the wrong impression" (Evans

117). It was an impression that Hamed's 1996 "Dime Bar" advertisement more than confirmed. To promote this commodity, the boxer smilingly exhibited a chocolate bar while in a state of undress. This further reinforced his erotic commoditizing by suggesting the selling of phallic fantasies. Over three million wrappers and posters of a mostly naked Naz littered a country eager to eat the boxer's bar.

This "wrong impression" of being a sex bunny was largely encouraged by the constant wearing and transformation of leopard-skin trunks in the 1990s. Sporting ever-changing animal prints helped turn Hamed into a hypersexualized object of desire. Until the beginning of 1995, Hamed boxed in the flimsy leopard shorts he wore for the *Loaded* cover. Swathes of brown around the waist and down the center contrasted with the otherwise light-colored background between the leopard spots. Starting in March 1995 at Edinburgh, he changed his spots and donned a new design. Sixty strips of leopard-skin material were stitched to a waistband to look like animal tails. When the boxer arrived for the fight in a kilt, sunglasses, and his new "hoola skirt," the reaction of female fans was instantaneous. Some vainly hoped that the regular flip over the ropes would reveal what was under the skirt. By the end of 1995, the tails gave way to a tasseled "skort" (half-skirt, half-short), a two-sided leopard invention revealing almost all of the boxer's upper thighs. The skort was then replaced by a new leopard-skin ensemble made up of a dark-colored fringed leopard top and matching leopard-printed shorts covered by eight rows of light-colored fringes. Sponsorship by Adidas in 1996 caused Hamed to change his wardrobe and thereafter he settled for a knee-length less elaborate version of leopard-patterned shorts decorated with his sponsor's three stripes. All these costume changes were an essential part of the prince myth, based on a proud, unbeatable, and savage "animal" who "slaughtered" everyone in its path. At the same time, the leopard spots turned Hamed into a permanent spectacle of erotic exoticism.

After Prince Naseem stopped professional fights, he was replaced as Britain's young Asian boxing hope by Amir Khan. This new sports celebrity followed in the footsteps of David Beckham when he became the object of a photo spread in the Autumn/Winter 2004–2005 issue of *Arena Homme Plus*. The *Arena* sequence of portraits fetishizes an athlete's physical attributes in order to help sell luxury accessories. Khan appears on the cover in a close-up boxing pose wearing a gold necklace and two gold chains. Another shot graces the Contents page. Here the post-workout boxer's sweaty head is covered by a veil-like Galliano sweatshirt and his neck harbors a Chopard chain. This jewelry prepares the reader for Tariq Goddard's article "The Kid" in which the young boxer models more necklaces. The opening black and white shot of Khan is a variation of the Galliano and Chopard pose. For this version, the boxer's lips are parted and his face streams with sweat. The emphasis on sweat obviously references intense physical effort while working out or boxing, but what is perhaps less evident is the sexual subtext of sweat, addressed by Kobena Mercer in "Imagining the Black Man's Sex." Here it is argued that "wherever naked black bodies appear in representation they are saturated with sweat, always already wet with sex" (187). This observation is of interest for how it informs Khan's eroticized wetness.

The boxer's eroticization is further aided by an accretion of fetishized body parts and clothes: full lips, long black eyelashes, and a sodden designer sweatshirt. Faint stubble on the chin provides evidence of a secondary sexual characteristic insisting on the model's youth and incipient virility. Over the page, another black and white full-page head and chest shot shows Khan's face at an angle, his eyes lowered and neck embellished by the Chopard gold chain. Three heads of chrysanthemum bring a note of floral beauty to harmonize with the boxer's natural beauty. Full-page color photographs follow in which a naked torso glistens with sweat. Khan's gold necklaces and chains help to fetishize his wet body, decorating it with exquisite taste.

If we now turn to France, an exceptional case of fetishizing the exotic is provided by Brahim Asloum who, more so than Hamed or Khan, offers some conventional evidence of metrosexual interests. He attended the 2003 and 2004 Francesco Smalto Autumn/Winter fashion shows in Paris. In June 2004, the boxer's grooming habits and taste for accessorizing were publicized in an illustrated article from the "Beauty" section of the French magazine *Gala*, which relayed the beauty tips of four representative Frenchmen. Asloum heads the piece with a two-page upper torso display in which he is naked, except for a Gucci necklace and ear studs. A description of his beauty treatment is followed by that of a company director, a pastry cook, and an actor. The idea behind the item was to convince the French, if they needed any convincing, that men's personal grooming does not detract from virility.

Asloum's self-care has become an almost banal phenomenon in the sports world. Of much more interest is his advertising of luxury watches in S/M-inspired poses for a photo spread which appeared in the Fall/Winter 2003–2004 issue of *Vogue Hommes International* (France). Ali Mahdavi's cover shot and six-page photo sequence "Brahim Time" present variations on the subject of bondage. There is an exploitation of accessories in these photographs, but not the ones metrosexual wannabes are used to wearing. Mr. Pearl, a French corsetier who has collaborated with Christian Lacroix and Thierry Mugler, provided the boxer with a body-modifying black corset. As well as the corset, a number of accessories are used to restrain Asloum. Here an athlete is blindfolded, restrained, choked, and gagged by diamonds, bezel, alligator, python, and mother of pearl watchbands. We always imagined that a metrosexual male is tied to accessories, but little did we suspect that a male could be tied *up* by accessories.

The *Vogue Hommes* photo spread fetishizes otherness by means of a religious metaphor. This series of advertisements is based on the idea of the chador, the garment used mostly in Iran to cover Muslim women from head to toe, leaving only the hands and part of the face visible. Referencing this religious practice is only possible because Asloum is here principally perceived of in terms of a religion, Islam. This means that his North African background and imagined religious beliefs are fetishized. Only one word accompanies Asloum's face on the magazine cover, the inscription "Ch'adore." This invented term is a pun combining the word "chador" and the French *j'adore,* meaning "I adore" or "I love." For the cover shot, Asloum looks straight into the camera lens. The only thing he is wearing, apart from makeup, is a customized Swarovski-crystal mouth guard. "Ch'adore" becomes a declaration that Asloum, a male Muslim, loves to be covered and have his movements restricted. This is also demonstrated in other photographs, not by a black outer garment covering the whole body, but by means of a black corset and black alligator straps.

Apart from foregrounding submission, the photograph featuring Asloum in a black corset, white Gucci briefs, and wearing a diamond-set bezel and platinum watch around his waist is also of interest as it highlights some general features of metrosexuality. The first feature concerns a combination of masculinity and femininity. Asloum's upraised arms and clenched fists emphasize his muscularity. His bulging muscular development tends to masculinize the representation, whereas the wasp waist and consequent hourglass figure add a feminizing dimension. The blond hair rinse is anyone's guess on the gender divide. Such a cohabitation of masculine and feminine gender markers demonstrates the way metrosexuality easily moves between and gathers together gender performances that have acquired cultural significance in terms of femininity and masculinity. Metrosexuality often reincorporates rituals that have become associated with femininity and brings them into the sway of normalized masculinity.

The second aspect of the corset photograph that has a more general significance is the ambiguous sexual context. The fact that Asloum is alone means that no attempt is made to heterosexualize or homosexualize the context of this bondage S/M scenario. Despite this absence of a second party, intrigued readers of *Vogue Hommes* will realize that the boxer could not have tied himself up with all these luxury watches without external help. Obviously there is a partner, albeit imaginary, who derives pleasure from restraining the movements and restricting the speech of a submissive male. The American tradition of homoerotic culturist photography sometimes used bondage themes to titillate its readers. Asloum's blindfolds, mouth gags, and modified waist reference this iconographic tradition based on homosexual desire. The largely male readership of *Vogue Hommes* reinforces this same-sex configuration.

However, a heterosexual configuration cannot be excluded. A similar ambiguity is present in the many photographs of pin-up model Bettie Page. One Movie Star News photograph of Page shows her gagged with her arms and wrists tied (Silke 37). Another photograph shows her gagged again, but on this occasion her legs are tied and her raised arms are hoisted onto ropes (Yeager 81). These images of Page also show her alone, so here, as in the Asloum photographs, there is still a doubt as to the sex of the restrainer and the sexual orientation of the person gagged. Other photographs of Page feature her pinned down or arm-locked in a wrestling tangle with another woman (Silke 34). The point I am making is that metrosexuality thrives on nonspecific sexuality. An excellent example is provided here in Asloum's publicity shots. The *Vogue Hommes* photographer encourages sexual ambiguity by refusing to provide a clearly defined heterosexual or homosexual context.

◯

From the evidence gathered in this chapter, it would appear that sports nudity, once normalized by the ancient Greeks, is fast becoming the norm again. The exposure and exhibition of denuded and at times fully naked sportsmen is one of the most visible and potentially stimulating aspects of metrosexuality. Mainstream sports magazines aimed at heteronormative males, women's magazines, and men's interest titles (including specialized gay magazines) are all intent on representing naked or semi-naked male bodies to attract the attention of readers. Advertising has been the principal motor behind commoditizing male bodies and exploiting their beauty for commercial purposes. The 2002 Yves Saint Laurent advertisement for the men's fragrance M7 featuring the French former Tae Kwon Do champion Samuel de Cubber posing in full frontal nudity is a spectacular sign of the spornographic times. It also points to a reticence in American sports culture to indulge in the unveiling of athletes' private parts. Characteristically, when the American *GQ* ran the ad, Cubber's genitals were cropped in order not to shock or excite readers.

Perhaps with time spornography may find generalized acceptance in the United States. If any single athlete is going to help America turn into a sporno consumer, it is going to be David Beckham whose five season contract with the LA Galaxy will most likely be an ideal springboard for the creation and exhibition of spornography. Beckham's status as the world's prime metrosexual male has been of vital importance in changing mentalities all over the world. The impact and importance of this athlete will be examined in the next chapter, devoted to making explicit the meaning of metrosexual masculinity.

8

Metrosexual Masculinity

The text in which metrosexuality was first mentioned as a concept was entitled "Here come the mirror men." This chapter focuses on three such men, Joe Namath, Ian Thorpe, and David Beckham, in order to build up a gradual and comprehensive picture of the characteristics which make up metrosexual masculinity. Beginning with football legend Joe Namath makes it possible to see in the playboy ethic a protometrosexual lifestyle. Namath is also of interest for the way in which he appears to adopt certain aspects of metrosexual masculinity: vanity, narcissism, dandyism, hedonism, self-care, and conspicuous consumption. However, Namath's status as a metrosexual precursor has its limits. Analyzing the exhibitionism of the football player reveals considerable qualms that put a damper on the pleasure he derived from showing off his body in public. Such doubts are a thing of the past when we turn to consider two contemporary male athletes who stand out as prime metrosexual models. Thorpe and Beckham provide us with the most rounded cases of metrosexual masculinity. Concentrating on Beckham, especially, helps define the clearest picture of metrosexual masculinity and see how an aesthetic of the body is a central preoccupation for a generation of "new males."

Joe Namath

If there is one American athlete who seems to fit the metrosexual mold before this term became fashionable, it is quarterback Joe Willie Namath. Throughout his time playing for the New York Jets from

1964 until 1975, especially after this team defeated the Baltimore Colts in the 1969 Super Bowl, Joe captured the imagination of America with his playboy activities and bar-loving bachelor lifestyle. In 1969, *Playboy* magazine referred to Super Joe as "a kind of Belmondo with a jockstrap" (Linderman 93), before comparing him to yet another film celebrity; "he was Errol Flynn swashbuckling his way into the hearts of every girl" (94). Namath's claim to protometrosexual status is considerably helped by his adopted New York background. New York, as chapter 3 showed, is where many contemporary metrosexual fantasies originate in the English-speaking world. Hailing from Beaver Falls in Pennsylvania, Joe won a scholarship to play for the University of Alabama before signing a record salary deal with the Jets in 1965. Even if Joe had other apartments in Alabama and Florida, New York was where he played, shopped, and visited nightclubs. It was here that he set up a cocktail lounge, Bachelors III, before it was closed down by the authorities for its alleged Cosa Nostra clientele. Whether he was out running in Central Park or prowling around the city's nightspots in his Lincoln Continental convertible, New York provided Namath with the commodities and services required by a young affluent athlete intent on living life to the full. Even his nickname "Broadway Joe" attached him forever to an urban environment. In 1965, a *Sports Illustrated* cover showed a uniformed Namath in the middle of Broadway. A fellow football player seeing the picture joked "There goes Broadway Joe!" Thereafter the name and the context stuck.

Joe's reputation as a Lothario helps situate him as a "swinging bachelor," an image prevalent in America in the late 1950s and early 1960s. Otherwise known as the "playboy ethic," this middle-class cultural phenomenon was available to Namath because of the salary he demanded as a successful quarterback. In *Playboys in Paradise,* Bill Osgerby describes the ethos which athletes such as Broadway Joe were able to put into practice. He argues that "By the mid-1960s, therefore, a new 'lifestyle' sensibility denoted by stylistic self-consciousness, sexual autonomy and leisure-oriented consumption was an established facet of American culture" (167). Joe's hedonistic consumption is evident in this declaration: "I wish I was born rich. I'd know how to spend money. Boats, planes, cars, clothes, brunettes, blondes, red-heads, brownheads, blondes [. . .] I love them all. What's there in life but to relax and have some fun. Man, if you don't have it, you're not living. And *I* like to live" (Bortstein 205). Women, especially blondes, are just an item of consumption on the list of life's luxuries. When asked by *Playboy* if the Broadway Joe lifestyle was just a myth manufactured by the press or had some basis in reality, the quarterback nonchalantly owned up to three hundred sexual conquests—before his graduation.

In the attention he gave to his personal appearance and wardrobe, Namath typifies the mod look of the 1960s. The *Playboy* interview mentions Joe's "skintight flashy attire" (Linderman 93). One biographer describes the quarterback as "impeccably mod" (Bortstein 3). Dan Jenkins's *Sports Illustrated* article of October 1966, "The Sweet Life of Swinging Joe" (the title of which recalls the bachelor playboy ethic), picks up on his "flashy tailoring" (42). Part of the "sweet life" meant whirling around New York in his car "wearing tailor-made suits with tight pants and loud print linings" (44), spending $25,000 a year "on nuthin', man" (44). In his autobiography, modestly entitled *I Can't Wait Until Tomorrow . . . 'Cause I Get Better Looking Every Day,* Namath provided evidence of his attention to grooming by claiming, "I get my hair cut fairly often. I want it to look right. I want the sideburns to come down to the right spot, and I want it all to look neat" (82–83). As for his wardrobe, Swinging Joe confidently asserted, "I think I dress pretty well—I'm up-to-date, I'm mod" (86). Given this special attention accorded to self-care, it is not surprising that the quarterback came out with a line that future heterosexually identified metrosexual athletes would imitate. He once claimed that "my only weaknesses are clothes and women" (Bortstein 60).

Joe Namath is the most flamboyant and historically significant protometrosexual athlete. He provides a template for the spate of athletes who expose their bodies in publicity internationally. Namath prefigured a generation of manscaped athletes by once shaving off his mustache on national television during an advertisement for an electric razor company. To compensate for the loss of hair he pocketed $10,000. Joe also collected six figures for lending his name to Arrow shirts. The company produced a Joe Namath signature range of shirts, slacks, and jackets. Another manufacturer came out with "The Playmaker Collection" of Joe Namath bed sheets. In November 1972, *Life* magazine published two photographs of the football star. A large close-up shows Namath with his face covered with shaving cream looking into a mirror. He is supposedly parodying a television commercial. A smaller photograph, again taken in front of a mirror, features a row of grooming products in Joe's bathroom. Joe has his hands raised "to primp his locks" ("Pain pays" 41), according to the editorial text. These two shots provide a prototype for David Beckham's three-year campaign advertising Gillette razors and blades which achieved worldwide attention thirty years later. The quarterback's self-care expertise reached a lucrative high point with the Fabergé Brut deal which lasted from 1975 to 1986. Brut already had a history of using athletes to sell their aftershave product. Along with Namath, Brut hired All-Star New York Yankees baseball champion Mickey Mantle, Lakers NBA player Wilt Chamberlain, baseball Hall of Fame player Hank Aaron, and even Mohammad Ali. Namath earned $250,000 a year promoting men's toiletries for television commercials. In 1975, the endorsement deal with Brut was the largest amount ever paid to a celebrity. According to the executive vice president of the firm: "In selecting Joe as 'our quarterback' we have chosen a man who epitomizes the American leisure lifestyle—a modern American hero" (Burke, *Joe Willie* 46).

As Namath epitomized success in sports, Brut declared in *Newsweek* that he would "remove the feminine stigma" from cosmetics and "masculinize" them (Langway 52). Exactly the same logic operated in Britain where Brut aftershave was promoted by heavyweight boxer Henry Cooper, motorcyclist Barry Sheene, and soccer player Kevin Keegan. The TV advertisement Cooper and Keegan did together for Brut deodorant in 1976 ended with a voice-over promising "the deodorant with muscle." A quarter of a century later, when metrosexual moisturizers for men exploded onto the global market, athletes were still being employed with exactly the same defeminizing intent, thus demonstrating the tenacity with which grooming products for men in the minds of advertisers still needed brawn to offset feminizing stigma. Two contemporary examples are the 2003 ads featuring Miami Dolphins star Jason Taylor lathering himself with a Neutrogena Men Power Scrub Deodorant Bar and XCD's endorsement of New Jersey Nets NBA player Jason Kidd, a spokesman for their Men's Skin Care line.

Broadway Joe's limitation as a protometrosexual model can be detected in connection to his legendary $5,000 mink fur coat. Photographs of Joe in a full-length mink coat were much publicized in 1968. Opinions diverge whether or not he wore mink in the streets of Manhattan. At the end of the introduction to his autobiography, Namath strongly denies ever having donned mink in public. "I was out

on the street wearing my $5,000 fur coat. That story is just plain ri-
diculous. I never wore that fur coat in public" (15). Ruth Lieder
began a *Sports Illustrated* article on the Green Bay Packers by recalling Joe's furry display. She claims that "Everyone laughed when Joe
Namath modeled a $5,000 mink coat in Shea Stadium last August"
(60). For the journalist, the laughter seemed to be linked to the excessive cost of the item and the nature of the fur. Joe's mink and another
player's $15,000 sea otter coat were signs that these men were "out-
and-out hedonists" (60). This ostentatious display of wealth by
sportsmen provoked laughter mixed with disapproval. It also elic-
ited unease on the part of the wearer himself.

It is worthwhile attempting to account for Joe's denial that he
wore his mink coat publicly. The expensive mink coat is again mentioned in Namath's autobiography in the context of yet another series of denials. Amid a torrent of contradictions, Joe wants to keep
and discard the fur:

> Some people got really shook up when I posed in that $5,000 fur
> coat. Hell, I didn't go out and buy the coat; I got it free for posing for
> the pictures. It's not the sort of thing I'd go out and buy—I don't
> have any need for a fur coat—but I don't think there's anything
> wrong with it. The coat was stolen during the week of the Super
> Bowl, but I might get another one, as long as I just have to pose for a
> picture for it. (Namath and Schaap 86–87)

This is one of the more interesting paragraphs in an otherwise unre-
markable sports autobiography. It appears that Joe thought there
was something "wrong" about a man, especially one of the country's
star quarterbacks, buying and wearing such a conspicuous sartorial
item. Rather than cost being the problem (as it appears to have been
for the *Sports Illustrated* journalist), Namath's misgivings can better
be explained by gender insecurity and perhaps an unconscious recognition that there is something incongruous about a man displaying such a spectacular garment. The incongruity arises from the
common idea that a person wearing mink is either a classy woman
or a sex worker. In either case, mink runs the risk of transforming the
wearer into an object of male desire. Joe seems sickened by the possibility of same-sex desire and must therefore distance himself from
having actively sought after the incriminating fur. Interestingly, he is
ready to be handed a mink for free like a prostitute, but will not
admit to having shopped for one like a bourgeois housewife.

Namath had misgivings about his mink coat, but the 1974 television commercial for Hanes Beautymist pantyhose caused the quarterback's doubts concerning gender and sexuality to considerably intensify. Viewers followed a camera caressingly as it panned up pantyhosed feet, calves, and thighs, moved along to green satin shorts and finally showed a number twelve football jersey. The female wearer of the pantyhose in the mind of spectators was then unexpectedly replaced by a reclining male saying: "Now, I don't wear pantyhose, but if Beautymist can make *my* legs good, imagine what they'll do for yours." After this memorable one-liner, a woman passed and gave Joe a kiss on the cheek.

Twenty-five years later, Joe's reminiscences about this notable event in the annals of American sports history provide a series of revealing contemporary reactions. In a *Newsweek* article, a negative response was voiced by a secretary when the idea was first presented to Joe with the help of storyboards. He recalled her saying: "It's cute, but my daddy wouldn't like it. He doesn't think football players should wear pantyhose" ("Cold War" 63). The secretary's father was not alone in disliking the subversion of a jock's hypermasculine image. Namath recalled in *Newsweek* that "This guy in Alabama came up to me and said, You know, Joe Willy, I don't mind you wearing those there pantyhose like that, but Lord, son, did you really shave your legs?" (63). Depilation hurt. Not only legs; it also offended nonmetrosexual sensibilities. What is significant about criticism of the Beautymist ad when it was broadcast is not so much what other people thought, but the model's feelings about his experience. Namath told *Newsweek* that "It was a lot of fun, though when I looked at it, my stomach turned; I didn't like anything about the way I looked" (63). Mark Kriegel's biography includes an even more virulent remark. Namath is quoted as having said: "I hated how I looked. I hated how I sounded. I almost got sick" (358).

In contrast to Namath's nausea, Marjorie Garber alludes to the pleasurable thrills of sheer tights in a quotation used to introduce a section of *Vested Interests*, "The Absolute Insignia of Maleness." Garber cites this advertisement for Surprise Pantyhose from a cross-dressing forum.

> Can you imagine the effect you will have on your partner as you enter a room dressed in the most elegant of feminine attire right down to these European stretch pantless pantyhose! These "surprise

pantyhose" will complete your web of intrigue as you slowly raise
your skirt to that delectable area where "lo & behold" your male
member will be anxiously awaiting introduction. (Garber 94–95)

What I find fascinating about this text is the fact that it has marked
resemblances with the Beautymist advertisement. The cross-dresser's
imagined partner mentioned in the forum finds a parallel in the millions of television viewers who are all coerced into a transvestic scenario. Like the wearer of the stretch pantyhose, Joe is also implicated
in a "web of intrigue" carried out on unsuspecting fans in front of
their TV. The panning shot of the camera slowly moving up Joe's
silky legs imitates the cock-teasing revelation described in the Surprise Pantyhose text. Both ads depend for their effect on a phallic
woman fantasy. Turning one of the country's most celebrated quarterbacks into a transgendered object of erotic desire for males (this is
what the Beautymist commercial momentarily achieved) constitutes
a dreadful moment of uncertainty for both Namath and television
viewers. If males watching the ad became excited seeing those misty
legs, even for a few seconds, if Broadway Joe was able to "pass" so
convincingly as a woman, then perhaps his masculinity might be as
flimsy and see-through as the pantyhose. The Beautymist commercial therefore effectively suggests that a male's masculinity and femininity are two forms of masquerade. A male can wear silky shorts as
naturally as silky hose.

Namath's feminine masquerade is especially understandable in
fetishistic terms. Whereas garter belts and stockings have been generally replaced by pantyhose, all three items are potentially valuable for fetishists. Valerie Steele identifies some of their fetishistic
appeal in the Underwear chapter of *Fetish* by pointing out that "The
legs are the pathway to the genitals. Stockings lead the viewer's
eyes up the legs [. . .] For many men, the effect is like arrows pointing to the promised land" (132). To understand this, we only have to
glance at some of Bunny Yeager's photographs of Bettie Page which
feature the pin-up model naked, except for long black gloves, black
high-heeled shoes, and sexy black stockings (Yeager 41–43). In other
photographs, only clad in fishnet pantyhose, Page looks lasciviously at the camera (Yeager 60–63). By dolling up in silky pantyhose, playboy Joe inadvertently transformed himself into a playboy
bunny. His sexy legs attracted the fetishistic gaze of the same men
who, twenty years before, had leered at Bettie Page's calves and

thighs. This potential eroticism between males helps to explain why Namath stressed his distaste and nausea after shooting the pantyhose ad. It was a way for Joe to distance himself from homoeroticism. It was also a means of denying any pleasure he may have felt slipping into those now famous silky hose.

Imitating the sexually inviting antics of a woman of leisure by donning pantyhose and a fur coat, Namath demonstrates the facility with which male body parts and the materials covering them can arouse desire. Rather than willingly embrace the sensuous comforts of silk and mink (as we would expect from a confident metrosexual male), Namath was plagued by doubts concerning how wearing these materials and items of clothing made him vulnerable to criticism. They were perceived to put into question his masculinity and his sexual orientation. Thirty years later, however, such doubts were more easily swept aside by other professional athletes who challenge conventional notions of masculinity with more audacity.

Ian Thorpe

After Euro RSCG Worldwide published their "Future of Men" reports in mid-2003, journalists worldwide began to look for token metrosexual males. Olympic swimmer Ian Thorpe had already been spotted by journalist Peter Gotting as typifying metrosexuality. Basing his March 2003 article "Rise of the Metrosexual" on Mark Simpson's Salon.com piece "Meet the Metrosexual," Gotting inaugurated the trend of nominating Thorpe as *the* representative Australian metrosexual. A few months previously, in November 2002, during a national radio interview, the swimmer was questioned about his sexual orientation. While denying that he was gay, Thorpe did say that he was "a little bit different to what most people would consider being an Australian male." But what exactly did Thorpe mean by claiming to be "different"?

Thorpe insisted that his sexual orientation was normative. He imitated some American athletes by staging a public outing. Providing an official explanation for being mistaken as gay was an unusual initiative. Normally, athletes who feel it necessary to have a heterosexual outing do not directly address why their sexual orientation might have been questioned. Thorpe, however, did exactly this by telling the radio interviewer, "I have an interest in things most people don't classify as being part of the macho male thing." This statement can be seen as problematic for several reasons. Already there is a mistaken assumption that male homosexuality and hypermasculinity are mutually exclusive. Furthermore, Thorpe implies that all homosexual males are interested in fashion and clothes, they are obsessed about their appearance, and they speak well. In telling the nation he was straight, Thorpe admitted that he did not look like or sound like what he called a "macho Australian." But this difference from traditional gender norms, he tried to convince radio listeners, should not be equated with a departure from sexual norms. In making this important distinction, Thorpe was attempting to disentangle gender from sexuality. Without knowing it, the swimmer was beginning to define metrosexual masculinity. It is *metrosexual* males who have interests not generally considered to be "part of the macho male thing."

Rather than fall into the trap of denigrating homosexuality, as some other athletes have done when publicly outing themselves as heterosexual, Thorpe said he was flattered at the suggestion he might be gay. This pro-gay stance was based on the argument that all minority groups have to show strength of character. If people thought he was gay, then they must think that he had good self-assertion skills. That, at least, was how Thorpe verbalized his lack of homophobia, while still insisting on his heterosexual orientation. Five years later, in a March 2007 interview, Thorpe made this declaration: "I don't have a problem being a gay icon" (Hawley 34). Such a pro-gay attitude is unusual in the context of repeated heterosexual outings.

Despite claiming in the 2007 interview, "You don't have to come out and declare you're straight" (Hawley 34), this is exactly what Thorpe has been doing on and off since 2002. Just after retiring from professional swimming in November 2006, the athlete told *GQ* (Australia), "People will tell you black and blue that I am gay, but there is no basis for what they are saying" (Scott 96). In fact, as Thorpe indirectly admitted in 2007 (when he again declared "I'm not gay"), there *is* a basis to explain why the media is so intent on probing into the private life of the country's principal swimming hero. The problem arises from confusing gender nonconformity with sexual nonconformity. It also comes from not making the necessary distinction between metrosexuality and homosexuality.

After publicly avowing interests which were not part of "the macho male thing," Thorpe developed a theory of gender in 2007 by arguing that "Some guys are more in touch with their feminine side, interested in design and quirky things, [whereas] some are blokey blokes" (Hawley 34). Here, Thorpe recycles the generally held, although unhelpful idea that gender "sides" exist. In a world of males who appear to express normative masculinity effortlessly, other "blokes" such as Thorpe also develop interests generally perceived to be feminine, or effeminate. It is interesting that the term "quirky" is used by Thorpe to characterize expressions of male femininity. The word is close to "queer" and this proximity leads us to the heart of Thorpe's dilemma. The athlete wants to be able to indulge what he calls "quirky" interests. And at the same time, he wishes to be identified as unqueer sexually.

Thorpe's "difference" lies partly in the importance he attributes to fashion, clothes, and accessories. This was publicized in the United States and in Australia following the swimmer's invitation to take part in the twenty-five-year retrospective of Giorgio Armani's work staged at the Guggenheim Museum in New York. It was here in late 2000 that the young athlete and Armani had their photograph taken together. The general manager for Armani in Australia was so impressed by Thorpe's enthusiasm for wearing designer labels that she contacted the Italian stylist in Milan and secured an invitation to the prestigious retrospective. For the occasion, Thorpe wore leather trousers and an open-necked black shirt, both designed by his host.

Following the Armani Retrospective, the *New York Times* provided readers with plenty of evidence concerning Thorpe's metrosexuality. Marion Hume accompanied the young medalist on a shopping expedition to Barneys. The exchange of dialogue between reporter and swimmer about styles, colors, and accessories forms the basis of Hume's article. Having only just turned eighteen, Thorpe showed an atypical preoccupation with jewelry, body products, and color coordination, even choice of fabrics. He wore bling jewelry, including one ring embedded with twelve diamonds. The swimmer clearly revealed his fashion intelligence several times, for example by recommending a more successful coordination of colors. A navy-blue, pink, and rosy Comme des Garçons T-shirt was criticized in favor of a more sober black and silver one. A Gucci leather jacket was mocked for looking more like a handbag. When Thorpe fell upon a black leather Prada coat, he expatiated on the choice of color for the lining, demonstrating the ability to distinguish similar shades by name: "Oh, look, it's even better with the brown, or I should say the tan lining." Hume's text helped situate the shopper in the role of wealthy aesthete. Laying hands on a $2,660 teal blue, waffle-knit sweater, said to be Thorpe's favorite piece of clothing in the store, the excited shopper was quoted as saying, "Umm, I love this—cashmere." The *Queer Eye* Fab Five would have been tickled pink to hear such discernment from a male before they set out to tell American men about the sensuous delights of cashmere.

Not long after this international coverage, Thorpe appeared on the cover of the Australian *Harper's Bazaar* in January 2001, wearing an Emporio Armani suit and nestled in between three long-haired brunettes in Armani swimsuits. The emphasis here is resolutely heterosexual. The cover promised "Ian Thorpe on Women, Fame, Armani and Life after the Olympics." Sharon Krum's article describes the Armani retrospective party where, according to one of the guests, "Thorpe could have charmed the beads off an Armani pantsuit, not to mention [. . .] the pants off every woman in the room" (122). Comments made by the star athlete about the cover photograph, "I had three beautiful girls around me for half a day. I don't think there are too many men who would complain, right?" (125) provided an obvious heterosexual context for Thorpe's "passion for fashion" (125), his "obsession" (125) for the brand Emporio Armani, and his love of clothes.

Contrasting with this overt heterosexualization, early spornographic representations of Thorpe emphasize his looked-at-ness and desirability, two aspects already celebrated by *Harper's Bazaar*. However, denuding the swimmer had consequences that the athlete may not have foreseen. The spornographic commoditizing of Thorpe's body fueled suspicions that there was something "feminine" or "gay" about the way the athlete stripped off for the camera and exhibited his body. This is what he did at the end of 2000 when he accepted the offer of a photo session in Los Angeles with the prestigious celebrity photographer Herb Ritts. In March 2001, shots from the Ritts photo session appeared in *GQ Style Directory*, a magazine included with the Australian version of *Vogue*. This photo shoot is particularly interesting for the way it queers the swimmer and departs from the overt heterosexualization relayed in *Harper's Bazaar*. The number of close parallels in *GQ Style* with the mid-century male physique photography of Bob Mizer and Bruce of L.A. is remarkable. These parallels anchor Ritts's portrayal of Thorpe in the tradition of West Coast homoerotic iconography.

One black and white shot used to illustrate the *GQ Style* article on the swimmer is clearly indebted to photographic precedents which insist on the desirability and sexual submission of a naked male body. This photograph captures Thorpe's muscled back. He stands facing a white screen or wall; his upright arms are out-stretched and his fingers splayed; the head is slightly at an angle. In his article on the swimmer, David Hay interprets this image by stating that Thorpe stood "as if he were being crucified" (100). Instead, I would argue that Ritts suggests an erotic tension in this pose by forcing the viewer to imagine the missing anatomy beneath the lumbar region. A very similar pose is evident in photographs taken by Bruce of Los Angeles and Bob Mizer. One of Bruce of L.A.'s photographs portrays a naked male standing with his back to the camera in front of a white doorway (Dolinsky 18). The arms, tilted head, and prominent back muscles featured here could easily have provided a source of inspiration for Ritts. The major difference is that Bruce of L.A. provides a full-length figure, thus restituting the cropped section of Ritts's photograph. In the older version, the model's heels are raised, the legs are apart, and firm buttocks jut out above muscled thighs. The end result is a highly eroticized stance that Ritts only hints at. At about the same time, Bob Mizer also used this pose in *Physique Pictorial.* An AMG photograph from the 1950s includes two male figures, one of whom is adopting Thorpe's stance. The other is a kneeling cowboy who is attaching a rope to the raised left heel of the standing, outstretched "prisoner" (Leyland 38). This uncropped bondage scene provides another homoerotic precedent for Ritts's photograph.

A second *GQ Style* photograph of Thorpe elicits more homoerotic parallels, but this time they can be traced to different sources. This photograph shows the athlete in a crouching position, wearing only black swimwear. The pose recalls Hippolyte Flandrin's painting, *Jeune homme nu assis au bord de la mer* (1835), a common motif used by early twentieth-century homoerotic photographers such as Baron Wilhelm von Gloeden (in "Kain," circa 1900) and Gaetano D'Agata (in "Caino," 1923). The seaside parallel may have been an appropriate allusion for a swimming champion. However, the previous use by these particular photographers puts the Thorpe version into a particular iconographic heritage. Thomas Waugh calls this tradition "the pictorialist ephebe" (91), which is based on bringing together a youth and an assumed older male spectator.

Spornography is also clearly noticeable in the "Our Olympic Heroes" calendar which appeared in Australia in 2001. This calendar invites a comparison with the ancient Greek idealization of winning athletes. James Houston produced a series of images featuring some of the country's celebrated male and female swimmers. For the calendar cover, a black and white portrait of Thorpe's head and naked chest attracted potential customers. The swimmer's slight frown, the distant glance averting the gaze of the lens and spectator, the cloud-like backdrop, and the erect nipples deify and eroticize this adulated youth. Ancient Greek Olympic athletes who triumphed were also deified. It was their nudity which acted as a reminder of the nudity of the gods. The nudity of Thorpe's upper torso and his gaze, which is turned away from the spectator in a disdainful glare, both suggest a god-like beauty and divine equanimity.

Covers of Australian style magazines since the turn of the century reinforce Thorpe's difference from "blokey blokes." In July 2002, just four months before his first heterosexual outing, the swimmer was chosen for the inaugural cover of *Autore Magazine,* an Australian publication dedicated to jewelry. For the occasion, the athlete wore an Emporio Armani wool mix, sleeveless zip jacket. Amid shots of gay icons such as Elizabeth Taylor and Joan Collins, a black and white photograph shows a cool and relaxed Thorpe clad in pearls. A white, unbuttoned-to-the-chest Emporio Armani cotton shirt offsets Armani jeans and a nylon mesh belt. Interviewed by Matt Preston, Thorpe proffered a personal definition of fashion: "[Armani] represents the way I feel about things [. . .] I'm not just to be stuck in a mould and come out looking a certain way. It lets me express what I am on the inside, on the outside. I think that's what fashion is about" (Preston 53). While not the most sophisticated of formulations, this reflection nevertheless does provide evidence that Thorpe has thought about personal identity and how this can be expressed through the sartorial. The lifestyle publication *Australian Men Magazine* featured an open-to-the-chest white Emporio Armani shirt on a bling-fingered and lip-glossed Thorpe for its first cover in 2004. The editor of the magazine wanted the swimmer to appeal to fashionable and style-conscious male readers. Interviewed, Thorpe reiterated his devotion to the Armani label: "I love the cut of Armani and know it's going to look good when I wear it" ("Ian Thorpe" 25). A more recent example of Thorpe's fashion cover status is the Australian *GQ's* summer 2007 "Sports Issue" featuring the swimmer wearing Giorgio Armani and items from the prestigious Ralph Lauren Purple Label.

The article dedicated to Thorpe in *Autore Magazine* drew attention to an important aspect of the swimmer's "difference," his enhanced aesthetic sense. Jeweler Sheridan Kennedy, who had done work featuring Autore's South Sea pearls, was entrusted with directing a new collection of pearl accessories for men. Realizing the potential feminization of men who wear pearls, she told *Autore Magazine:* "There's an interesting dichotomy about a masculine man wearing what are perceived to be feminine things" (Preston 57). In order to convince male customers that wearing pearls could be manly, Thorpe was asked to design and model a collection of neck and wrist pieces incorporating pearls for Autore. His thoughts on the subject, quoted in *Autore Magazine,* demonstrate the extent to which Thorpe's interest in aesthetics and his ability to produce discourse on the subject separated him from the stereotypical preoccupations of "blokey bloke" Australians. He told the journalist: "I wanted something that was strong, clean and classical but with a really contemporary feel. I also wanted it to be quite urban, very young and edgy, yet at the same time it would show off the pearl's true beauty. The look also had to be quite androgynous" (Preston 57). This concern with embellishing the body, even at the price of encouraging gender ambiguity, fueled preexisting suspicions that the sexual orientation of the swimmer might be as nonnormative as his choice of body accessories.

Thorpe's launching of a signature range of underwear in late 2003 is another instance of a preoccupation which has traditionally not been seen as "part of the macho male thing." In Australia, underwear promotion carrying the name of a celebrity was particularly associated with women's lingerie before Thorpe inaugurated his own label. His celebrity predecessors were Kylie Minogue and Elle Macpherson. Kylie Minogue's "Love Kylie Lingerie" range, launched in Australia in 2000, then in Britain three years later, included such collections as Vamp, Seduce, Sheer Escape, Fever, Diva, and Cheekies. Elle Macpherson's "Intimates" offered designs called Dentelle, Luminesque, Toujours, and Titania. Thorpe imitated his fellow compatriots when he introduced and modeled the more banally named Oxygen T-shirts, boxer shorts, briefs, and hipsters.

Thorpe's signature underwear line emphasizes corporeal aesthetics and an eroticization of the sartorial. A spokesperson from the designers of the IT brand of men's underwear commented that "This is something that Ian believes in passionately and he has involved himself in every step of the process, even to the point of designing his own logo. Ian pushed construction techniques, fabrication and styling to a new level" ("Thorpie's Dax" 5). Not to be outstaged, the swimmer was quoted as saying: "It was exciting because what we were doing design-wise was unique and cutting edge, the ultimate test was the wearing of the garments—and I'm confident in saying that the range certainly delivers" ("Thorpie's Dax" 5). Claims such as these about what men's underwear could "deliver" to the wearer served to reinforce the idea that Thorpe was somehow "different."

There is a potential problem area concerning Thorpe's underwear publicity: it draws attention to the male body as the object of a sexually indeterminate gaze. This is characteristic of metrosexuality. James Houston again demonstrated the appeal of a desirable male body when he photographed the launching of Thorpe's underwear line in a prestigious Sydney downtown store. Similar to the Olympic calendar, there is also a noticeable beefcake quality in this spornographic display, especially the swimmer's pose which shows his open arms extended and hands placed behind his head to reveal his armpits. Thorpe's pose here depends on homoerotic and heteroerotic traditions. These iconographic precedents are coded according to two distinct conventions (one based on a male homoeroticized object and the other on a female heteroeroticized object). Such a pose is typical of American postwar muscle magazines. The March 1962 issue of *Physique Pictorial* with cover model Art Byman in skimpy underwear features the same bodybuilder pose that Houston employs to emphasize an athlete's musculature. As well as referencing homoerotic culturist photography, this particular pose also situates the Australian underwear model in the pin-up tradition of Bettie Page, who adopted exactly the same posture in many of her photographs.

Since 2000, Ian Thorpe has cultivated interests which seemingly distinguish him from "blokey bloke" Australian males. This can be seen in his preoccupation with style, clothes, and accessories. His launchings of a fragrance line and an underwear collection reinforce the perception that he has always privileged corporeal aesthetics. Coverage in the style press invariably portrays Thorpe as an aesthete. Three labels have been used to specify Thorpe's difference. One facile label is "gay." The swimmer's interests and his exhibitionism in the style press are taken as evidence of effeminacy and gayness. This label has been systematically repudiated by Thorpe. He prefers a second label: a heterosexual male in touch with his "feminine side." This way of interpreting Thorpe's difference from "blokey bloke" males is also somewhat facile. In addition, a third label, "metrosexual" has been used. In 2007, Thorpe revealed that he found this descriptive offensive "because metrosexual is a marketing term" (Hawley 34). Despite the disclaimer, I find "metrosexual" to be the most appropriate label when attempting to describe the twenty-first-century masculinity that Thorpe became the figurehead for in Australia. This masculinity is based on masculinizing and heterosexualizing expressions of gender formerly associated with femininity and same-sex desire. Metrosexuality allows Thorpe and others like him to express their masculinity and identify as heterosexual.

David Beckham

David Beckham is the athlete who best incarnates the contemporary cultural changes that we call metrosexuality. Factors which allow Beckham to be perceived as the person who most explicitly represents changing norms include the player's autobiographic writings, his interviews, and the large number of fashion photo shoots which have been published in many different types of magazines. In these sources we find evidence of conspicuous consumption (clothes, jewelry and cars), a taste for sartorial flamboyance, close ties with Italian fashion houses, and an openness of mind which extends to a positive portrayal of nonnormative sexualities. We also find information concerning multiple endorsement deals promoting beauty products and body accessories. Beckham offers an excellent means to map out the revision of gender and sexual mythologies that is conveniently referred to as metrosexuality.

Beckham is particularly noteworthy in a study of metrosexuality because of his exceptional self-awareness and the reactions that he provokes from a wide variety of areas. Beckham is conscious that he is different; he provides evidence to suggest that this difference is intentional and he produces discourse describing how and why he departs from conventional gender norms. More than any other athlete associated with metrosexuality, Beckham has attracted extensive comments and reactions in Britain and abroad for his looks, clothes, and defiance of traditional gender norms. These observations have come from journalists, fashion editors, designers, and academics.

Beckham defies jock culture's expectations concerning how a male athlete is supposed to look, behave, and dress. Aware of this defiance, Beckham noted in his 2000 autobiography: "Because I'm a footballer, people expect me to wear the same sort of clothes as other footballers and go out and get drunk and be a man" (Beckham 94). He distances himself from jock culture by not equating drunkenness with virility. Photographs taken surreptitiously have often caught the "buysexual" laden, not with containers of beer, but with bags of couture. England's former soccer captain prefers to shop for clothes rather than pub crawl. By replacing one masculinity ritual with another, hitherto not especially considered normative for males, he helps in the normalization of the same activity for heterosexual and homosexual males alike.

One obvious manifestation of Beckham's metrosexuality is his intense interest in clothes and in how he looks. A preoccupation with appearance is sometimes interpreted as a sign of vanity or narcissism. In his *Marie Claire* 2002 interview, Beckham refused this somewhat simplistic explanation to account for his concern with external appearance. When asked if he were vain, Beckham replied, "I just like to look good. I don't love myself and I don't think I'm vain" (Thornton 74). In one autobiography, the soccer player provided a more complex explanation for his fascination with clothes and his scrupulous care for outward appearance. He saw the sartorial as a sign of individualism and personal aesthetics, claiming that "Clothes are just one way of expressing your individuality, but it's an important one for me. I also think of dressing as a way of being artistic" (Beckham 94). This use of the word "artistic" is important because it expresses a fundamental aspect of metrosexuality. It shows that Beckham was aware that an aesthetic of the body was something that could provide substantial pleasure for himself and for anyone interested enough to look at him.

Interviewed about the allure of expensive designer wear in June 2000, Beckham situated his interest in clothes as far back as his childhood.

> "I do like to be a bit different, but I always have," he agrees. "Once when I was little I was chosen to be a page boy. I was shown a couple of outfits and I chose one with maroon velvet trousers which stopped at the knee, long white socks and ballet shoes. My mum said, 'You're going to look silly, people will laugh at you,' but that was what I wanted to wear. I take pride in my appearance." (Pattenden 24)

This episode has been retold in interviews so many times that it has become part of the self-perpetuated Beckham myth. It therefore needs to be examined more closely. In later versions a frilly Spanish shirt and a matching velvet waistcoat were added to the list of sartorial items, the trousers were described as knickerbockers, and the age of seven given. Beckham remembers his father not having cared about the fact that his son was parading around the house in an outfit that satisfied the young boy's early exhibitionist tastes, even at the price of provoking derision elsewhere due to the camp nature of the attire. Although Beckham was already playing soccer at this age, he had obviously not yet learned the single-track vision of gender and sexuality with which his mother was familiar and which was entrenched in British sports culture. Oblivious to these behavioral constraints, Beckham was only guided by his precocious desire to feel and look good. Such an early pride in appearance signifies a predisposition for metrosexuality.

The desire to look good, combined with a love of clothes and a desire to shop for them, constitutes a cornerstone of metrosexual masculinity. In 2000, Beckham wrote: "I do buy a lot of clothes for myself. I have a real passion for clothes and I have always taken a lot of care with my appearance" (Beckham 92). This self-care and concern for appearance would express itself more fully once he married the media-savvy Victoria Adams. Beckham was first attracted to his future wife because of her dress sense. He later wrote that upon seeing the singer on television, he found her clothes and appearance to be "unbelievable" (93). Within a year of his marriage, Beckham was able to match his wife in "unbelievable" sartorial styles which he paraded on the pages of the world's fashion magazines.

Beckham created a precedent in British sports culture when he posed for the British gay magazine *Attitude* in June 2002. This format for exposing an athlete's body is diametrically opposed to the homophobic norms of jock culture. Despite this ambient homophobia, Beckham did a fashion spread for *Attitude* wearing a Roberto Cavalli caftan and showed a plunging neckline in a Dolce & Gabbana silk print shirt. One of the shots is pure beefcake, since Beckham's upper torso is shown naked. Beckham's poses in *Attitude* resemble those he was used to doing for mainstream magazines. The novelty is that Beckham's body is intentionally offered as an object of desire for gay spectators. For jock culture, this is unthinkable. Unlike the vast majority of sportsmen, Beckham actively sought the gay gaze.

The soccer star's open-mindedness concerning nonnormative sexualities is characteristic of metrosexual masculinity. Beckham has always demonstrated a total absence of homophobia. When asked by a *Marie Claire* journalist in June 2002 how he felt about being considered a "gay icon," the athlete replied: "I'm flattered. I'm very comfortable with it" (Thornton 74). Confirming this gay-friendly sentiment, Beckham smilingly confided to another magazine the same month: "I've got a big fan zone in the male area" and added "I think it's a good thing" (Flynn 36). The question of a numerous gay following was broached by the American *W* magazine in August 2007 just after Beckham's arrival in Los Angeles. There Beckham reacted to this possibility by saying: "I feel it's an honor" and "It's nice to be loved" (Reginato 235). Such positive portrayals of homosexuality are in stark opposition to jock culture's vilification of nonnormative sexualities.

Photo shoots featuring Beckham have been published by an increasing number of magazines since the beginning of the twenty-first century. They greatly contribute to his celebrity as a fashion model, while insisting on his being the object of the male and female gaze. This media frenzy came to a head in June 2002 when Beckham achieved a moment of iconographic glory by appearing simultaneously on the covers of three British publications. The women's interest magazine *Marie Claire*, the gay magazine *Attitude*, and *GQ* each devoted space to the player. *Marie Claire* had never had a male on the cover before. It was unusual, to say the least, for the captain of a national sports team to be seen on the cover of a gay publication. And unlike the American version, the British edition of *GQ* was unused to putting a sportsman on the cover. This media interest revealed that Beckham was becoming more extravagant in his Continental sartorial tastes. The *pièce de résistance* occurred when the then captain of the English soccer team posed for New York photographer David LaChapelle. Beckham provoked a sellout of the June 2002 British *GQ*, turning it into a "special collector's issue." For one of the *GQ* covers (two different cover shots of Beckham were published) a reclining aesthete appears wearing a £1,870 cream cashmere coat with £355 cream wool trousers both designed by Tom Ford for Yves Saint Laurent Rive Gauche. Beckham is shirtless, proudly exhibiting his chest and abdomen. One eye is sexily covered by a Monte Cristi wide-brim Panama hat. A white gold diamond stud in his ear, Beckham also sports a yellow gold diamond pavé and a sapphire bombé ring complementing the nine carat gold curb bracelet on one wrist. His fingernails are painted with mauve nail varnish. For the other cover, an oiled, bare-chested Beckham in a mock-crucifixion pose stands with his arms outstretched in front of a red cross recalling Saint George. He wears a £450 pair of Richard James beaded boxer shorts which are highly visible over a pair of Michiko Koshino baggy jeans.

It may have been the *GQ* pin-up cover of Beckham wearing cashmere that led George Wayne in *Vanity Fair* to refer to Beckham two years later as Queen Louis XIV. Mark Simpson reacted more quickly. Upon seeing the sportsman in such French finery, he put "Meet the Metrosexual" online in July 2002. In this text, Simpson provided a new word to describe such flamboyant sartorial exhibitionism. Simpson "outed" the soccer player for being "a screaming, shrieking, flaming, freaking metrosexual." Beckham was the world's first professional athlete to be identified as a metrosexual. In the years since, his reputation as the leading spokesman to typify metrosexual masculinity has been consolidated. Understandably, Beckham has become the world figurehead of metrosexuality.

In his 2000 autobiography, Beckham had recourse to the simplistic "side theory" to explain his metrosexuality when he stated, "I suppose I get the male side out by playing football" (Beckham 95). After mentioning that he watched fashion programs on television, read fashion magazines, and loved to cook, the player opined, "I think it's good for men to be in touch with their feminine side" (95). As we saw in chapter 2 and as noted in connection with Ian Thorpe, this interpretation of gender identity based on "sides" is unhelpful. It has the unfortunate result of perpetuating essentialized notions of femininity and masculinity. Still, Beckham's way of seeing gender identity endorses a desire to express a more comprehensive and all-encompassing human potential that is unchecked by stigmatization in terms of feminization or homosexualization.

Metrosexuality refers to a palette of masculinity which incorporates a concern for the aesthetic together with more conventional expressions of masculinity. This explains why journalists, fashion writers, and a brand consultant interpret Beckham's metrosexuality in terms of a binary opposition based on the athletic and the aesthetic. For Paul Flynn, Beckham is "the bridge between two supposedly separate streams of masculinity" (36), one "stream" represented by the rough and tumble heteronormative world of soccer and the other by an immaculate personal presentation. David Thomas conceived of the contrast in terms of "the hairy-arsed machismo of traditional sport" and "the homoerotic iconography of men's fashion" (49). Andy Milligan found reason to believe that Beckham was "the first footballer to have straddled the worlds of football and fashion and not looked awkward in either" (72). This habit of reading Beckham as straddling two "worlds," genders, or even sexualities, spread to the Continent. In the French magazine *Le Nouvel Observateur*, it was noted in September 2003 that Beckham pleased everyone by mixing categories. This was shown by means of three contrasts expressed as a football side and a face-cream side, simultaneous status as ideal father and gay icon, or else wearing studded soccer boots and having perfectly manicured hands (Reynaert 50). For Flynn, the result of encompassing different and what were perceived to be contradictory masculinities is that Beckham "has become emblematic of the thoroughly modern male" (36). Likewise, the French journalist dubbed Beckham the incarnation of the modern man.

Comments included with an *Arena Homme Plus* article on England's soccer hero provide a rare opportunity to see how different designers interpret Beckham's metrosexuality. More so than journalists and fashion writers, designers congratulate Beckham for his aesthetic sense. Dolce and Gabbana, Beckham's favorite Italian designers, declared their love for the soccer player and complimented him on his "great sense and feeling for fashion." Armani was as impressed by Beckham's talent on the pitch as he was by the athlete's "underlying sensitivity and vulnerability" as well as his "innate sense of style." Likewise, Donatella Versace admired the player's athletic capacity and his equally beautiful sense of style. Reactions from another two designers offer more substantial reflections on Beckham's metrosexuality. Lothar Reiff from Hugo Boss saw Beckham's influence extending to "a new generation of soccer players," each competing to be "handsome, talented and stylish." Finally, Tom Ford saw a parallel with Beau Brummell and highlighted the links between metrosexuality and dandyism by complimenting Beckham for being a "total modern dandy." Ford went on to refer to the influence the soccer player was having on changing gender norms, not just in sports, but in society at large. He said: "I think men will continue to change when they see a man like Beckham, a macho role model who is not afraid of fashion or of being attractive and showing off his body" (Healy 186). In noticing these aspects of Beckham's personality, Ford provided a neat summary of key metrosexual characteristics. Designers commend Beckham's exceptional preoccupation with aesthetics. They realize that he can be a powerful marketing tool in influencing other males, notably heterosexual males, to copy his example. Academics who write on Beckham are more interested in gender than aesthetics. In 2002, Garry Whannel devoted a chapter to the player in *Media Sport Stars: Masculinities and Moralities*. Seemingly unaware of the term "metrosexual," Whannel still partly analyzed the idea when he spoke about Beckham's "narcissistic self-absorption" and his "departure from the dominant masculinised codes of footballer style" (202). The first use of "metrosexual" as a label for Beckham in academic discourse dates from 2003 when Ellis Cashmore and Andrew Parker published "One David Beckham? Celebrity, Masculinity, and the Soccerati." As an example of subversive trends and behaviors, the authors referred to the soccer star as a "cosmetically conscientious 'metrosexual'" (225). However, reducing metrosexuality to makeup and putting it in quotation marks did little to show the full import of Beckham's subversion. Strangely, Cashmore's biography *Beckham* (first published in 2002, then revised and expanded for republication in 2004) has no mention of the word "metrosexual," despite having a chapter devoted to sex and masculinity.

A more challenging analysis of Beckham can be found in the work of sociologist Momin Rahman, who has focused on gender, sexuality, aesthetics, and class. In 2004, he published "Beckham as a Historical Moment in the Representation of Masculinity." This was followed the same year by an online piece, "Is Straight the New Queer?: David Beckham and the Dialectics of Celebrity." Interested in how representations of Beckham both reiterate and potentially subvert traditional codes of masculinity by queering them, Rahman argues in the earlier article that the soccer star shows how there has been an "expansion of cultural possibilities around masculine identity which incorporates elements previously antithetical to working-class masculinity" ("Beckham" 228). One of these elements is the fact that Beckham has intentionally encouraged the gay gaze and become the willing object of gay desire. Another element concerns Beckham's aesthetic sensibility, an aspect of the soccer player that was emphasized by the designers quoted in the *Arena* article. An intense interest in the aesthetic is potentially subversive for a heterosexual male because it is stereotypically linked with women or homosexual males. Rahman concludes his first analysis on the celebrity star by asserting that "representations of Beckham do not reflect progressive social change but rather, they push at the boundaries of it" ("Beckham" 229). For Rahman, the emphasis in the press on the player's traditional masculinity means that "the resignifications deployed within constructions of Beckham are easily recuperated before they effect a subversive destabilisation of masculine or heterosexual culture" ("Beckham" 228). This is why, despite the testing of these cultural boundaries, traditional working-class masculinity may have been re-marked or expanded with the help of Beckham, but according to Rahman, there has been "no fundamental destabilisation of the traditional referents of heterosexual masculinity" ("Beckham" 228). A similar idea ends the later analysis on Beckham where Rahman affirms that queer constructions of the soccer player are "only fleeting materializations," the fate of which is to be "recuperat[ed] into the heterosexual subject" ("Straight" 4).

Beckham's status as a major metrosexual model depends on the way he *has* helped destabilize traditional referents of heterosexualized masculinity. One means the celebrity does this is by showing how sexual passivity is not incompatible with hypermasculinity. Rahman's analysis on representations of masculinity is based on magazine articles devoted to Beckham which were published in 2002. However, other magazine coverage provides representations which clearly destabilize and queer heterosexualized masculinity. Beckham once characterized the attention of photographers who constantly had their lenses pointed at him in terms of a sexual metaphor. In his 2000 autobiography, he complained, "I have a camera up my backside almost 24 hours a day" (Beckham 85). This claim, taken literally, perfectly illustrates how metrosexuality foregrounds the passivity and the desirability of the male body.

Beckham conspicuously subverted traditional codes of heterosexualized masculinity in the Autumn/Winter 2000 issue of the British fashion publication *Arena Homme Plus*. The photographer, Steven Klein, often takes inspiration from a range of sexual fantasies such as rape, bondage, sadomasochism, or master-slave relations. The skinhead fantasy lies at the center of the Beckham photo shoot, fully justifying Mark Simpson's observation that sport has become the new gay porn. The cover of this issue of *Arena Homme Plus* features a highly eroticized portrait of Beckham. He is naked except for a diamond ear stud, a pair of Calvin Klein boxer shorts, and a leather wristband. The accompanying text "Hot and Hard" is more than justified by Beckham's turf-strip Mohawk buzz-cut and three-day growth. One hand is resting on his crotch. "Cash In," the two-word title in white print, and the black-print subtitle "The New Money Culture," both provide a commercial context for this glaring figure. With the addition of gay fetish items (especially the CK underwear and the leather accessory), Beckham, to all intents, looks like rough trade, an expression used to signify male prostitutes (who may identify as heterosexual) looking for male customers.

The first photograph chosen to start Murray Healy's text, "David Beckham: Made in Britain," foregrounds Beckham's butt. It is so obviously the center of focus in this *mise-en-scène* of skinhead erotics that one is tempted to retitle the article "Bend Over Like Beckham." This photograph is a one-and-half-page image of the athlete and features the same ear stud and band as the ones shown on the cover. The two accessories, diamonds and leather, insist that the wearer is pierced and strapped, perhaps for cash. The leather lace of the band here would seem to be potentially useful as a bondage tool. The waistband of the CK boxers peeks out of a pair of tatty Levi's jeans beneath a Gothic script tattoo. Beckham is kneeling on a bed facing the wall, one arm extended onto the headboard, the other touching his leg. He leers at the camera, adopting what Richard Dyer (with the help of Freud's work on the taboo of anal eroticism) interprets as a "castrating" or "penetrating" (269) look. Such a posture unequivocally situates the sitter as a potentially passive sexual partner about to be penetrated by a paying client. The accompanying text used to introduce this first photograph provides typographic evidence to justify this reading:

> And David Beckham takes it
> to a new level in these pictures.
> What better way to tease?
> A pop-culture icon turns his back
> on pretty labels and toughs it out
> on his own turf
> (Healy 177)

The divisions between lines provide an alternative meaning informing the adjacent scenario. Given the erotic coding controlled by the photographer, the phrase "takes it" acquires a sexual dimension. Beckham literally turns his back to prepare for a sexual act. He renounces his "pretty boy" image by adopting a skinhead persona. And his turf, if not pubic, is the public beat where he attracts potential clients.

Other shots in the eighteen-page photo spread provide variations on the rough trade theme and reinforce the homoerotic focus. Two cropped naked shots show Beckham's arms extending backward, as if he had his hands tied outside of the frame. Dressed in khaki trousers and a sleeveless Versace shirt, he is reclining on a couch with one booted foot lying on a cushion. In this photo, Beckham's look can only be described as a sneer. There are two shots of Beckham sitting on a motorbike wearing a khaki cotton boiler suit open to the waist. Klein is reworking a commonplace gay fantasy here. For example, in *Physique Pictorial* from April 1960, a Tom of Finland drawing shows an almost naked male astride a motorbike. In one photo, Beckham sits on a bed with his knees upright, wearing a green MA-1 bomber jacket, popularly worn by skinheads. He gives another hard-faced sneer at the camera. He is then shown kneeling in front of a closet mirror wearing camouflage trousers in a pose of narcissistic submission. More semi-naked bedroom scenes are included in which Dolce & Gabbana jeans replace the Levi's. He gives the impression of being a rent boy ready to sell his body to a male client. This sequence in *Arena* vividly demonstrates how metrosexuality queers major codes of traditional masculinity. Here masculinity is manifestly passive (not active), desired (not desiring), and looked at (not looking).

Passivity was further demonstrated in July 2003 when Beckham was the subject of another eroticized scenario provided by Steven Klein. He photographed the celebrity alone and in the company of his wife Victoria for the men's fashion magazine *L'Uomo Vogue* (Italy). Shots from the series later reappeared elsewhere, for example in the summer 2004 issue of *GQ* (Australia) where the player was referred to as a "sex God" (Iley 74). In this series of photographs, Beckham showed that he could give the impression of performing active and passive heterosexual roles as convincingly as he had evoked homosexual passivity in *Arena* three years earlier. The Australian version opens with a two-page photograph of the Beckhams. Victoria is lying face down on a bench, her arms extended and her buttocks poised near David's waist. She is wearing a hat, a bra, and briefs. David is standing behind her in a mesh top and a Dolce & Gabbana black satin jumpsuit with his hand on his wife's neck forcing her not to move. In a reversal of situation, another shot from the series (not reproduced in the Australian *GQ*) shows Beckham kneeling, his head thrown back and controlled by Victoria who is straddling her husband in a sexually suggestive posture. This pose demonstrates how Beckham's masculinity is not to be exclusively equated with an exertion of power. The *Vogue* photographs show a sexual politics based on an equal sharing of power between the sexes.

Beckham posed again for Steven Klein in his first major photo shoot for an American magazine after the move to Los Angeles. "American Idols," the impressive twenty-eight-page fashion shoot published in *W* magazine, was subtitled "Stripped Down, Sexy and Worth a Fortune." In the company of his wife, America's new sex idol modeled Italian fashion items (Dolce & Gabbana white cotton briefs, Just Cavalli black leather pants) as well as garments from New York shops, including latex pants from New York Fetish. With these images of the LA Galaxy player wearing skimpy designer underwear and fetish gear, Klein helped launch a new sporno star into American sports culture.

Speculation arose in June 2007 concerning whether David Beckham should be knighted. *Times'* journalist Matthew Syed attempted to convince readers that this athlete should be awarded a knighthood for his services to masculinity. The writer was correct to argue that Beckham should be honored, not for his sports achievements, but more importantly because he "has been the single most significant catalyst in the metrosexual revolution, changing the contemporary notion of masculinity, softening it, smoothing it, widening it, diversifying it" (101). This observation demonstrates an increased acknowledgment of Beckham's role as an instrument of change globally. It is especially in the widening and diversifying of what is considered normative masculinity that Beckham is important.

Beautiful Bodies

The many male athletes discussed in this book share a common feature: their bodies are aesthetically pleasing. Males who can be described as metrosexual all practice self-beautifying, but a discursive problem arises when analyzing the male body made beautiful. It is not easy to find the right words to refer to metrosexualized bodies. This problem is evident, for example, in magazine coverage of David Beckham, The Rock, and the professional boxer Oscar De La Hoya. Journalists find it problematic to lexically capture in a single word the physical attributes of these males. This is obvious in the August 2005 *Details* article on Beckham. After complimenting his subject in the opening line as "better looking and better dressed than most women" (Blasengame 134), the journalist proceeds to interpret the athlete's features as "frustratingly pretty" or "Beautiful, even, in a way usually reserved for runway models and gay men" (137). In the case of The Rock, one journalist tries "beautiful," insisting this "*is* the correct word," then adjusts the description to "ruggedly handsome," before settling on a hesitant, but forceful "quite . . . *pretty*" (Corsello 264). To justify the italicized epithet the journalist provides "long eyelashes, soft eyes and a certain roundness to his features" (264) as evidence of prettiness. It is noteworthy observing the progression of descriptive terms here, beginning with "beautiful," changing to "handsome," and finally climaxing in "pretty." The addition of "ruggedly" seems to be there to offset the feminizing connotations of "beautiful" and "pretty." De La Hoya also found himself called a "pretty boy" by a men's fashion writer, before being compared to "a member of a boy band" (Bhattacharya 116). "Pretty" has frequently been used in the press to describe young male athletes who pose for the fashion press. It implies the sort of gender and sexual ambiguity that is often associated with boy band idols.

There is a terminological problem in English due to the connotations of the terms "beautiful" and "pretty." "Beautiful" is normally only used to characterize females; "pretty" when used for males can suggest homosexuality or feminization; and "handsome" is judged to be a term reserved for males. The restrictive application of all these adjectives is not present in other languages. In his research on ancient Greek athletics, Thomas Scanlon speaks about the ideal of athletic beauty by drawing attention to *kalos* inscriptions written on baths, city walls, and vase paintings. These inscriptions refer to male athletes. Revealingly, Scanlon has a problem translating the term *kalos* (the Greek adjective for beautiful) when using it in a male context. When discussing its use to describe Greek athletes, he sometimes translates it as "handsome" (205), other times as "good-looking" (205). The Greeks used the same word for both sexes. So does modern French and Italian, for example, where the equivalents of "beautiful" are employed for females and males. This lexical dilemma is therefore specifically linked to the English language which depends on a culturally learned, but as other languages show, unnecessary division based on sexual differentiation. English terms to characterize made-better or physically pleasing bodies insist on a bipolar separation which imposes the use of "beautiful" and "pretty" as possibilities for females, while keeping "handsome" or "good-looking" for males. Metrosexuality is based on the dissolving of such bipolar logic concerning gender. The terms habitually used to refer to women need to become a lexical possibility in English without any feminizing or homosexualizing connotations. Physically striking males who attract the male gaze thus reveal generalized tensions especially discernible when males compliment each other. A lexical realignment is required whereby "beautiful" and "pretty" can be normalized terms to describe aesthetically pleasing male bodies. Journalistic hesitation to employ these words in a male context suggests that such normalization has not yet taken place.

Conclusion

In 2003, when journalists were scratching their heads trying to work out what metrosexuality was all about, Dolce and Gabbana opened a three-story extravaganza in the heart of Milan's fashion quarter at the intersection of Corso Venezia and Via della Spiga. Sam Grobart's *GQ* (U.S.) July 2003 article "Do Real Men Exfoliate?" covered the event. Dolce and Gabbana's Mecca for men included a new clothes shop, a barbershop, a Martini Bar and a grooming spa. Details of the shop décor (basaltina floors, travertine fireplaces, and black Murano-glass chandeliers) prepare the reader for a description of what lay outside. Beyond the eighteenth-century courtyard there was a "Playboy Mansion grotto" (168) dedicated to male vanity. Grobart enthuses about this temple of pleasure by declaring that "every man wants to be from Milan" (168). One illustration features a Milanese customer lying on his stomach, while a shower of water is streaming onto his back. The accompanying text begins with a sexual pun, "Take It Lying Down," which is somewhat lessened in the next line, "Or sitting, if you prefer" (167). The journalist is at pains to point out that in Milan a man can be "exfoliated, peeled, waxed, filed, tanned and massaged" (168), and still feel like and be considered a "real man."

While fascinating, and in a limited way instructive, the journalist's highlighting of Milan is indicative of analyses which give the impression that metrosexuality is a specifically Western concept. Concentrating on Milan also takes away attention from other Western centers. However, an increasing amount of evidence suggests that the growth of metrosexuality is becoming the rule rather than the exception in Western and non-Western countries. Metrosexuality may have been first noticed in Britain and its transformation into a household buzzword may be largely dependent on a U.S. marketing machine. However, this should not make us oblivious to the cultural transformations that are captured by the term "metrosexual" in Europe, Australia, and Asia.

Adopting grooming habits similar to those of Western metrosexual males, Indian athletes have taken a leading role in the popularization of metrosexuality. A case in point is the cricketer Yuvraj Singh, who was chosen as the brand ambassador to advertise an aftershower hair cream in August 2005. Another case is the former captain of the Indian hockey team, Dhanraj Pillay, who frequently had facials and carried lotions and scrubs when on tour. Changes in Indian urban masculinities and their transmission in the media are easily comparable to the processes involved in the growth of metrosexuality elsewhere. Significantly, the 2004 article providing the information on Pillay was entitled "The Age of the New Man" (Pishatory).

On an academic level, interest generated by the "New Man" compelled Himanshu Verma, the author of the pamphlet *The Metrosexuals*, to organize a ten-day interdisciplinary festival in Mumbai entitled "Met-Fest: Masculinities in the City." Exploring Indian metrosexuality through talks, films, visual art, music, and plays, this festival brought to light different facets of Indian masculinities. As the festival suggests, changing notions of masculinity have become so entrenched in Indian urban centers that an online article by Mangesh Kulkarni entitled "Is there such a thing as the metrosexual male?" argued that "an unprecedented transformation of Indian masculinity is occurring in the vast grey zone between the media-bolstered façade of metrosexuality and the deep-rooted structures of hetero-patriarchy."

Metrosexual males are so common in all of Asia that *Time* magazine did a cover story on the subject in October 2005. Ling Liu's extensive article "Mirror, Mirror . . ." began with the observation that "in Asia nowadays, the definition of masculinity is undergoing a makeover—and narcissism is in" (39). Such an observation clearly interprets the metrosexual revolution as taking place in Asia. Liu informed readers that "Asian males are preening like peacocks, perming, plucking and powdering themselves to perfection" (39). While the term "metrosexual" is not necessarily used to describe these Asian narcissists (in China, Liu revealed, they are called "love beauty men" and in Korea the equivalent is "flower men"), the phenomenon was said to be similar to events in the West. And like her

New York colleagues, Liu was struck by the high number of "primp-ing fops who accessorize with designer bling and faux fur" (40). Major Asian cities, like their American, European, and Australian equivalents, offer men-only spas and grooming salons.

As in Western countries, Asian athletes participate in promoting the boom of men's grooming products. One such case is the "David Beckham of South Korea," long-haired soccer player Ahn Jung-Hwan, who in 2002 starred in a publicity campaign for the men's liq-uid foundation Color Lotion. Ultimately, the effects of changes in the realm of male self-care can be seen in fashion writer and male jew-elry director Jung Soon-Won's book *Cut Off Your Necktie Right Now* (an analysis of metrosexuality in Korean society) as well as in local Korean versions of men's lifestyle magazines such as *GQ, Esquire* and, since 2006, *Men's Health.*

This brief cross-cultural survey shows that metrosexuality cannot be reduced to what John Harris and Ben Clayton dismiss as "an ef-fect of consumerism and media proliferation on Western definitions of masculinity." "Metrosexuality is more of a media construction," these authors argue, not "a brand of masculinity" (152). Countering such observations, I see the worldwide changes taking place in tradi-tional masculinity norms as deep-rooted and somehow fundamental in their nature. Athletes are the catalysts of these important changes. It is due to sportsmen being identified as model metrosexuals that their example has been followed so effectively by other males inter-nationally. This book has shown that on one level metrosexuality can be described as a series of self-care and beautifying practices that have been encoded as "feminine" or "gay." We have seen that iden-tifying athletes as prime metrosexuals has enabled the destigmatiza-tion of the cultivation of the self. The immediately obvious hyper-masculine and generally assumed heterosexual status of most sportsmen has been vital in changing attitudes about exposing, eroti-cizing, and taking care of the male body. Without some of the most celebrated heterosexual athletes in the world endorsing and embod-ying different facets of metrosexuality, it is uncertain if masculinity norms would have changed so rapidly in so many different cultures. Metrosexuality, in a way, is indebted to sportsmen for its very exis-tence. This is one of the most interesting paradoxes at the heart of metrosexual masculinity.

Another paradox can be identified concerning the self-improvement rituals represented by the Fab Five in *Queer Eye* or by

Michael Flocker's advice in his little handbook *The Metrosexual Guide to Style*. While these aspects of metrosexuality undeniably help to transform normative masculinity, they also inevitably restrict and limit its potential importance. The *Queer Eye* television series was primordial in transmitting metrosexuality to a wide audience. However, limiting the "queer eye" to five domains, as the series did, gave the misleading idea that metrosexuality is only or mostly about activities such as grooming, decorating, and fashion. Having five gay men take charge of metrosexualization reinforced the stereotypical idea that male self-care is evidence of homosexuality.

Contrasting with the interpretation of metrosexuality transmitted by the Fab Five, the significance of metrosexuality can be perceived on a more profound level. Metrosexuality tells us something about the relations between the sexes, about nonnormative sexualities, and about how gender and sexuality are used as interpretative tools to label individuals and as markers of self-identity. Changing attitudes in these areas is where metrosexuality has the most potential importance as a cultural phenomenon. Metrosexual males may look prettier and more beautiful than their nonmetrosexual brothers, but metrosexuality is the motor behind more decisive changes in the realm of sexual politics; it influences how heterosexual males interact with homosexual males and it is in the process of replacing traditional categories of sexual orientation.

If males no longer have to persistently exert power or dominate in order to prove their masculinity, if compulsory heterosexuality is no longer synonymous with virility, if power and heterosexual conquests are deprived of their capacity to define a male's sense of worth, then these reinterpretations of masculinity have vast implications for relations between the sexes and for how nonnormative sexualities are perceived. Metrosexuality is based on the idea that power can be shared between the sexes, rather than be exclusively seen as a sign of virility or naturally pertain to the male sex. Metrosexuality means that passivity can be shared by men and women rather than be confused with femininity. It also implies a destigmatization of homosexuality and a consequent decrease of homophobia, since metrosexuality is blind to sexual orientation and privileges no single sexual identity. As well, the fact that metrosexuality can replace conventional categories of sexual orientation means that less attention is being paid to the traditional binary opposition separating males into two discrete categories, heterosexual or homosexual.

It defeats the point of inventing this new word "metrosexual" if we still insist on deciding whose sexual orientation is heterosexual and whose is homosexual. "Metrosexual" obviates the need to make this distinction. Using "metrosexual" by itself puts the question of sexual orientation into the background and concentrates on other issues as being more significant to describe a male. Metrosexuality is replacing traditional and conventional masculinity norms. It may in time become itself the new norm, transforming the way men treat their bodies, how they interact with women, and how they perceive nonnormative sexualities. The metrosexual future is one in which men demonstrate more human and more humane values.

Works Cited

Aldrich, Robert. *The Seduction of the Mediterranean: Writing, Art and Homosexual Fantasy.* London: Routledge, 1993.

Allen, Ted et al. *Queer Eye for the Straight Guy: The Fab 5's Guide to Looking Better, Cooking Better, Dressing Better, Behaving Better, and Living Better.* London: Weidenfeld & Nicolson, 2004.

Amaechi, John, and Chris Bull. *Man in the Middle.* New York: ESPN, 2007.

Anderson, Eric. *In the Game: Gay Athletes and the Cult of Masculinity.* New York: State University of New York Press, 2005.

Armani, Giorgio. *Facce da sport: Faces of Sport.* Milan: Skira, 2004.

Baraquin, Jérémy. "Hidé Cadeau." *Préférences Mag,* September–October 2004: 20–21.

Beckham, David. *David Beckham: My World.* 2000. London: Hodder & Stoughton, 2001.

Beland, Nicole. "So What Do You Do Art Cooper?" 19 November 2002, http://www.mediabistro.com/content/archives/02/11/19/.

Bell-Price, Shannon, and Elyssa Da Cruz. "Tigress." *Wild: Fashion Untamed.* Ed. Andrew Bolton. New York: The Metropolitan Museum of Art, 2004: 116–43.

Belsky, Gary. "Esquire, GQ Fashionably Ahead." *Advertising Age,* 18 April 1988, Special Report: S2.

Benedict, Jeff. *Out of Bounds: Inside the NBA's Culture of Rape, Violence, and Crime.* New York: HarperCollins, 2004.

———. *Public Heroes, Private Felons: Athletes and Crimes Against Women.* Boston: Northeastern University Press, 1997.

Benedict, Jeff, and Don Yaeger. *Pros and Cons: The Criminals Who Play in the NFL.* New York: Warner, 1998.

Bhabha, Homi. "The Other Question: Stereotypes, Discrimination and the Discourse of Colonialism." 1983. *The Location of Culture.* New York: Routledge, 1994: 66–84.

Bhattacharya, Sanjiv. "Icon Oscar De La Hoya." *GQ* (UK), September 2003: 116–17, 119–20, 122.

Blasengame, Bart. "David Beckham Is the Most Famous Athlete on Earth." *Details,* August 2005: 134–39.

Bordo, Susan. *The Male Body: A New Look at Men in Public and in Private.* 1999. New York: Farrar, Straus and Giroux, 2000.

Borrows, Bill. "Little Ali." *Loaded,* November 1994: 20–24, 27.

Bortstein, Larry. *Superjoe: The Joe Namath Story.* New York: Tempo, 1969.

Boston, Lloyd. *Make Over Your Man: The Woman's Guide to Dressing Any Man in Her Life*. New York: Broadway, 2002.

Boswell, Thomas. "The Wizardry of Ozzie." *GQ* (U.S.), April 1988: 246–48, 298.

Bowlby, Rachel. *Carried Away: The Invention of Modern Shopping*. London: Faber & Faber, 2000.

Boyd, Randy. "When Will the Walls Come Tumbling Down?" 15 March 2002, http://www.outsports.com/ballin/20020219walls.htm.

Boyd, Todd. *Young, Black, Rich and Famous: The Rise of the NBA, the Hip Hop Invasion and the Transformation of American Culture*. New York: Doubleday, 2003.

Breward, Christopher. *The Hidden Consumer: Masculinities, Fashion and City Life 1860–1914*. Manchester: Manchester University Press, 1999.

Brigham, Roger. "The Importance of Being Earvin." *The Advocate*, 21 April 1992: 34–39.

Bronski, Michael. "Blatant Male Pulchritude: The Art of George Quaintance and Bruce Weber's *Bear Pond*." *Art Papers*, 16.4 (July–August 1992): 26–29.

Brown, Laura. "The Rock." *Details*, January–February 2005: 124–29.

Burke, Jason, Denis Campbell, and Anushka Asthana. "Football's Nemesis." *Observer*, 12 October 2003, Observer's News Pages: 16.

Burke, Jim. *Joe Willie*. New York: Belmont Tower, 1975.

Butler, Judith. "Imitation and Gender Insubordination." *Inside/Out: Lesbian Theories, Gay Theories*. Ed. Diana Fuss. Routledge: New York, 1991: 13–31.

Buzinski, Jim. "Jeff Garcia: I'm Not Gay." 4 February 2004, http://www.out sports.com/nfl/2004/0204garcia.htm.

Cashmore, Ellis. *Beckham*. 2002. Cambridge: Polity, 2004.

Cashmore, Ellis, and Andrew Parker. "One David Beckham? Celebrity, Masculinity, and the Soccerati." *Sociology of Sport Journal*, 20 (2003): 214–31.

Chapman, David, ed. *Adonis: The Male Physique Pin-Up 1870–1940*. 1989. Swaffham, England: Éditions Aubrey Walter, 1997.

Chrisafis, Angelique. "Neutered Modern Man to Be Offered Back His Missing Pride in Exchange for His Wallet." *Guardian*, 16 June 2003, Home Pages: 6.

Clark, Matthew. *Playing Away: The A-Z of Soccer Sex Scandals*. Edinburgh: Cutting Edge, 2004.

Coad, David. *Gender Trouble Down Under: Australian Masculinities*. Valenciennes: Presses Universitaires de Valenciennes, 2002.

"Cold War at the Pool, Shaking a Leg, in Pantyhose." *Newsweek* (U.S.), 25 October 1999: 63.

Collins, Patricia Hill. *Black Sexual Politics: African Americans, Gender, and the New Racism*. New York: Routledge, 2004.

Corsello, Andrew. "I Am The Rock." *GQ* (U.S.), October 2003: 206–11, 264–65.

———. "The Quiet Man." *GQ* (U.S.), September 1997: 350–59.

Croft, Claudia. "Men Who Flirt with Skirts." *Evening Standard*, 4 June 1998: 3.

Davies, Laura Lee. "Swede Little Mystery." *Time Out*, 7–14 August 2002: 12–14.

Davis, Melody. *The Male Nude in Contemporary Photography*. Philadelphia: Temple University Press, 1991.

Deeny, Godfrey. "Becks: Soccer's Reigning Style King Strikes an Unexpected Pose." *Sepp,* Summer 2004: 36–42.

Di Drusco, Fabia. "Sheva." *Vogue Sport* (Italy), January 2005: 205.

Dolce & Gabbana. *A.C. Milan Dressed by Dolce & Gabbana.* Milan: Dolce & Gabbana, 2005.

———. *Calcio.* Milan: Dolce & Gabbana, 2004.

———. *Milan.* Milan: Electa, 2006.

Dolinsky, Jim, ed. *Bruce of Los Angeles.* Berlin: Bruno Gmünder Verlag, 1990.

Dyer, Richard. "Don't Look Now: The Male Pin-up." 1982. *The Sexual Subject: A* Screen *Reader in Sexuality. Screen.* London: Routledge, 1998: 265–76.

English, Peter. "String of Sex Scandals Turns Spotlight on Macho Culture in Australian Sport." *Guardian,* 30 March 2004, Sport Pages: 25.

Entine, Jon. *Taboo: Why Black Athletes Dominate Sports and Why We're Afraid to Talk about It.* 1999. New York: PublicAffairs, 2001.

Eskenazi, Gerald. "Gastineau & Co. Cash In." *New York Times,* 15 June 1982: D27.

Euro RSCG Worldwide. "The Future of Men: U.K." June 2003.

———. "The Future of Men: U.S.A." June 2003.

Evans, Gavin. *Wicked: The Prince Naseem Phenomenon.* London: Robson, 1999.

Fachet, Robert. "You'd Run Too if You Saw Carl Lewis in Heels." *Washington Post,* 15 April 1994, Sports: F2.

Feldman, Loren. "A Cardinal in Peacock's Plume." *GQ* (U.S.), April 1988: 249, 298, 300.

Fish, Mike. "Olympic Watch the Countdown to 1996 Atlanta Games XXVI Olympiad 817 Days Left." *Atlanta Journal-Constitution,* 24 April 1994, Sports: F4.

Flocker, Michael. *The Hedonism Handbook: Mastering the Lost Arts of Leisure and Pleasure.* Cambridge, MA: Da Capo, 2004.

———. *The Metrosexual Guide to Style: A Handbook for Modern Man.* Cambridge, MA: Da Capo, 2003.

Flynn, Paul. "And God Created . . . DAVID." *Attitude,* June 2002: 32–43.

Foucault, Michel. *The Care of the Self. The History of Sexuality: Volume Three.* Trans. Robert Hurley. Harmondsworth: Penguin, 1990. Trans. of *Le Souci de soi.* 1984.

Foy, Chris. "Dan Is the Man to Steal Jonny's Spot at the Top." *Daily Mail,* 3 December 2004: 100.

Freud, Sigmund. *On Sexuality: Three Essays on the Theory of Sexuality and Other Works.* Trans. James Strachey. Harmondsworth: Penguin, 1991.

Funches, Tracy, and Rob Marriott. *Pimpnosis.* New York: HarperEntertainment, 2002.

Furnish, David. "Captain Fantastic." *GQ* (UK), June 2002: 140–55.

Galvin, Peter. "Dennis the Menace." *The Advocate,* 21 January 1997: 26–28, 30, 32, 34.

Garber, Marjorie. *Vested Interests: Cross-Dressing and Cultural Anxiety.* 1992. New York: Penguin, 1993.

Goddard, Tariq. "The Kid." *Arena Homme Plus,* Autumn/Winter 2004–2005: 284–93.

Gotting, Peter. "Rise of the Metrosexual." *The Age,* 11 March 2003, The Culture: 1.

Gottlieb, Andrew. *In the Paint: Tattoos of the NBA and the Stories Behind Them.* New York: Hyperion, 2003.

"*GQ*'s NBA All-Star Style Team." *GQ* (U.S.), February 1991: 184–89.

Greer, Germaine. *The Whole Woman.* 1999. London: Anchor, 2000.

Grobart, Sam. "Do Real Men Exfoliate?" *GQ* (U.S.), July 2003: 166–68.

Guidi, Mark. "Football: Milan's Model Pro." *Sunday Mail* (Scotland), 26 September 2004, Sport: 68–69.

Guttmann, Allen. *The Erotic in Sports.* New York: Columbia University Press, 1996.

Hall, Stuart. "What Is This 'Black' in Black Popular Culture?" *Black Popular Culture: A Project by Michelle Wallace.* Ed. Gina Dent. Seattle: Bay Press, 1992: 21–37.

Harper, Phillip Brian. *Are We Not Men? Masculine Anxiety and the Problem of African-American Identity.* New York: Oxford University Press, 1996.

Harris, John, and Ben Clayton. "The First Metrosexual Rugby Star: Rugby Union, Masculinity, and Celebrity in Contemporary Wales." *Sociology of Sport Journal,* 24:2 (June 2007): 145–64.

Hausman, Ken. "America Finds Its Values in the Locker Room." *Psychiatric News,* 39.13 (2 July 2004): 19.

Hawley, Janet. "Fish Out of Water." *Good Weekend (Sydney Morning Herald),* 24 March 2007: 26–34.

Hay, David. "Thorpedo." *GQ Style Directory* (Australia), Autumn/Winter 2001: 100–101.

Healy, Murray. "David Beckham: Made in Britain." *Arena Homme Plus,* Autumn/Winter 2000–2001: 176–93.

Hirshey, Gerri. "The Frosted Flake." *GQ* (U.S.), September 1989: 416–21, 492–96.

hooks, bell. "Feminism Inside: Toward a Black Body Politic." *Black Male: Representations of Masculinity in Contemporary American Art.* Ed. Thelma Gordon. New York: Whitney Museum of American Art, 1994: 127–40.

———. *We Real Cool: Black Men and Masculinity.* New York: Routledge, 2004.

———. *Yearning: Race, Gender, and Cultural Politics.* Cambridge, MA: South End Press, 1990.

Hooven, F. Valentine. *Beefcake: The Muscle Magazines of America 1950–1970.* 1995. Cologne: Taschen, 2002.

Howarth, Peter. "Beautiful Game." *Financial Times,* 24 January 2004, FT Weekend—Shopping: 15.

———. "European Designers Kick Grass." *National Post,* 2 February 2004, Arts & Life: B12.

———. "The Beautiful Game." *Observer,* 13 June 2004, Observer Magazine: 10.

Hruby, Patrick. "Ice, Ice Baby." *Washington Times,* 1 November 2002, Sports: C1.

Hume, Marion. "Teenage Olympian Learns to Wear Fame." *New York Times,* 29 October 2000, sec. 9, Sunday Styles: 8.

Hurt, Jessica. "Designers Mix and Match Wild Ideas and Accessories." *Advertiser* (Adelaide, South Australia), 16 March 2005: 40.

Hyde, Nina. "Underwear Joe." *Washington Post,* 18 November 1984, final ed., Style: K3.

"Ian Thorpe." *Australian Men Magazine,* Autumn/Winter 2004: 22–25.

Iley, Chrissy. "The Beckhams." *GQ* (Australia), Summer 2004: 70–83.

Isaacs, Neil D. *Jock Culture, U.S.A.* New York: Norton, 1978.

Jackson, Ronald L. II. *Scripting the Black Masculine Body: Identity, Discourse, and Racial Politics in Popular Media.* New York: State University of New York Press, 2006.

Jenkins, Dan. "The Sweet Life of Swinging Joe." *Sports Illustrated,* 17 October 1966: 42–44, 47, 48, 50, 55.

Jenkins, Sally. "Advantage Skunky." *GQ* (U.S.), July 1999: 107–13, 174.

Jobling, Paul. *Man Appeal: Advertising, Modernism and Men's Wear.* Oxford: Berg, 2005.

Johnson, E. Patrick. *Appropriating Blackness: Performance and the Politics of Authenticity.* 2003. Durham: Duke University Press, 2004.

Johnson, Magic, and Roy S. Johnson. "I'll Deal with It." *Sports Illustrated,* 18 November 1991: 16–26.

Kamp, David. "Don't Hate Me Because I'm Ghetto-Fabulous." *GQ* (U.S.), August 1999: 139–45, 206–209.

Kay, Karen. "Everything for the Man." *Times,* 29 October 1994, Features.

Kirkpatrick, Curry. "Devilishly Different." *Sports Illustrated,* 25 November 1991: 62–64, 69–70, 73.

Kriegel, Mark. *Namath: A Biography.* New York: Viking, 2004.

Krum, Sharon. "Like a Duck to Water." *Harper's Bazaar* (Australia), January–February 2001: 120–25.

Kuchta, David. *The Three-Piece Suit and Modern Masculinity: England, 1550–1850.* Berkeley: University of California Press, 2002.

Kulkarni, Mangesh. "Is There Such a Thing as the Metrosexual Male?" http://www.infochangeindia.org/agenda4_08.jsp.

La Ferla, Ruth. "Are Diamonds Now a Man's Best Friend?" *New York Times,* 4 January 2004, sec. 9, Style Desk: 6.

Lafrance, Mélisse, and Geneviève Rail. "Excursions into Otherness: Understanding Dennis Rodman and the Limits of Subversive Agency." *Sport Stars: The Cultural Politics of Sporting Celebrity.* Ed. David L. Andrews and Steven J. Jackson. London: Routledge, 2001: 36–50.

Langway, Lynn. "Cosmetics: The Rub-Off." *Newsweek* (U.S.), 28 July 1975: 52.

Lapointe, Joe. "Pro Basketball." *New York Times,* 13 May 1990, late ed., sec. 8: 1.

Lawton, James. "No Flowers, Please, for a Game That Lost Its Soul." *Independent,* 8 October 2003, Features: 2–3.

———. "Football: Pampered Players Defraud Fans." *Independent,* 5 March 2004, Sport: 56.

Lehman, Peter. "In an Imperfect World, Men with Small Penises Are Unforgiven: The Presentation of the Penis/Phallus in American Films of the 1990s." 1998. *Men's Lives*. Ed. Michael Kimmel and Michael Messner. Boston: Allyn & Bacon, 2001: 494–504.

Leyland, Winston, ed. *Physique: A Pictorial History of the Athletic Model Guild*. San Francisco: Gay Sunshine Press, 1982.

Lieder, Ruth. "Fur Coats for Frigid Days in Green Bay." *Sports Illustrated*, 9 December 1968: 60–61.

Linderman, Lawrence. "Playboy Interview: Joe Namath." *Playboy*, December 1969: 93–94, 100, 102, 104, 106, 108, 110, 112, 114, 118.

Liu, Ling. "Mirror, Mirror. . . ." *Time* (Asia), 31 October 2005: 38–43.

Lipsyte, Robert. *SportsWorld: An American Dreamland*. New York: Quadrangle, 1975.

———. "Surviving Jock Culture." *Rush Hour: A Journal of Contemporary Voices*. Ed. Michael Cart. New York: Delacorte, 2004: 177–95.

Lomartire, Paul. "Jim Palmer's Still Got It." *Palm Beach Post*, 23 March 2003, Accent: D1.

Lorelle, Véronique. "Les 'métrosexuels' ou la mode sur impulsion." *Le Monde*, 31 January 2004: 26.

Mackay, Duncan. "Athletics: Lewis Still Plans to Cut a Dash." *Observer*, 10 July 1994, Sports: 10.

Maggio, Serge. "Unseen Cri Cri." *Vogue Sport* (Italy), January 2005: 234–37.

Mansfield, Stephanie. "Jim Palmer's New Pitch." *Washington Post*, 18 June 1985, Style: D1.

Marks, Kathy, and David Randall. "And They Call It the British Disease." *Independent on Sunday*, 7 March 2004, News: 17.

Marks, Kathy, and David Randall. "Why Do Good Sports Turn Bad?" *Canberra Times*, 10 March 2004: A35.

Masseret, Catherine. "Pascal Gentil." *C&G*, Winter 2004–2005: 32–37.

Massey, John. *American Adonis: Tony Sansone, the First Male Physique Icon*. New York: Universe, 2004.

McBride, Dwight A. *Why I Hate Abercrombie & Fitch: Essays on Race and Sexuality*. New York: New York University Press, 2005.

McCarron, Anthony. "A Chat with Baseball's Best Player." *Gazette* (Montreal), 18 March 2004, Sports: C4.

McClintock, Anne. *Imperial Leather: Race, Gender and Sexuality in the Colonial Conquest*. New York: Routledge, 1995.

McDowell, Colin. *The Man of Fashion: Peacock Males and Perfect Gentlemen*. London: Thames & Hudson, 1997.

McGee, David. "I Fondled Freddie's Panther . . . and Turned into a Wildcat." *News of the World*, 4 January 2004.

McNeil, Peter. "Macaroni Masculinities." *Fashion Theory: The Journal of Dress, Body & Culture*, 4.4 (2000): 373–404.

Melly, George. "Why the Tables Have Turned on Macho Males." *Campaign*, 18 July 1986: 40–41.

Mercer, Kobena. *Welcome to the Jungle: New Positions in Black Cultural Studies.* New York: Routledge, 1994.

Meyers, William. "What's New in Marketing; Jim Palmer Pitches 'Style' for Jockey." *New York Times,* 29 August 1982, late city final ed., sec. 3: 23.

Miller, Toby. *Sportsex.* Philadelphia: Temple University Press, 2001.

Milligan, Andy. *Brand It Like Beckham: The Story of How Brand Beckham Was Built.* London: Cyan, 2004.

Mills, Simon. "Nemesis." *GQ* (UK), June 2002: 174–76.

Milner, Christina, and Richard Milner. *Black Players: The Secret World of Black Pimps.* London: Michael Joseph, 1973.

"Mix It Up." *GQ* (U.S.), July 2004: 128–31.

Montgomery Ward Catalog of Winter Underwear and Outerwear. Chicago: Montgomery Ward & Co., 1915.

Montre, Lorraine Kee. "Gay or Nay?" *St. Louis Post-Dispatch,* 4 April 1992, Sports: 1C.

Morgan, Piers. "We Shoot He Scores." *GQ* (UK), February 2004: 106–14.

Mulvey, Laura. "Visual Pleasure and Narrative Cinema." 1975. *The Sexual Subject: A* Screen *Reader in Sexuality. Screen.* Routledge: London, 1998: 22–34.

Namath, Joe Willie, and Dick Schaap. *I Can't Wait Until Tomorrow . . . 'Cause I Get Better Looking Every Day.* 1969. New York: Signet, 1970.

"NZ Guys Fess-Up about Their Undie Habits." 5 July 2004, http://www.thread.co.nz/article/952.

Oh, Minya. *Bling Bling: Hip Hop's Crown Jewels.* New York: Wenner, 2005.

Osgerby, Bill. "A Pedigree of the Consuming Male: Masculinity, Consumption and the American 'Leisure Class.'" *Masculinity and Men's Lifestyle Magazines.* Ed. Bethan Benwell. Oxford: Blackwell, 2003: 57–85.

———. *Playboys in Paradise: Masculinity, Youth and Leisure-Style in Modern America.* Oxford: Berg, 2001.

"Pain Pays the Bills for Joe's Good Life." *Life,* 3 November 1972: 36–42.

Palmer, Jim. *Jim Palmer's Way to Fitness.* New York: Harper & Row, 1985.

Pattenden, Mike. "David Beckham Esq." *Esquire* (UK), June 2000: 18–26.

Pisharoty, Sangeeta Barooah. "The Age of the New Man." *The Hindu,* 20 September 2004, http://www.hindu.com/mp/2004/09/20/stories/2004092002890100.htm.

Platt, Larry. *Only the Strong Survive: The Odyssey of Allen Iverson.* 2002. New York: Regan Books, 2003.

Preston, Matt. "Racing His Shadow." *Autore Magazine,* July 2002: 52–57.

Pronger, Brian. *The Arena of Masculinity: Sports, Homosexuality, and the Meaning of Sex.* London: GMP, 1990.

Quinn, Eithne. *Nuthin' but a "g" Thang: The Culture and Commerce of Gangsta Rap.* New York: Columbia University Press, 2005.

Raab, Scott. "Dennis Rodman in the Pink." *GQ* (U.S.), February 1997: 136–41.

———. "Wild Thing." *GQ* (U.S.), January 1995: 94–101.

Rahman, Momin. "Beckham as a Historical Moment in the Representation of Masculinity." *Labour History Review,* 69.2 (August 2004): 219–34.

———. "Is Straight the New Queer?: David Beckham and the Dialectics of Celebrity." *M/C Journal*, 7.5 (2004), http://journal.media-culture.org.au/0411/15-rahman.php.

Raphael, Amy. "Freddie Ljungberg." *Room Service*, April 2005: 26–30.

Reginato, James. "American Idols." *W*, August 2007: 206–35.

Reilly, Rick. "Counter Point." *Sports Illustrated*, 9 March 1998: 82–93.

Resch, Scott. "King David." *Player Magazine*, January 2005: 70–76.

Reynaert, François. "Beckingham Palace." *Le Nouvel Observateur*, 25 September 2003: 50.

Richmond, Peter. "Pat Riley Is Still Looking for a Fight." *GQ* (U.S.), January 1998: 120–27.

———. "The Height of Fashion." *GQ* (U.S.), October 2003: 238–43.

Robins, Stephen. *How to Be a Complete Dandy*. London: Prion, 2001.

Rodman, Dennis, and Michael Silver. *Walk on the Wild Side*. New York: Delacorte, 1997.

Rodman, Dennis, and Tim Keown. *Bad as I Wanna Be*. 1996. New York: Dell, 1997.

Rodrick, Stephen. "No Rebound." *New York Times*, 1 June 2003, late ed., final: 36.

Rodrigues, João Rui. "Ronaldo Só Há." *GQ* (Portugal), April 2005: 62–70.

Rose, Michael S. "Metrosexual Goes America." Cruxnews.com. 16 September 2003, http://www.cruxnews.org/rose-metrosexual.html.

Rousseau, François. *Dievx dv stade*. Paris: www.stade.fr, 2004.

"Rugby Hero 'Boxers' into Fame." 2 August 2004, http://www.thread.co.nz/article/985.

Sabo, Donald F. Jr., and Ross Runfola, eds. *Jock: Sports and Male Identity*. Englewood Cliffs, NJ: Prentice-Hall, 1980.

Salzman, Marian, Ira Matathia, and Ann O'Reilly. *The Future of Men*. New York: Palgrave Macmillan, 2005.

Samuels, Allison, and Mark Starr. "Ready for His Close-Up." *Newsweek*, 9 April 2001: 54.

Scala, Gina. "L'Homme nouveau est arrivé!" *Femme en Ville*. N° 11. September 2005: 26–31.

Scanlon, Thomas F. *Eros and Greek Athletics*. New York: Oxford University Press, 2002.

Scott, Nick. "Total Immersion." *GQ* (Australia), Summer 2007: 92–97.

Schulian, John. "Jock Style." *GQ* (U.S.), January 1986: 110–13, 158–59.

Sedgwick, Eve Kosofsky. *Between Men: English Literature and Male Homosocial Desire*. 1985. New York Columbia University Press, 1993.

Shah, Diane K. "Magic's Kingdom." *GQ* (U.S.), March 1987: 250–53, 292–95.

———. "The Transformation of Pat Riley." *GQ* (U.S.), January 1989: 136–41, 188–90.

Silke, Jim. *Bettie Page: Queen of Hearts*. Milwaukie, OR: Dark Horse, 1995.

Silva, Horacio. "Goal Oriented." *New York Times*, 21 September 2003, late ed., sec. 6: 80.

Silver, Michael. "In Control." *Sports Illustrated*, 14 January 2002: 41–46.

———. "Rodman Unchained." *Sports Illustrated,* 29 May 1995: 20–27.

Simpson, Mark. "Here Come the Mirror Men." *Independent,* 15 November 1994, Metro Page: 22.

———. *Male Impersonators: Men Performing Masculinity.* London: Cassell, 1994.

———. "Meet the Metrosexual." Salon.com, 22 July 2002.

———. "MetroDaddy Speaks." Salon.com, 5 January 2004.

———. "Metrosexuals: Male Vanity Steps Out of the Closet." 1994. *It's a Queer World: Deviant Adventures in Pop Culture.* New York: Harrington Park Press, 1999: 207–10.

———. "Sporno." *Out,* July 2006: 45–49.

Smalls, James. *The Homoerotic Photography of Carl Van Vechten: Public Face, Private Thoughts.* Philadelphia: Temple University Press, 2006.

Smith, Richard. "Game On." *Gay Times,* July 2004: 52–65.

"Soccer Stud." *Out,* August 2004: 50–53.

Stanford, Peter. "Sport's Ugliest Taboo." *Independent,* 10 Febuary 2004, Features: 6–7.

Steele, Valerie. *Fetish: Fashion, Sex and Power.* 1996. New York: Oxford University Press, 1997.

St. John, Warren. "Metrosexuals Come Out." *New York Times,* 22 June 2003, sec. 9, Style Desk: 1.

Stratton, Jon. *The Desirable Body: Cultural Fetishism and the Erotics of Consumption.* 1996. Urbana: University of Illinois Press, 2001.

Sullivan, Nick. "Forza England!" *GQ* (UK), October 2003: 182–85.

Sullivan, Robert. "Dream Team." *Vogue* (U.S.), May 2004: 264–67.

Syed, Matthew. "Knighthood Would Be Fitting Reward for New Man Who Changed Old Ideas." *Times,* 28 June 2007, Sport: 101.

Tatchell, Peter. "Come Out Fighting, Lennox Lewis," *Guardian,* 16 November 2001.

Teague, Matthew. "Kevin Garnett Has Everything." *GQ* (U.S.), October 2002: 242–45, 298–99.

Thomas, David. "Netting a Fortune." *Business Life,* September 2001: 44–49.

———. "We All Knew That If We Didn't Go to Turkey Our Careers Would Be Wrecked." *Mail on Sunday,* 19 October 2003, Night & Day: 18–24.

Thornton, Kate. "Becks Father Lover Icon Hero." *Marie Claire* (UK), June 2002: 69–76.

Thorpe, Ian. Interview with Monica Attard. *Sunday Profile.* ABC Local Radio, Australia. 17 November 2002.

"Thorpie's Dax Take Off." *Sydney Star Observer,* 30 October 2003: 5.

Veblen, Thorstein. *The Theory of the Leisure Class.* 1899. New York: Penguin, 1994.

Verley, Frédérique, and Leïla Smara. "Brahim Time." *Vogue Hommes International,* Fall/Winter 2003–2004: 242–47.

Verma, Himanshu. *The Metrosexuals: Exploring the Unexplored.* New Delhi: Red Earth, 2004.

Vidal, Gore. *Sexually Speaking: Collected Sex Writings.* San Francisco: Cleis, 1999.

Walden, George. *Who Is a Dandy?* London: Gibson Square, 2002.

Walton, A. Scott. "Beefcake Ads Go Beyond 'Boxers or Briefs?'" *Atlanta Journal-Constitution,* 28 February 2002, home ed., Features: F1.

Ward, Susan. "Earrings." *Encyclopedia of Clothing and Fashion.* Ed. Valerie Steele. Vol. 1. Farmington Hills, MI: Thomson/Gale, 2004: 391–95.

Waugh, Thomas. *Hard to Imagine: Gay Male Eroticism in Photography and Film from Their Beginnings to Stonewall.* New York: Columbia University Press, 1996.

Wayne, George. "Ready Freddie." *Vanity Fair,* April 2004: 116.

Whannel, Garry. *Media Sport Stars: Masculinities and Moralities.* London: Routledge, 2002.

White, Shane, and Graham White. *Stylin': African American Expressive Culture.* 1998. Ithaca: Cornell University Press, 1999.

Williams, Ann. "Soccer Mad." *South China Morning Post,* 13 September 2004: 46.

Yeager, Bunny. *Betty Page Confidential.* New York: St. Martin's Press, 1994.

Zeigler, Cyd Jr., and Jim Buzinski. "John Amaechi to Come Out Publicly." February 2007, http://www.outsports.com/nba/20062007/0207amaechi.htm.

Index